Accounting Terms

Financial Education Is Your Best Investment

Published February 27, 2020

Revision 2.2

Financial Terms Dictionary

Copyright And Trademark Notices

Limits of Liability and Disclaimer of Warranties

The materials in this book are provided "as is" and without warranties of any kind either express or implied. The Author disclaims all warranties, express or implied, including, but not limited to, implied warranties of merchantability and fitness for a particular purpose.

The Author does not warrant that defects will be corrected, or that that the site or the server that makes this eBook available are free of viruses or other harmful components. The Author does not warrant or make any representations regarding the use or the results of the use of the materials in this book in terms of their correctness, accuracy, reliability, or otherwise. Applicable law may not allow the exclusion of implied warranties, so the above exclusion may not apply to you.

Under no circumstances, including, but not limited to, negligence, shall the Author be liable for any special or consequential damages that result from the use of, or the inability to use this eBook, even if the Author or his authorized representative has been advised of the possibility of such damages.

Applicable law may not allow the limitation or exclusion of liability or incidental or consequential damages, so the above limitation or exclusion may not apply to you. In no event shall the Author's total liability to you for all damages, losses, and causes of action (whether in contract, tort, including but not limited to, negligence or otherwise) exceed the amount paid by you, if any, for this eBook.

Facts and information are believed to be accurate at the time they were placed in this book. All data provided in this book is to be used for information purposes only. The information contained within is not intended to provide specific legal, financial or tax advice, or any other advice whatsoever, for any individual or company and should not be relied upon in that regard. The services described are only offered in jurisdictions where they may be legally offered. Information provided is not all-inclusive and is limited to information that is made available and such information should not be relied upon as all-inclusive or accurate.

You are advised to do your own due diligence when it comes to making business decisions and should use caution and seek the advice of qualified professionals. You should check with your accountant, lawyer, or professional advisor, before acting on this or any information. You may not consider any examples, documents, or other content in this eBook or otherwise provided by the Author to be the equivalent of professional advice.

The Author assumes no responsibility for any losses or damages resulting from your use of any link, information, or opportunity contained in this book or within any other information disclosed by the author in any form whatsoever.

About the Author

Thomas Herold is a successful entrepreneur, mediator, author, and personal development coach. He published over 35 books with over 200,000 copies distributed worldwide and the founder of seven online businesses.

For over ten years Thomas Herold has studied the monetary system and has experienced some profound insights on how money and wealth are related. After three years of successful investing in silver, he released 'Building Wealth with Silver - How to Profit From The Biggest Wealth Transfer in History' in 2012. One of the first books that illustrate in a remarkable, simple way the monetary system and its consequences.

He is the founder and CEO of the 'Financial Terms Dictionary' book series and website, which explains in detail and comprehensive form over 1000 financial terms. In his financial book series, he informs in detail and with practical examples all aspects of the financial sector. His educational materials are designed to help people get started with financial education.

In his 2018 released book 'The Money Deception', Mr. Herold provides the most sophisticated insight and shocking details about the current monetary system. Never before has the massive manipulation of money caused so much economic inequality in the world. In spite of these frightening facts, 'The Money Deception' also provides remarkable and simple solutions to create abundance for all people, and it's a must-read if you want to survive the global monetary transformation that's underway right now.

In 2019 he released an entirely new financial book series explaining in detail and with practical examples over 1000 financial terms. The 'Herold Financial IQ Series' contains currently of 16 titles covering every category of the financial market.

His latest book "High Credit Score Secrets" offers the most effective strategies to boost the average credit score from as low as 450 points to over 810. It teaches the tactics to build excellent credit, repair credit, monitor credit and how to guard that good score for a lifetime. It reached bestseller status in 2020 in three categories.

For more information please visit the author's websites:

High Credit Score Secrets - The Smart Raise & Repair Guide to Excellent Credit
https://highcreditscoresecrets.com

The Money Deception - What Banks & Government Don't Want You to Know
https://www.moneydeception.com

The Herold Financial IQ Series - Financial Education Is Your Best Investment
https://www.financial-dictionary.com

The Online Financial Dictionary - Over 1000 Terms Explained
https://www.financial-dictionary.info

Please Leave Your Review on Amazon

This book and the Financial IQ Series are self-published and the author does not have a contract with one of the five largest publishers, which are able to support the author's work with advertising. If you like this book, please consider leaving a solid 4 or 5-star review on Amazon.

Herold Financial IQ Series on Amazon

Table Of Contents

Accountant

Accountants are professional financial personnel whose careers are centered on dealing with money and figures. Their responsibilities cover compiling financial records, certifying them, and recording them for businesses, individuals, government organizations, and not for profit organizations. As such, they track a company or individual's money through the development of reports.

Managers of companies and organizations and other individuals read these accounting reports. The managers learn the state and progress of their company from them. Governments utilize these reports to determine the taxes that companies are required to pay. Investors and other businesses look at them to determine if they wish to work with a company. Banks and others investigate these reports in their decisions of lending money to a company.

The majority of accountants are specialized. Four main types of accountants practice their trade. Management accountants follow the money that is both earned and spent by their employing companies.

Public accountants work at public accounting firms. Here, they perform auditing, accounting, consulting, and tax preparation work. These types of accountants perform numerous tasks for individuals who are clients of the accounting firm. Some public accountants have their own small business.

Government auditors and accountants ensure that the accounting records of government agencies are correct. Besides this, they double check the record of those individuals who transact business with the government. This helps to keep governments responsible.

Internal auditors are accountants who ensure that the accounting records of their company are correct. In this role, they are investigating to make certain that no person within the firm is stealing. Besides this, they investigate to make certain that no individual in the company is wasting the firm's capital.

Accountants perform their tasks in offices. Those accountants who work for public companies and government groups often travel to perform audits of their own company's other branches or outside companies. Regarding their hours, accountants typically work for a normal forty hours per week. Some accountants ply their trade for more than fifty hours each week. Especially in tax season that runs from January through April, tax accountants commonly work incredibly long hours.

The outlook for accountants is exceptionally strong. Their field of work is anticipated to grow substantially faster than the average occupation through at least 2018. The reasons for this have much to do with the complex nature of both income tax laws and mandatory financial reporting. Because of the nature of these laws and rules, the demand for accountants will always exist. Working as an accountant entails a wide variety of requirements and prerequisites. Some very important positions mandate advanced degrees. Other accountant positions only need an ability and compliance to learn the trade, along with the necessary patience to see the training through.

Adjusted Gross Income (AGI)

Adjusted Gross Income (AGI) refers to a means of calculating income off of an individual's actual gross income. People use this figure in order to determine the amount of their income which the Internal Revenue Service will subject to tax assessment. It is ultimately the United States tax code which creates this AGI figure. This number should never be confused with the actual gross income. Gross income is merely the total amount of all money individuals realize and earn over a year long period.

The Adjusted Gross Income considers a range of deductions which it subtracts from the individuals in question's actual gross incomes. The result is the basis off of which the person's individual income taxes become calculated at the end of the tax year. Where tax activities and the Internal Revenue Service are concerned, this figure generally proves to be more useful than gross income alone.

All relevant deductions that apply to gross income and turn it into Adjusted Gross Income come from above the line deductions. This simply signifies that they must be reflected on the tax calculations ahead of dependents, military service, and other exemptions. There are a number of such deductions which count in the compiling of this AGI. Among the best known and most common are the following: contributions to retirement plans, business expenses which are not reimbursed, medical expenses, losses from property sales, and alimony or child support.

To calculate up individuals' Adjusted Gross Income, it is first necessary to figure up all reported income in the year being considered. Additional taxable income sources also have to be added in to the total. This includes any compensation for unemployment, property sales' profits, Social Security payments, pensions, and other sources of income that did not become reported on the tax return. Once this complete earnings' total has been figured up, it is necessary to subtract out all relevant deductions to come up with the appropriate AGI.

The Internal Revenue Service makes it easier to come up with all of the potential deductions pertaining to gross income by going to their IRS website. Here they provide a rules list for all potential deductions' requirements. Some of these prove to be extremely specific. This is why people have to carefully study the tax code in order to be certain of their eligibility for any and all deductions that they take.

Once individuals have figured out their AGI, they are able to then add in the government's normal federal tax deductions to finish calculating their taxable income. For some tax payers, this will mean itemizing out their various expenses to come up with the itemized deductions alternatively. Sometimes this works out better for taxpayers. One thing that a tax payer must be careful to never do is to not confuse their Adjusted Gross Income with their MAGI modified adjusted gross income.

In fact the modified adjusted gross income is supposed to be totally separate from the AGI. It is utilized to figure out the deductible dollar amount from the person's IRA individual retirement account. It will also be employed to decide if the private parties are eligible for specific tax deductions. In order to figure up this MAGI, tax payers have to add back in some items like foreign housing deductions, foreign earned income, IRA contribution deductions, higher education cost deductions, and student loan deductions.

In many cases, the MAGI is often much the same as the AGI for a given individual. Yet it is important to be aware that even tiny differences can significantly impact the overall tax return for an individual. In particular, such variances will impact a person's eligibility to receive particular benefits allowed under the ACA Affordable Care Act.

Amortization

The word amortization is one that is commonly utilized by financial officers of corporations and accountants. They utilize it when they are working with time concepts and how they relate to financial statements of accounts. You typically hear this word employed when you are figuring up loan calculations, or when you are determining interest payments.

The concept of amortization possesses a lengthy history and it is currently employed in numerous different segments of finance. The word itself descends from Middle English. Here amortisen meant to "alienate" or "kill" something. This derivation itself comes from the Latin admortire that signified "plus death." It is loosely related to the derivation of the word mortgage, as well.

This accounting principle is much like depreciation that diminishes a liability or asset's value over a given period of time through payments. It covers the practical life span of a tangible asset. With liabilities, it includes a pre-set amount of time over which money is paid back. Like this, a certain amount of money is set aside for the loan repayment over its lifetime.

Even though depreciation is similar to amortization, they are not the same concepts. The main difference between them lies in what they cover. While depreciation is most commonly employed to describe physical assets like property, vehicles, or buildings, amortization instead covers intangibles such as product development, copyrights, or patents. Where liabilities are concerned, it relates to income in the future that will be paid out over a given amount of time. Depreciation is instead a lost income over a time period.

Several different kinds of amortization are presently in use. This varies with the accounting method that is practiced. Business amortization deals with borrowed funds and loans and the paying of particular amounts in different time frames. When used as amortization analysis, this is the means of cost execution analysis for a given group of operations. Where tax law is concerned, amortization pertains to the interest amount that is paid over a given span of time relevant to payments and tax rates.

Amortization can also be employed with regards to zoning rules and regulations, since it conveys a property owner's time for relocating as a result of zoning guidelines and pre-existing use. Another variation is used as negative amortization. This pertains specifically to increasing loan amounts that result from total interest due not being paid up at the appropriate time.

Amortization can also be employed over a widely ranging time frame. It could cover only a year or extend to as many as forty years. This depends on the kind of loan or asset utilized. Some examples include building loans that span over as many as forty years and car loans that commonly span over merely four to five years. Asset examples would be patent right expenses that commonly are spread out over seventeen years.

Assets

Assets are any thing that can be owned by a company or an individual person. These are able to be sold for cash. Commonly, assets produce income or give value to the owner.

In the world of financial accounting, assets prove to be economic resources. They can be physical objects or intangible concepts that can be utilized and owned to create value. Assets are deemed to have real and positive value for their owners. Assets must also be convertible into cash, which itself is furthermore considered to be an asset.

There are several different types of assets as measured by accountants and accounting processes. These might be current assets, longer term assets, intangible assets, or deferred assets. Current assets include cash and other items that are readily and easily able to be sold to raise cash. Longer term assets are those that are held and useful for great periods of time, including such physical items as factory plants, real estate, and equipment. Intangible assets are non physical rights or concepts, like patents, trademarks, goodwill, and copyrights. Finally, deferred assets are those that involve monies spent now for the costs in the future of things like rent, insurance, or interest.

Though tangible, physical assets are not hard to conceptualize, intangible assets are often confusing for people to understand. Even though these are not physical items that may be touched, they still have value that can be controlled and sold to raise cash. Intangible assets include rights and resources which provide a company with a form of marketplace advantage. These can cover many different elements beyond those listed above, such as computer programs, stocks, bonds, and even accounts receivable.

On balance sheets, tangible assets are commonly divided into further categories. These include fixed assets and current assets. Fixed assets are objects that are immobile or not easily transported, such as buildings, office locations, and equipment. Current assets are comprised of inventory that a business holds. Balance sheets of companies keep track of a firm's assets and their value as expressed in monetary terms. These assets are both the cash and other items that the business or person owns.

Assets should never be confused with liabilities. Assets create positive cash flow that represents value or money coming into a business, organization, or individual's accounts. Liabilities are obligations that have to be paid and that create negative cash flow, or take money out of a business, individual, or organization's accounts. As an example of the difference between the two, assets would be houses that are rented out that bring in more rent every month than the expenses, interest, and upkeep of the houses. Liabilities would be homes that have payments that must be paid every month and do not provide any income stream to effectively offset this.

Audit

An audit refers to a third party evaluation and review of a business or individual's financial statements. The goal is to ensure that the financial records are both accurate and reflective of the transactions for the entity they represent. Such a review can be carried out by an external auditing firm or by accounting employees within an organization itself.

There is also the possibility for the Internal Revenue Service itself to conduct audits in order to confirm the veracity of a business or individual's tax payer returns and transactions. As the IRS engages in such audits, this usually creates a dark cloud over the victim organization or individual. This is because such IRS audits come with a negative connotation. It is as if the government suspects the taxpayers in question have engaged in illegal activities with their taxes or income declarations.

For those audits which an external company performs on behalf of corporations, these are often very useful in taking away the tendency towards personal bias. It means that the final picture of the corporation should be more complete, unbiased, and accurate. Such audits are often seeking any inadvertent material error in the corporations' statements or activities. They reassure shareholders of the company that the financial statements are accurate. As third parties undertake audits, the bias of the internal accountant who would otherwise be engaging in the auditing tasks is eliminated.

This could be regarding a company subsidiary or division, the entire corporation or one system within it, or the financial books of the business. There is also no pressure that a member of management will think negatively of the employee for producing less than stellar outcomes from the audit when the corporation engages and retains an external accounting firm.

The majority of publicly traded firms become audited one time each year. Enormous corporations can be audited even every month. There are companies in industries where their oversight organization requires legally that the firm receive routine audits so as to eliminate any temptation to deliberately misrepresent financial information. Such misrepresentation is literally called fraud. Still other large corporations look at audits and auditors as a valuable tool to ascertain how effective their financial reports and associated internal controls of them actually are.

Two different types of auditors exist in the realm of external audits. These are statutory auditors and external cost auditors. The statutory varieties independently labor to consider the quality of the financial statements and reports. The external cost auditors consider and review the cost sheets and statements to make certain they do not contain any errors, misrepresentations, or fraudulent facts or figures. Each of the two different kinds of auditing personnel work with a range of varying standards that are different than those which the corporation hiring them would engage in otherwise.

Such internal auditors will be hired by the firm or other organization on whose behalf they are engaging in the audit in the first place. They do their fiduciary best to deliver reliable and accurate information and certification to the management of the company, the board of directors, and shareholders regarding the books and all internal operating systems and procedures of the company in question.

Other auditors will be consultants. They will still utilize the standards of the corporation which they are auditing instead of an independent set of standards, even though they are not internal employees of the organization. Such consultants are brought in when the corporation or other organization lacks the necessary resources to perform their own internal operational audits.

Auditors must meet certain specified standards which their jurisdictional governments lay out when they conduct these audits. The American Institute of Certified Public Accountants has its respected external audit standards which they call the GAAS Generally Accepted Auditing Standards. Internationally, the International Auditing and Assurance Board maintain their International Standards on Auditing. The U.S. also has a regulatory body dating back to 2002 called the PCAOB, or Public Company Accounting Oversight Board.

Bad Bank

A Bad Bank refers to a special bank which a government agency typically establishes in order to purchase the failing loans from one or more banks that possess a large number of non-performing assets. They purchase these at the market price in order to not wreck the bank. Through the action of transferring such toxic assets from the institution's balance sheet over to the new bad bank, such damaged banks are able to free up their balance sheet from the toxic assets that they would eventually be writing down otherwise.

Bondholders and shareholders alike will likely lose money off of such a solution, not the bank depositors. These banks which devolve into insolvency from such actions can be liquidated, nationalized by the government authorities, or recapitalized and kept going on life support (hoping that their situation will improve with time).

There are countless examples of bad banks. In 1988, Mellon Bank created its own bad bank which it named Grant Street National Bank. The 2008 global financial crisis renewed the old interest in this solution for dealing with the assets of bad banks. The managers of many of the world's largest banks started thinking seriously about segregating out the toxic assets into these bad banks.

It was the then Chairman Ben Bernanke of the Federal Reserve Banking System who put forward the idea to set up a government administered and backed bad bank following the recession created by the subprime mortgage crisis. He wanted to clean up the balance sheets of the commercial banks which were suffering from devastating levels of poorly performing assets so that they could start over with their lending. Another competing strategy they contemplated was issuing a guaranteed form of insurance plan that could allow the banks to maintain their toxic assets on the books. At the same time it would pass the risks from the banks on to the taxpayers.

Banks can easily build up a massive portfolio position of financial instruments and debts that can suddenly grow in risk. This makes it far harder for the banks in question to raise additional fresh capital by selling more bonds. In such scenarios, the bank may decide it is a good idea to separate out their bad assets and good assets with the bad banks concept. This goal lies in permitting the investors to contemplate the financial health of the bank with more certainty. The bad bank could be set up in order to help deal with a worsening financial situation, or alternatively by a government agency as part of their official government response to the various financial problems in a range of financial institutions throughout the financial sector.

Besides removing these debilitating assets off of the balance sheet of the parent bank, the bad bank will allow them to have special management teams to work on the problems of the badly performing debts. This concept helps the banks to do what they do best, which is to concentrate their efforts on the primary business model of lending. Meanwhile, the bad bank itself will be able to concentrate on delivering the optimal value which it can from the remaining high risk assets.

Thanks to the global financial crisis which raged from 2007 through 2010, a number of nations established their own bad banks. The Emergency Economic Stabilization Act of 2008 suggested a bad bank to deal with the subprime mortgage crisis across the United States. Over in Europe, Ireland set up its own bad bank the National Asset Management Agency in 2009 to deal with the financial crisis as it spread in Ireland.

Balance of Payments

The balance of payments refers to a statement whose purpose is to explain the transactions of an economy with the other countries of the world. Such a statement covers a particular time frame. This is also referred to as the balance of international payments. It covers every transaction that occurs between the inhabitants of the nation with the remainder of the world. This includes income, goods, and services; liabilities and financial claims to the world; and transfers and remittances (like gifts).

A balance of payments tabulation will group all types of transactions into two different accounts. These are the current account and the capital account. In the current account are services, goods, present transfers, and income from investments. The capital account is mostly made up of financial instrument transactions. These are combined with a nation's IIP international investment position to make up its complete international accounts.

The phrase balance of payments is somewhat of a misnomer as it does not pertain to any payments which an economy receives or makes. Instead it is only concerned with transactions. A great number of such international transactions do not have money payments involved with them. This explains how the number can be substantially different from the net payments a country affects to foreign countries, companies, and individuals.

The balance of payments is seldom an even zero sum figure without adjustments being made. There are typically either current account deficits or surpluses. When a current account deficit exists, this would mean that it had to be counterbalanced by net inflows to the capital and financial account. Current account surpluses would match capital and financial account outflows. Either situation balances out the number. Reality is that this data comes from a number of divergent sources so that there is always some error in measurement.

This combined data for balance of payments and international investment positions informs international and domestic economic policies. A country will use various economic policies to attempt to address imbalances in the payments as well as direct foreign investment levels.

There are also a range of economic policies that governments utilize to achieve particular objectives that pertain to the balance of payments. Examples of this abound. Countries may be interested in generating a larger amount of direct foreign investment in specific sectors of the economy. They could implement a series of policies that would encourage such investment.

Other countries may be more concerned with increasing their exports. To do this, they may try to lower the exchange value of their currency. By maintaining their currency value at lower depressed levels, they can make their exports less expensive to foreign customers. As exports grow, this would help them to increase their currency reserves as a consequence. How successful such policies prove to be and the impacts they have become clear in the BOP information.

The balance of payments should never be confused with the balance of trade. Balance of trade is the single biggest component which makes up the nation's BOP. It only includes the variance between the country in question's exports and imports over a particular time frame.

Balance of Trade

Balance of Trade refers to a nation's difference between the value of its exports and imports in a particular time frame. It also represents the biggest part of the nation's BOP balance of payments. Economists often utilize the BOT as their statistical tool for grasping the comparative strength of any national economy against another national economy. It also helps them to effectively understand the bigger picture trade flow between different countries. Other names for the BOT are the International Trade Balance and simply the Trade Balance.

Those countries (like the United States) whose imports of goods and services are larger than their exports possess what is called a trade deficit. On the other extreme, those nations (like Germany) which export far more goods and services than they actually import in return possess a trade surplus. It is entirely possible to figure up the Balance of Trade in a simplified format of imports minus exports. The true calculation is made up of a few different items though. In order for the number to make any meaningful sense, the trade deficit or alternatively surplus raw number has to be measured up against the GDP gross domestic product of the nation. This is because bigger economies are better prepared to absorb and handle larger amounts of surpluses or deficits.

There are many debit ledger items in this formula. These include foreign aid, imports, overseas domestic spending, and overseas domestic investments. On the credit side of the ledger are foreign spending within the domestic economy, exports, and foreign investments made within the domestic economy. When analysts subtract out the credit ledger items off of the debit ledger items, they come to the appropriate trade surplus or trade deficit on the nation in question during the time frame of year, quarter, or month.

In some countries, one can almost assume that they will have a trade deficit. The U.S. is a prime example of this. It has experienced a large trade deficit since 1976. This is largely due to its continued reliance on expensive oil imports as well as its insatiable lust for foreign consumer goods. At the same time, China the nation which produces and then exports a plurality of the consumer goods in the world has boasted a comfortable trade surplus since the year 1995.

By itself, such deficits or trade surpluses do not mean that an economy is doing well or poorly. Such numbers have to be viewed relative to the various economic indicators of the business cycle. Countries will likely export more in recessions in order to stimulate demand for the economy and to develop additional jobs. During powerful expansions, nations usually import larger amounts of goods and services which help to induce price competition to limit the ravaging effects of inflation.

For the year 2015, Germany, The EU as a whole, Japan, and China all enjoyed enormous trade surpluses at the same time as the United Kingdom, the United States, Australia, Canada, and Brazil had the biggest trade deficits.

Nations attempt to develop trade policies to foster a potential trade surplus. This is because favorable trade balances enable nations to amass profits on a national scale. It is always preferable to bring in a higher level of capital and to sell more goods. This equates to a greater standard of living. National firms also obtain competitive advantages of expertise when they produce large amounts of good for export. They are able to bring on more staff, generate higher levels of income, pay out higher dividends to their national investors, and to lower the unemployment level in consequence.

This explains why political leaders will often stoop to trade protectionist policies to encourage a trade surplus with other key trading partners. They do this through assessing quotas, tariffs, and putting subsidies on their imports.

Balance Sheet

Balance Sheet refers to a corporate financial statement. The purpose of it is to thoroughly summarize the liabilities, assets, and shareholders' equity in the firm at a fixed moment in time. The statement provides a revealing glimpse into the things the corporation owns and the money it owes, along with the total amount which shareholders have invested in the going concern. Where these financial statements are concerned, the formula for assets is liabilities plus shareholders' equity.

Balance sheets ultimately derive their names from the equation which pits the assets on one side while the shareholders' equity and liabilities remain on the opposite site. They have to balance out, which provides the concept behind the name. It makes perfect sense that corporations have only two choices when paying for their assets. They might either borrow the money through assuming liabilities or obtain it off of investors, which happens when they issue shareholder equity.

Consider an example to better understand what is involved with this concept. If a corporation obtains a $40,000 bank loan to be repaid in five years, then its assets (cash account section) will rise by the $40,000. At the same time, the total liabilities (long term debt section) will also rise by the $40,000 amount. This restores balance to the equation. Should the firm then receive $80,000 from investors, the assets will also increase by that same amount. On the other side of the equation, the shareholder equity rises by the same $80,000. When the company earns revenues which are greater than the liabilities, these go into the so called shareholder equity account. It is that category that stands for all net assets the owners of the corporation hold. The offsetting revenues balance out on the assets side in the form of inventory, investments, or cash categories.

The three main categories of the balance sheet equation--- assets, liabilities, and shareholder equity each break down further into a few of their own sub accounts. These sub accounts actually reveal the particulars of the corporate finances. Every industry will have its own range of sub accounts. Many of the sub account terms will mean different things from one type of business to another. In general, there are always several sub account categories that different industries have in common.

As an example, under the assets category, such sub accounts are broken out from top down to bottom according to which is most liquid. This simply means the ease of selling them for cash. The divisions for all sub accounts will be by current assets and long term assets. The current ones may be changed to cash in under a year. Longer term ones obviously may not be converted so quickly. Current assets generally list top to bottom according to the following precedence: cash or cash equivalents, marketable securities, accounts receivable, inventory, and prepaid expenses. Longer term assets have the following general top down order: long term investments, fixed assets, and intangible assets such as goodwill, trademarks, and intellectual property.

Under the liabilities category will be the total amount firms owe to other entities. These include building rent, salaries, utilities, supplier invoices, and interest on loans or bonds. The current liabilities will be due in under a year, while the longer term ones are due after a year. Some sub accounts for current liabilities include: currently due part of longer term debt, interest payable, bank debts, wages payable, rents/utilities/taxes, dividend payments, and customer prepayments. Under longer term liabilities there are pension fund liabilities, long term debts, and deferred tax liabilities. There can also be off-balance sheet liabilities, like operating leases.

Shareholders' equity includes money from the owners of the business, the stake holding shareholders. This includes the net assets like treasury stock, retained earnings, preferred stock, and additionally paid in capital.

Blockchain

Blockchain refers to a technology that serves as a means of structuring and storing data. As such it is the ultimate foundation of the revolutionary crypto-currencies such as Bitcoin and Ether. The true breakthrough in coding capability permits participants to share digital ledgers back and forth over a computer network. Its genius and appeal lies in the fact that it does not require a central authority to run or oversee it. Since there is no meddling central authority like a central bank or boss to the system, no one party can interfere with the financial records.

In other words, the straight math makes sure that all the parties who participate are honest with each other. Blockchain is made up of concatenated transactions blocks. Nowadays, the technology has become so important and offers so many future possibilities for real world applications that over forty of the world's biggest and most important financial firms are experimenting with uses for it.

Blockchains are also public record ledgers of all transactions in a crypto-currency which have ever taken place. For this reason, the chain is always expanding as every new record adds additional completed blocks to it. These become a part of the blockchain via a chronological and linear fashioned order. Every participating node receives a copy of this blockchain as it is updated. Nodes are computers which share a Bitcoin network connection that utilizes the system to validate and relay such transactions which were performed in it. The chain comes as an auto download once a computer network joins up to the Bitcoin network. This chain maintains full information on all balances and appropriate addresses from the very first transaction ever all the way to the latest one which has been performed utilizing the block.

In the end, it is this blockchain that represents the primary technological advance offered by Bitcoin. It amounts to the proof and record of every transaction performed using the network. The blocks represent the current record in the chain that will ultimately record all or at least some of the recent transaction. After it is finished, this block will join the chain as part and parcel of the current and permanent database. Once a block is spoken for, a new block will become generated. Myriads of such blocks exist in the chain. They are linked one to another, much like a physical chain, in their correct chronological and linear order. Each block contains the hash of the prior block in it.

It is always helpful to consider a real world example to better understand a somewhat complex concept like this one. Traditional banking is a solid analogy. This blockchain is much like a complete history of banking records and transactions. Bitcoin transactions must be chronologically entered in the blockchain as real world banking transactions are at financial institutions. Such blocks are something like the statements recording individual bank accounts and banking transactions.

The protocol of Bitcoin is based upon all nodes in the system sharing the blockchain's database. A complete and unaltered copy of the chain will include records of all the transactions in Bitcoin which have ever been executed. This delivers useful insights into the quantity of value that a specific address owned at any time in the past.

The problem with the ever growing nature of the chain is that it has become so very large with over a decade of increasing size that synchronization and storage have become serious issues. These days, the average time of a new block appearing on the chain amounts to only ten minutes. Mining, the process of unlocking new BTC, is adding the majority of new blocks to the chain these days.

Book Value

The book value refers to the tangible asset value of any company. Tangible value here is used to refer to any assets that can be felt, seen, or touched, such as inventory, plants, equipment, cash, offices, or properties. Because of this tangible factor to book value, it is often referred to as Net Tangible Assets.

Finding a company's book value is not particularly hard if you have a company's balance sheet. To determine this number, all that you have to do is to look at the shareholder's equity. From this number, you simply subtract out all of the intangible items' values, such as goodwill. What remains is the book value of tangible assets that the company has.

Book value, or the net tangible assets, that companies possess proves to be extremely important. You ought to analyze a company's balance sheet directly from them, not from a third party website. This means that the book value figure may not be determined on the balance sheet. Coming up with the figure is just a matter of taking all of a company's assets and subtracting the intangible types of assets from the figure. You will then be looking at the company's true components, including properties, office buildings, phones, computers, chairs, etc.

In the past, this book value represented the ultimate measurement for value investors who were looking for bargains on stock prices of companies. This meant that higher assets, and thereby book values, proved to be the principal measurement for making value investing decisions. During the last twenty or so years, investors who seek out value have shifted away from the importance of the dollar values of assets to preferring companies that create higher earnings using a smaller base of assets.

As an example of why book value is less valuable than smaller asset bases with earnings creation, consider a company that possesses thirty million dollars in physical assets and earns $10 million per year. Look at another company that makes the same $10 million in earnings while having $50 million in asserts. Relationships between the asset base of a company and its earnings are well known and established.

This means that doubling the earnings of the company with $30 million would require investing another $30 million. This would leave the business with $60 million in assets and $20 million in earnings. Doubling the earnings of the company with $50 million in assets would similarly require adding another $50 million in assets. The business would then own a $100 million of assets and create the same $20 million in earnings per year.

The new company with $100 million in assets has the higher book value to be sure. But the smaller asset company only needed to retain $30 million in earnings in order to double its profits. The $20 million difference could be used for expansion of the business, paying dividends, or buying back shares. So while higher book values are still important, higher returns on assets are actually more significant and beneficial.

Bookkeeper

A bookkeeper is an individual who maintains a business' important financial records. These are typically kept in journals or ledgers format. This is where the word books derives from, which is used in the title of bookkeeper.

Although bookkeepers typically engage in basic levels of accounting tasks, they are still not labeled as fully qualified accountants. This is because bookkeepers are given substantially less amounts of training than are accountants. On top of this, bookkeepers do not have the requirements of legal certification applied to them. Bookkeepers could perform their duties as employees of a single business. They might also become a small sole proprietorship, working on the behalf of several small groups or individuals. In such a capacity, bookkeepers actually keep the books of a number of different clients at a time.

An individual who labors as a bookkeeper has important responsibilities. They must dutifully record each and every financial transaction in which a business engages. Bookkeepers make notes of every payment received or made, and for what each of these amounts represented. Monies that are both spent and received have to be carefully tracked. All entries placed into the ledger books have to be balanced at the end of the period, so that a company's expenses and income are accurately and precisely detailed in the accounting.

Bookkeepers are not expected to do all of the financial tasks of a business. When an accounting period that is either a quarter or a month is reached, they will often carry the books over to a qualified accountant. Such an accountant will handle the tasks of figuring up the taxes that need to be paid to the IRS. They also create official accounting reports. There are a number of larger or mid-sized firms that simply engage their own accounting staff and accountant rather than have a bookkeeper as well. This is generally considered to be more efficient financially. Smaller companies will tend to have their own bookkeeper on staff then engage an accountant on a basis of need. Such accountants are generally used for reporting taxes, as well as profits or losses.

Bookkeeping tasks, like with accounting, can become very complicated. This is especially true as companies expand. Capable bookkeepers are able to work flexibly, handling a constant barrage of data and even unexpected issues. A reliable bookkeeper will also have to possess people skills. This is because bookkeepers actually interact with other employees through the company to make certain that the company is able to keep track of every expense, ranging from ink and paper for the copy machine to hotel stays for business related to work.

Bookkeeping can occasionally involve a bookkeeper in activities that are against the law, like with creating incorrect records on the ledgers in order to make a company look to be in better financial health than it truly is. When this happens, it is casually referred to as cooking the books. No only is such activity in bookkeeping immoral, but it is highly illegal.

Budget Deficit

Budget deficits are accounting positions in which revenues are not sufficient to cover expenditures. As such they involve spending more than the entity takes in from receipts. This term is most often utilized to address government accounting and spending instead of individual or business spending.

This concept can also be applied to a number of government deficits that have been built up over time. In this case, the phrase national debt is employed. A budget surplus is the opposite of the budget deficit. Budgets are balanced when money coming in equals money being spent. Budget surpluses are rare and have occurred for only 6 times since World War II in the United States.

When economic conditions improve and become prosperous budget deficits may decrease as a share of GDP. This happens because tax revenues rise while the economy is growing and unemployment becomes reduced. It also lowers the government expenditures on programs like unemployment. If economic conditions instead deteriorate then budget deficits can grow as a percentage of the country's GDP. This is because government spending rises to help stimulate the economy and cover higher unemployment while tax revenues typically decline at these times.

Nations are able to fight budget deficits with some efforts. They can do this by encouraging economic growth. They might also choose to raise taxes or lower government spending. One easy way to promote better economic conditions is by decreasing the burdensome regulations and complicated tax rules for businesses. This boosts business confidence and results which inevitably increase tax inflows to the national treasury. Lowering the amount of government expenditures such as defense and social programs and improving the efficiency of entitlement programs like state pensions can also help countries to borrow less money.

The United States has been struggling with deficits since its founding in the 1780s. Alexander Hamilton served as Secretary of the new Treasury in the 1790s. He suggested that the states pay back their Revolutionary War debts via the Federal government using bond issues to assume them and pay them off.

The interest payments on these bonds caused deficits which were not finally eradicated until they paid off the debts in the 1860s. This set a precedent for the U.S. Every war the country fought after the Revolutionary War the nation paid for using debt. This led to increasingly larger deficits.

In the early years of the twentieth century, there were not many industrial countries that struggled with larger budget deficits and debt. This financial position changed dramatically during the First and Second World Wars. In these years, governments were forced to borrow extensively to pay for the expensive conflicts as they ran down their financial reserves.

The United States ran up enormous deficits of 17% of national GDP in World War I and 24% in World War II. The industrial nations were able to reduce their deficits into the 1960s and 1970s thanks to many years of consistent economic growth.

High budget deficits consistently will lead to high national debt. As a percentage of GDP, President Franklin D. Roosevelt earned the record for the largest national budget deficit. By 1949, he had amassed a national deficit of $568 billion that equated to nearly 130% of GDP.

While his deficits remained high because of the New Deal and war costs, they did decline to $88 billion under President Harry Truman. President Barack Obama holds the distinction of having the first $1 trillion deficit in all of history. He ran these up with stimulus programs to battle the Great Recession. In the full first four year term of his time in office, these deficits remained at over $1 trillion per year.

C Corporation

C Corporations refers to the primary subchapter under which American businesses decide to incorporate themselves in order to restrict the total financial and legal liabilities of the owners. Such C Corporations prove to be the principle alternatives to S Corporations, whose profits are able to pass directly through to the owners and so only become taxable on the individual level. Limited liability companies are the other main choice to the C corporations. They deliver all of the legal safeties of corporations yet become tax treated as if they were sole proprietorships.

Unfortunately for C Corporations, they do suffer the effects of double taxation. Yet they do also permit the businesses to reinvest their profits back into the firm with a lower corporate tax rate penalty. The majority of incorporated companies within the United States turn out to be C Corporations.

Organizing a corporation starts with the new owners selecting the new entity's name (and in many states registering or reserving it with the secretary of state) of the new business enterprise. The owners must draft up the articles of incorporation and file them with the appropriate state business department. The first shareholders will then be issued their stock certificates once the business is established. Every C Corporation has to first file the Form SS-4 in order to get their EIN employer identification number. Every jurisdiction has its own varying requirements for these obligations, yet the corporations generally must file income, state, payroll, disability, and unemployment taxes for their employees.

Such C Corporations must hold minimally one meeting per year for the benefit of both the directors and the shareholders. These must have meeting minutes kept in order to transparently display the ways and means in which the business functions. There will have to be voting records maintained of the company directors as well as a full list of all owners' names and their ownership percentages in the firm. The company bylaws are required to be kept on the business headquarter premises at all times. Such enterprises also have to file all necessary financial disclosure reports, annual reports, and relevant financial statements with the SEC.

There are many benefits to such C Corporations. Most importantly for owners, they first limit the liability of all shareholders, directors, officers, and employees. It is not possible for the legal and debt obligations from the company to transfer over to one or more individuals under this type of corporate structuring. Even if each of the company owners become changed out, the corporation continues its existence. There is no limit to the numbers of shareholders and owners with this kind of corporation either as there would be with an S Corporation. Yet these must be registered properly with the SEC Securities and Exchange Commission once they reach a certain number of shareholders.

The primary downside to the C corporations centers on the idea of double taxation. As the firm generates its income, it will have to file a corporate tax return with the IRS Internal Revenue Service. Once the appropriate business expenses (including salaries) have been deducted from the gross income, the rest becomes subjected to corporate income taxes. Much of the remaining net income will then be distributed out to shareholders in what is called dividends. The income to the shareholders must be reported on the recipients' tax returns. This means that the C Corporation profits are being twice taxed, once at the corporate tax rate level and a second on the individuals' tax rate level. That income which is retained earnings will avoid double taxation only. It helps to explain why mega corporations like Apple hold on to billions of dollars in retained earnings routinely.

Cap Rate

Cap rate refers to the real estate property and its rate of return. Investors figure this out by utilizing the income which they anticipate the property will generate. The cap rate is also referred to as the capitalization rate. Realtors utilize it to gauge how much return investors will realize on their investments.

The way people determine this cap rate is by using an easy to understand formula. Investors take the property's NOI net operating income and divide it by the current fair market value of the property. This NOI turns out to be the annual return less all operating costs. The capitalization rate formula can be written as Capitalization Rate = Net Operating Income / Current Market Value. Investors and realtors express it as a percentage.

Investors consider the cap rate to be very helpful because it summarizes information regarding real estate investments. It is also simple to understand. This important rate discerns the profitability of a given piece of property. In order for it to remain consistent, the net operating income and current market value have to be constant compared to each other. If the NOI goes up when market value remains constant, the capitalization rate rises. If instead market value increases while NOI remains the same, then this rate will go down.

Real estate investments only stay profitable if the NOI goes up at the same rate as or a greater rate than the increase in the value of the property. This is another way that the capitalization rate is helpful. It can be employed to track the performance of real estate investments through time to learn if their performance is increasing. When the rate declines instead, investors may decide to sell the property so that they can reinvest the capital in some other place.

The cap rate is especially practical because it allows individuals to measure different investments in property. It permits them to compare and contrast a number of different investment possibilities against each other. Sometimes it is not easy to compare operating income or market values of radically different properties. Comparing percentages to one another is simple and intuitive. The rate is at its most useful when either the current market value or NOI are similar. This is because investments where the cost is vastly different can create a variety of other considerations that interfere with effective comparison.

Many times investors will come up with a minimum capitalization rate which they are willing to take so that the investment is practical. They might set 12% as their minimum rate. This helps them to sift through the various possibilities to rule out the ones that do not measure up to their desired minimum.

Investors may also employ the capitalization rate to figure out the amount of time it will take for the investment to reach its payback point. They can find the payback period by taking 100 and dividing it by the capitalization rate. This will provide an estimate of the payback period and not a fixed number. Most investments will see their capitalization rate change during significant amounts of time.

Another useful way of determining the value for a real estate investment is to utilize direct capitalization. To find this number, investors simply divide their NOI by the cap rate. This provides them with the capital cost of the real estate investment in question.

Investors should realize that the capitalization rate is not so helpful for shorter time frame investments as it is for longer ones. Figuring up NOI requires some time to determine a cash flow number that is reliable.

Capital Account

Capital Account demonstrates the net changes in the financial asset ownership for any country. When added in with the national current account, this makes up the given country's balance of payments. This capital account will always include such things as portfolio investment and FDI foreign direct investment as well as any changes in the reserve account. It is also possible for the capital account to refer to any account which displays a company's net worth at a particular moment and snapshot in time.

On a macro-economic scale, what the capital account actually figures up is the total economic production for a region or entire nation. With corporations it is different. Here the capital account is actually a general ledger account that the firm will utilize to record the sums of money which any investor provides the company with in exchange for a stake. It also shows the accumulative amount of the earnings of the firm less the accumulative distributions to the various stakeholders in the firm. These balances become reportable in the owner's equity section, the stockholder's equity section, or the partner's equity section on balance sheets.

Where nations are concerned, the capital accounts total up all of the economic affairs of the nation as a whole. Markets are particularly concerned with this figure as it reveals the total picture and general direction of the nation economically. It also delivers a range of sell and buy signals for a number of different portfolio strategies and particular industries.

The balance of trade for a nation is a component of the national balance of payments. Take the United States as an example. The balance of payments within the U.S. is comprised of three subaccounts. These are the capital account, the current account, and the financial account. Each of these possesses its own special outflows and inflows.

Analysts and economists like to use the balance of trade. It helps them to more effectively grasp the national economic strength as measured against other competing nations. Take another example. Nations that possess huge trade deficits like the United States and Great Britain will generally borrow money in order to purchase foreign-produced goods and services. Those countries like Germany with enormous trade surpluses usually engage in the opposite activity. Such a balance of trade often corresponds to the political situation in a nation as it reveals how much foreign investment occurs in the receiving nation.

With corporations, it is once again different. They will have a great number of capital accounts. Those capital accounts which are for paid-in capital include preferred stock, common stock, and paid-in capital that stands in excess of par. These sums report in the money which the firm receives in as they float their share of capital stock to various investors. Retained earnings represent the accumulative earnings less accumulative dividends which they have paid out to stake holders. The account for treasury stock reports the sum of money the firm pays out to buy back shares of its stock (which are not retired).

Where sole proprietorships are concerned, there will be a capital account that shows the initial investment of the owner. This will grow every year by the amount of the annual earnings less the yearly withdrawals. There will also be a drawing account, many times referred to as a contra account. Its debit balance will equate to the amount of assets of the firm that the owner draws down in a given accounting year for his or her personal use. When the conclusion of the accounting year arrives, this drawing account becomes closed through transferring over any debit balance to the company capital account. It is a requirement that the balances in the various capital accounts have to equal the as-reported sum of all assets less liabilities of the firm.

Capital Adequacy Ratio

The Capital Adequacy Ratio refers to a metric for sizing up the capital of a given bank. It is usually written out in terms of a percentage of the risk weighted credit exposures of a bank. This formula is also referred to as CRAR or capital to risk weighted assets ratio. It is commonly employed to help ensure that the money from depositors is safeguarded while promoting the efficiency and stability of the globe's various financial systems.

There are two different types of capital which this ratio measures. The first is Tier One Capital, able to absorb significant losses without causing a bank to stop trading. Tier Two Capital instead refers to those losses which will be sufficient to see through a bank wind down which actually offers less protection to the bank depositors. The official expression of CAR takes the form of Tier One Capital plus Tier Two Capital divided by the amount or Risk Weighted Assets.

Government regulators have determined that such minimum capital adequacy ratios are crucial in order to be sure that the various banks maintain a large enough cushion to suffer a reasonable sum in losses before the y fall into insolvency, having lost the funds of their depositors. By reducing the risks of banks sinking into insolvency, the Capital Adequacy Ratios make certain that the financial system of the nation are both providing stability and efficiency. When even one good-sized bank becomes officially insolvent, this shatters the financial system confidence potentially in a move that upsets the whole financial market system of the nation in which it occurs.

When such an insolvent bank is being wound down, the depositors' funds receive the highest possible priority as compared to the capital of the bank. This means that depositors only have their savings at risk if the losses which the bank experiences are higher than the level of capital which it claims on its balance sheet. In other words, the larger the Capital Adequacy Ratio of the bank proves to be, the greater the amount of protection exists for the monies deposited by the bank depositors.

The Tier One Capital turns out to be that money which is constantly available and readily liquid in order to offset any losses which the bank suffers without having to cease operations. Ordinary share capital is considered to be a fine example for such Tier One Capital.

The Tier Two Capital by contrast is the amount which cushions depositors from losses when the bank winds down. It offers a significantly lower amount of protection to both the depositors and especially to the creditors. If the bank were to suffer the devastating loss of all of its Tier One Capital, this Tier Two Capital would be the one the bank fell back on subsequently.

Actually measuring the banks' credit exposure requires making necessary adjustments to the asset values declared on the balance sheet of the lender. Every one of the loans the bank made will be weighted according to its degrees of risk. Loans which were made to the government or one of its agencies weight at zero percent. Those made to individuals receive a weighting of 100 percent for maximum potential risk.

There are also off-balance sheet agreements, foreign exchange guarantees and contracts that pose credit risks to the banks. These will be converted over to their credit equivalent amounts before being risk weighted according to the same design of the on-balance sheet credit kinds of exposures. Both on-balance and off-balance sheet credit exposures will finally be combined in order to come up with the final risk weighted credit exposures.

The United States sets its own minimum Capital Adequacy Ratio depending on the tier which the regulators assign to the individual bank in question. They do not allow the Tier One Capital for the bank as divided by its total risk weighted exposure to drop below four percent. The total capital requires that the full risk weighted credit exposure remains higher than eight percent.

Capital Expenditures

Capital expenditure refers to money that a firm employs to purchase physical assets. This can also be used to upgrade existing assets. These can include items such as equipment, industrial buildings, and property. It is also known as CapEx. Companies often use this CapEx to make new investments or to begin a new project.

Other corporations utilize capital expenditures to build up their operations' size and scale. Such expenditures can cover many different items like buying a new piece of equipment, fixing the roof on a company building, or constructing a new factory for the company.

Accounting procedures utilize this capital expenditure concept regularly. Expenses will be labeled as CapEx if the item the company buys is a new purchase of a capital asset. They also fall under this category when the purchase is some type of investment that extends the practical life of an already owned capital asset.

When a purchase falls under the capital expenditure's category, the accounting department will be required to capitalize it. They do this when the fixed cost of the purchase is spread out over the asset's useful life. In other cases, the money they spend will only keep the capital item in its present condition. For these scenarios the company and accountants may simply deduct the entire expense for the year in which they spend the money.

Different industries will employ varying levels of capital expenditures. Some use very little, while others are more capital intensive. Among the most intensive capital industries in the world are the exploration and production of energy such as oil or natural gas, manufacturing businesses, telecommunications, and electricity, gas, and water utilities.

It is important to not confuse capital expenditures with other ideas like operating expenses, known as OPEX, or revenue expenditures. Operating and revenue expenses are money that companies pay to cover the daily cost of running the business. Revenue expenses are different from CapEx in another significant way. The former can be completely deducted from taxes in the year in which the company spends them.

Capital expenditures can be used to help come up with the relative value of a company also. Cash flow to capital expenditure ratio is one such measure. It is commonly referred to as CF/CapEx. This explains the ability of a company to purchase assets for long term use by utilizing its free cash flow. This ratio commonly goes up and down for businesses as they engage in cycles of small capital versus large capital expenses.

Ideally a business wants to have a higher multiple in this ratio. Higher numbers signify that the company is in a position of solid financial health and strength. This is because firms that possess the financial capabilities to invest in their future with capital expenditures can expand with greater ease and flexibility.

Cash flows to capital expenditures are ratios that are specific to every industry. Each segment's ratio will be different. This means that the ratio of one company in one business should not be compared to a second company in another industry. Instead, the ratio is only useful for comparison when two companies that possess comparable CapEx requirements are examined. Comparing various CapEx ratios from two oil firms or utility companies makes sense. Holding up the CapEx ratios of an oil company or telecom firm against a consulting business or advertising agency does not.

The higher a company's capital expenditure is, the lower its other measures of financial health may be. As an example, firms with high CapEx will often show less free cash flow to equity.

Capital Loss

Capital Loss refers to a type of loss that companies or individuals experience as one of their capital assets decreases by value. This includes a real estate or investment asset. The loss only becomes realized when the asset itself sells for less than the price for which it was originally purchased. Another way of looking at these capital losses is that they represent the difference from the asset's purchase price and the asset's selling price. In other words, for it to be a loss the selling price must be less than the original price. As an example, when investors purchase a home for $300,000 and then sell the same home six years later for only $260,000, they have taken a capital loss amounting to $40,000.

Where income taxes are concerned, capital losses often offset capital gains. Capital losses in fact reduce the personal or business income in a like dollar for dollar amount. When net losses are higher than $3,000, then the overage amount can not be applied. Instead, this amount higher than net $3,000 simply carries over against any other gains or taxable income to the following year when they will similarly offset capital gains and income. When losses are multiple thousands, they continue to carry forward as many years as it takes for them to be fully exhausted.

Both capital losses and capital gains will be reported using a Form 8949. This form helps taxpayers to determine if the sale dates allow for the transactions to be counted as long term or short term losses or gains. When such transactions are deemed to be short term gains, they become taxable by the individual's ordinary income tax rates. These ranged from only 10 percent to 39.6 percent as of 2015. This is why the shorter term losses when paired off against shorter term gains give significant tax advantages to higher income earning individuals. It benefits them when they have earned profits by selling off any asset or assets in under a year from original purchase point.

With longer term capital gains, investors become taxed by rates of zero percent, 15 percent, or 20 percent. This occurs when they take a gain which results from a position they possessed for over a year. Such capital gains also can only be offset by capital losses which they realize after holding the investments for over a year. It is also on form 8949 that these assets become reportable. Here investors list out both the gross proceeds from the sales and assets' cost basis. The two figures are compared to determine if the total sales equate to a loss, gain, or wash. Such losses become reported on Schedule D. Here the taxpayer is able to ascertain the amount that may be utilized to lower overall taxable income.

These wash sale rules can be confusing to individuals without an example. Consider an investor who dumps his IBM stock on the last day of November in order to realize a loss. The taxing authority of the Internal Revenue Service will disallow such a capital loss if the exact stock was bought again on the day of December 30th or before this. This is because investors have to wait at least 31 days before such a security can be repurchased then sold off once more in order to realize another loss.

Yet the regulation does not affect sales and re-buys of different mutual funds that possess similar positions and holdings. As an example, $10,000 worth of Vanguard Energy Fund shares may be entirely reinvested in the Fidelity Select Energy Portfolio at any point. This would not forfeit the investors' ability to recognize another loss even as they continue to own an equity portfolio (through the mutual fund) that is similar to their earlier mutual fund holdings.

Capital Stock

A business' capital stock is the up front capital that the founders of the firm invest in or put into the company. This capital stock also proves useful as security for a business' creditors. This is because capital stock may not be taken out of the business to disadvantage the creditors in question. Such stock is separate from a business' assets or property that can rise and fall in value and amount.

A company's capital stock is segregated into shares. The complete number of such shares have to be detailed when the business is founded. Based on the entire sum of money that is put into the company when it is started up, each share will possess a particular face value that must be declared.

This value is referred to as par value of the individual shares. These par values are the minimum sums of money that may be issued and sold in stock shares by the business. It is similarly the capital value representation in the business' own accounting. In some countries, these shares do not contain any par value period. In this case, the capital stock shares would be termed non par value stock. Such shares literally represent a portion of an ownership in the business in question. These businesses may then declare various classes of shares. All of these could have their own privileges, rules, and share values.

The owning of such capital stock shares is proven by the possession of a certificate of stock. These stock certificates prove to be legal documents that detail the numbers of shares each shareholder owns. Other particular data of the capital stock shares, including class of shares and par value, is similarly detailed on these certificates.

These owners of the firm in question may decide that they need more capital in order to invest in additional projects that the company has in mind. Besides this, they might decide that they want to cash out some of their own holdings in order to release a portion of capital for their own private needs. They can do this by selling all or some of their capital stock to many partial owners. The ownership of one such share gives the share owner an ownership stake in the company. This includes such privileges as a tiny portion of any profits that may be paid out as dividends, as well as a small part of any decision making powers.

These shares sold from the capital stock each represent a single vote. The owners could decide to offer various classes of shares that could then have differing rights of voting. By owning a majority of the shares, the owners can out vote all of the little shareholders combined. This permits the original owners to maintain effective control of their company even after issuing shares of their capital stock to investors.

Cash Flow

Cash Flow is either an incoming revenue or outgoing expense stream that affects the value of any cash account over time. Inflows of cash, or positive cash flows, typically result from one of three possible activities, including operations, investing, or financing for businesses or individuals. Individuals are also able to realize positive cash flows from gifts or donations.

Negative cash flow is also called cash outflows. Outflows of cash happen because of either expenses or investments made. This is the case for both individuals' finances, as well as for those of businesses.

Where both individual finances and business corporate finances are concerned, positive cash flows are required to maintain solvency. Cash flows could be demonstrated because of a past transaction like selling a business product or a personal item or investment. They might also be projected into a future time for some consideration that a company or individual anticipates receiving and then possibly spending. No person or corporation can survive for long without cash flow.

Positive cash flow is essential for a variety of needs. Sufficient cash flow allows for money for you to pay your personal bills and creditors. It also allows a business to cover the costs of employee payroll, suppliers' bills, and creditors' payments in a timely fashion. When individuals and businesses lack sufficient cash on hand to maintain their budget or operations, then they are named insolvent. Lasting insolvency generally leads to personal or corporate bankruptcy.

For businesses, statements of cash flows are created by accountants. These demonstrate the quantity of cash that is created and utilized by a corporation in a certain time frame. Cash flows in this definition are calculated by totaling net income following taxes with non cash charges like depreciation. Cash flow is able to be assigned to either a business' entire operations or to one particular segment or project of the company. Cash flow is often considered to be an effective measurement of a business' ongoing financial strength.

Cash flows are also used by business and individuals to ascertain the value or return of a project or investment. The numbers of cash flows in to and out of such projects and investments are often utilized as inputs for indicators of performance like net present value and internal rate of return. A problem with a business' liquidity can also be determined by measuring the entire entity's cash flow.

Many individuals prefer investments that yield periodic positive cash flow over ones that pay only one time capital gains. High yielding dividend stocks, energy trusts, and real estate investment trusts are all examples of positive cash flow investments. Real estate properties can also be positive cash flow yielding investments when they provide greater amounts of rental income than their combined monthly mortgage payments, maintenance expenses, and property management upkeep costs and outflows total.

Cash Flow Quadrant

The cash flow quadrant is a diagram that shows four types of individuals involved in a business. These four people make up the entire business world. The four quadrants are E, S, B, and I.

The E quadrant stands for employees. Employees have the same core values in general. This is security. When any employee sits down with a manager or a president, they will always tell them the same thing. This is that they are looking for a secure and safe job that includes benefits.

The S in the cash flow quadrant represents a small business owner or a self employed person. They are generally solo actors or one person outfits. These types would rather operate on their own, as their motto is always to have something done right, you should do it yourself.

On the right side of the cash flow quadrant are the B's. B stands for Big Business people. Big businesses have five hundred or greater numbers of employees. They are completely different from the others in the quadrants, as they are constantly looking for the most intelligent and capable people, networks, and systems to aid them in running their large business. They do not want to micro manage the company themselves, rather they want good people to do it on their behalf.

The last quarter of the cash flow quadrants is the I, which stands for Investor. Investors are those individuals who make money work effectively and efficiently for themselves. The main difference between them and the B quadrants it that the investors have their money working hard while the Big Business people have other people working hard for them. Both groups of B's and I's represent the wealthy. The employees and the self employed are the people who work hard for the business people and investors on the right, or wealthy side of the quadrant.

The cash flow quadrant explains the differences between the rich and the working poor. It is useful to describe four types of income that a person can generate as well. The smartest people in the cash flow quadrant are the ones who manage to make the other people and their money work hard for their benefit. That is why they are the wealthy, while the hard working members of society on the left side are the ones who do all of the working on the wealthy people's behalf. Learning to become wealthy means effectively changing which square of the cash flow quadrant a person occupies.

Cash Flow Statement (CFS)

The Cash Flow Statement (CFS) proves to be one of three critical components in any corporation's financial reports. The other two are income statements and balance sheets. From 1987, the SEC Securities Exchange Commission has mandated that such cash flow statements be included with all corporate financial reports. This statement details the quantities of cash and cash equivalents that come into and flow out of a firm. Such a CFS permits the stake holders and potential investors alike to comprehend the way corporations' operations are functioning, how they are effectively spending the money, and from where their money originates in the first place.

There are differences that separate these Cash Flow Statements from the balance sheets and income statements. The principal one is that CFSs do not cover the future anticipated outgoing and incoming cash amounts which have already been recorded under the credit sales category. It explains why the component cash is never identical to net income. Both balance sheets and income statements cover not only cash sales, but also sales that happen on credit. In the end, a firm's cash flow is derived from three separate means of money coming in and leaving a corporation. These are cash from operations, cash from financing, and cash from investing.

Cash from Operations comprise both the cash inflow and outflow which result from the mainstay operation of the business. This means that they show the quantity of cash that the firms' services and products actually accrue to the business. Cash from operations would usually include changes to cash, depreciation, accounts receivable, accounts payable, and inventory.

The Cash from Financing component includes loans, changes in debt, and dividends. As capital becomes raised, this is a cash-in accounting item. As dividends pay out, it becomes marked as a cash-out event. As an example, when firms sell bonds on the markets, the firm obtains cash financing. As the corporation pays the associated interest out to the holders of the bonds, then the firm reduces its cash by the corresponding amount.

The final category of Cash from Investing covers all changes in assets, equipment, or company investments. These are commonly considered to be cash out events. This is because cash will be utilized to purchase new buildings, buy factory or other production equipment, and acquire other types of assets which are short term (like securities which are easily marketable). It is not always the case that these are cash negative events though. As any firms choose to sell off one or more of their assets, this creates a cash-in transaction. It would then be notated as a positive accounting item under the cash from investing category. When companies sell shares they hold in another firm, the revenue this generates becomes accounted for under the Cash from Investing.

Cash flow becomes calculated by adjustments that accountants make to net income. They simply add in (or alternatively subtract out) any differences in expenses, revenue, and credit types of transactions that appear on the income statements and balance sheets since the last accounting period. Such transactions happen every accounting period. These adjustments will be reviewed and amended as non-cash items go into the income statement under net income while liabilities and total assets go on to the balance sheet. Since not every type of financial transaction of a firm relates to real cash items, a great number of items must be reconsidered when the accountants are figuring up the cash flow from operations.

Company accountants deduce the cash flow statement calculations and compile them into official corporate report documents every reportable quarter. The SEC requires that they make this a part of every quarterly report and also each annual report which they must divulge to analysts and members of the investing public by law.

Cash Management

Cash management refers to the corporate functions of gathering, handling, and short term investing cash. This represents a critical part of making certain a firm is financially viable and stays solvent. In many cases, the business managers of a company or corporate treasurers of a large corporation will handle the aggregate cash management responsibilities. This means they will be responsible for ensuring the firm continues to be financially viable and solvent on a week to week basis.

There is more to successfully handled cash management than simply sidestepping financial problems or even bankruptcy. This job also involves bringing in invoice payments and account receivables, boosting the rates and speed of collection, improving the level of available cash at hand, and picking out relevant short term investment instruments which will all contribute to better profits and a stronger cash position for the firm in question.

Those small business managers and developers must learn to manage cash flow well since they do not enjoy low cost access to easy credit. They also encounter many ongoing running costs that they have to stay on top of while they are waiting for their customers to pay their receivables. By properly and prudently managing their cash flow, firms are able to cover unanticipated costs and to effectively cover their routine financial events like payroll on a bi-weekly or semi-monthly basis. The point of cash management is to effectively balance out two main corporate counteracting forces. These are the receivables for incoming cash and the outflows of payables.

Part of the dilemma for many companies struggling to effectively run their cash management operations is that invoices and receivables are positive cash flow on the books, yet in practice they are not always received immediately. Some invoice terms allow for the customer to wait from 30 to 60 to even 90 days to settle their invoices. This is how businesses can actually find themselves in the uncomfortable position of their sales growing even rapidly and still have cash flow problems because their receivables come in slowly or even unfortunately late.

Businesses have a variety of tools and means to speed up their receivables so that their payment float becomes reduced. Some of these are to deploy an auto billing service that immediately invoices the customers electronically, to make clear the billing and payment terms to the clients, to keep on top of all collections with an aging receivables spreadsheet, to offer incentives for same as cash 10 day invoice payments, and to collect payments via electronic payment processing at a bank.

Businesses which are successful in controlling their payables will be better capable of maintaining positive cash flows. Through streamlining the efficiency of the payables operations, firms are able to lower their costs all the while holding on to more cash which they can put to work in the company operations. There are a wide variety of effective payable management solutions available today. Some of these include direct payroll deposits, payment processing which is handled electronically, and closely and carefully controlled cash disbursements. Each of these processes will help to both automate and make efficient all of the payout operations.

Thanks to the variety of digital age offerings, the vast majority of payable management and receivable operations may be simply automated through current day solutions in business banking. Smaller companies are now able to operate with the same big scale technologies for cash management as the mega corporations. This is in no small part due to the rapid march of technological advances across business solutions and banking. Such cost savings created by these cutting-edged cash management techniques effectively more than offset the costs of utilizing them. The best part of the process nowadays is that a firm's management is capable of allocating critical resources to expanding the core business better than ever before possible.

Cash On Cash Return (CCR)

Cash on cash return, also known by its acronym CCR, is an investing term. It describes a ratio of the yearly cash flow before taxes against the total sum of cash invested. This cash on cash return is expressed as a percentage.

Cash on cash return is mostly utilized to analyze any income generating asset's actual cash flow situation. This percentage is commonly applied as a simple and quick test to decide if an asset under consideration is worthy of additional study and analysis. An investor who believed that cash flow is the greatest goal would be most interested in an analysis based on cash on cash return. Others employ it to discover if a particular property or asset turns out to be under priced. This would mean that equity in a property would exist immediately upon purchase.

Cash on cash return formulas do not figure in any deprecation or appreciation of an income producing asset. This means that the cash on cash return number may be skewed to the high side if some of the cash flow produced turns out to be a return on capital. This is because return on capital is not income.

Another limitation to cash on cash returns as a measurement lies in the fact that the calculation is more or less one of simple interest. This means that it does not take into consideration the compounding of interest. As a result of this, investments that provide a lower compound interest rate might be better over time than those that provide greater cash on cash returns, which is only a simple interest calculation.

A last downside to using cash on cash returns as a means of evaluating an investment centers around the fact that they are only pre tax cash flow evaluations. This means that your tax situation as a unique investor will not be considered in the formula. Varying tax situations can determine if an investment is a good match for you or not.

Consider an example of figuring up out a cash on cash return. You could buy an apartment complex for $1,200,000 using a down payment of $300,000. Every month, the resulting rental cash flow after expenses for this property is $5,000. This means that in a year, the income before tax would amount to $60,000, as $5,000 was multiplied by twelve months. This would make the cash on cash return the cash flow for the year before taxes of $60,000 over the entire amount of money invested in the asset of $300,000. This results in an actual twenty percent cash on cash return.

Cash Operating Cost

Cash Operating Cost refers to a cash flow statement which effectively follows all cash types of business expenditures. It is in the first section of a cash flow statement, the operating activities, that keeps all relevant and pertinent information regarding the cash operating costs. Such expenses are derived from the firm's information on financial accounting. It does not matter if the expense items are variable or fixed.

The cash flow statement merely details the quantity of such cash operating costs as well as if the firm had a cash outflow or inflow over a particular time frame. This section covers a variety of cash expenditures. Among these are payables, assets, and various other current liabilities.

Payables are those things that corporations buy on account. They promise to pay the vendor later on in the arrangement. There are a wide variety of items which will be detailed in this section. Among them are wages, notes, interest, payroll, and any taxes due. Cash utilization happens as a company pays off the prior balance on any such items in the current month period. There will be a single line that refers to the repayment of these types of liabilities in the cash operating costs. Payables accounts increasing mean that cash flow for the firm is decreasing to match. This is because these are money the company has spent.

Assets prove to be among the most significant category of these cash operating costs. This is particularly the case with retail and manufacturing businesses that will be heavy on assets especially. Such assets detailed out here would include inventory, prepaid assets, supplies, accounts receivable, and other forms of current assets. Such items are typically utilized in the day to day business operations. The anticipation is that the various individual groups will not last for over 12 months. For these, the statement of cash flows shows real money which the firm pays for such items. Each particular category will have its own line on the statement along with the aggregate amount the category spend in a particular time frame.

The categories of other current liabilities will be a last section of the cash operating costs. Such items can be revenue that is unearned or various other current liabilities which firms incur in the normal course of business operations. Every item which does not adhere to the above two criterion will be listed out by the accountants in this category section. This includes special and one time items. It allows for the company accountant to make shareholders aware of substantial types of expenses which the normal business operations are costing. Sometime special disclosures will be required to be made to the various stock holders when major cash position reductions occur as a result of them.

Such statements of cash flow are useful for external and internal stake holders in a given corporation alike. The company accountants can also put together various other types of reports to show the cash operating costs for the firm. Such reports would be less formal yet still official. They explain the relevant cost items for the internal stakeholders such as upper level management and the board of directors. So long as the accountant utilize standard accounting processes, any range of statistics and figures could be included in the informational reports. In these cases, they may use whatever format they wish to produce the additional illuminating report.

Cash Reserves

Cash reserves refer to money which an individual person, a company, or a corporation saves in order to be ready to cover any emergency funding or short term requirements. They can also be utilized to refer to a kind of extremely liquid, short term investment which usually garners a poor rate of return (under three percent in a year).

An example of this would be Fidelity Cash Reserves, one of the Fidelity mutual families of funds particular investments. Sometimes individuals will hold money they need rapid access to in such a fund which can be instantly liquidated on the same day they issue the order. Possessing a major amount in a cash reserve fund provides corporations, companies, individuals, families, or communities with the necessary capability to engage in a significant purchase right away.

There are various reasons why firms wish to maintain some cash reserves. They need to have sufficient money on hand in order to cover all of their costs which may be anticipated or even unanticipated over the short term time-frame. Besides this, they often prefer to have enough cash readily available for such interesting possible investments which could arise with little to no warning.

Though cash is always considered to be the most liquid type of wealth and assets, there are also short term kinds of assets like three month U.S. Treasury bills which investors also deem to be a type of a cash reserve because of the ease and frequency with which they can exchange them and their close proximity to maturity date. Major corporations like Alphabet (Google), General Electric, IBM, and Apple keep enormous cash reserves available. These typically range from fifty billion dollars to one hundred and fifty billion dollars.

At the beginning of 2016, Apple boasted such cash reserve ranging from fifty billion to one hundred fifty billion dollars. At the same time, Alphabet (Google) counted $75.3 billion in their immediate cash on hand reserves. This permitted Google to buy out major corporate purchases like their acquisition of Nest, which they bought for a hefty $3 billion price tag back in 2014.

With banks, governmental oversight agencies require that they maintain a minimum quantity of cash reserves on hand. This is because their operations are critical for the functioning of any economy. In the United States, it is the American Federal Reserve that determines these cash reserve amounts for the banks. In other countries, it is often the national central bank or some other governmental oversight regulator who makes the call.

Banking cash reserves will typically be set as a certain percentage of the banks' liabilities or net transaction accounts. With those banks which contain in excess of $110.2 million in their net transaction accounts, this amount within the U.S. proves to be 10 percent of such liabilities. This amount became effective on January 1st of 2016. Such bank reserves have to be kept in either deposits at a Federal Reserve Bank or in their own vaults as cash on hand. With euro currency liabilities or time deposits of a non-personal nature, these liabilities are not subjected to such a cash reserve requirement.

Economists and personal finance gurus generally state that individuals are wise to keep minimally sufficient cash on hand to cover from three to six months of expenses in the event they suffer a family emergency. Such an emergency fund is a form of a cash reserve. These reserves would be kept in either their local bank accounts or otherwise in a stable and short term time frame investment which will maintain its value regardless of what happens in the markets. In this way, individuals are able to draw on their own emergency funds or alternatively to sell such investments at a moment's notice without taking a financial loss. This needs to be the case no matter how the financial investment markets are performing.

Other forms of personal cash reserves could be held in a savings account, checking account, money market account, money market fund, or even CDs and Treasury Bills. For those businesses or individuals who do not plan ahead with enough cash reserves, they may have to instead to fall back on credit, loans, or in some drastic cases, declaring bankruptcy.

Certified Public Accountant (CPA)

CPA's, or certified public accountants, are accountants who have taken and successfully completed a series of demanding exams that are given by the American Institute of Certified Public Accountants. Many states also have their own state level exams that have to be passed along with the national one.

CPA'a are accountants in every sense of the word, but not every accountant is qualified as a CPA. Because of the difficulties in becoming a CPA, there are many accountants who either never attempt or never succeed in successfully passing the Certified Public Accountant exam. This does not mean such an accountant is not qualified to practice accounting tasks, only that he or she will not be allowed to do tasks that require specific CPA credentials.

Such Certified Public Accountants do a number of varying tasks and jobs. Many will provide advice and simple income tax preparing for various clients who might be comprised of corporations, small companies, or individuals. Besides this, Certified Public Accountants practice many other tasks that include auditing, keeping the records of businesses, and consulting for business entities.

Keeping a CPA license is not accomplished through automatic renewal. Certified Public Accountants are required to engage in a full one hundred and twenty hours of courses on continuing education in every three year period. This is so that they will be on top of any and all changes going on in the field of their chosen profession.

The opportunities for Certified Public Accountants are many and varied. The FBI seeks to hire them routinely, preferring applicant candidates with either such a CPA background or alternatively an attorney background. Numerous state and Federal government agencies offer CPA's opportunities by providing CPA positions. Businesses ranging from small companies to large corporations also seek them out. With these firms, CPA's can occupy positions ranging from controllers, to CFO or Chief Financial Officers, to CEO's or Chief Executive Officers.

Among the most significant parts that CPA's can play proves to be one of a consultant. As a consultant, Certified Public Accountants can be looking into possible means of saving small businesses or even enormous corporations money on expenses or putting together specific financial plans that permit a corporation or business to appear more appealing to investors or possible buyers. Certified Public Accountants are sworn to a particular code of ethical conduct. They are required to provide their clients with honest and reliable advice that is also ethical.

Certified Public Accountants who do not stay within the bounds of their ethical code can lead to the total financial failure of a firm. This turned out to be the case in recent years at Enron, the energy trading and producing giant. Not only were Enron corporate executives charged for illegal accounting activities, but also a number of CPA's from nationally renowned accounting firm Arthur Anderson were charged with unethical practices of accounting.

Chapter 7 Bankruptcy

Chapter 7 bankruptcy is a form of protection from creditors. Unlike Chapter 13 bankruptcy, it does not have any repayment plan. In the Chapter 7 a bankruptcy trustee determines what eligible assets the debtor individual or company has. The trustee then collects these available assets, sells them, and distributes proceeds to the creditors against their debts. This is all done under the rules of the Bankruptcy Code.

Debtors are permitted to keep specific property that is exempt, such as their house. Other property that the debtor holds will be mortgaged or have liens put against it to pledge it to the various creditors until it is liquidated. Debtors who file chapter 7 will likely forfeit property in partial payment of debts.

Chapter 7 bankruptcy is available to corporations, partnerships, and individuals who pass a means test. The relief can be granted whether or not the debtor is ruled to be insolvent.

Chapter 7 bankruptcy cases start when debtors file their petitions with their particular area's bankruptcy court. For businesses, they use the address where the main office is located. Debtors are required to give the court information that includes schedules of current expenditures and income and liabilities and assets.

They are also required to furnish a financial affairs statement and a schedule of contracts and leases which are not expired. The debtors will also have to deliver the trustee tax return copies from the most current tax year along with any tax returns which they file while the case is ongoing.

Debtors who are individuals also have to furnish their court with other documents. They are required to file a credit counseling certificate and any repayment plan created there. They must also file proof of income from employers 60 days before their original filing, a monthly income statement along with expected increases in either, and notice of interest they have in tuition or state education accounts. Husbands and wives are allowed to file individually or jointly. They must abide by the requirements for individual debtors either way.

The courts are required to charge debtors who file $335 in filing, administrative, and trustee fees. Debtors typically pay these when they file to the clerk of court. The court can give permission for individuals to pay by installments instead. When the income of debtor's proves to be less than 150% of the amount of the poverty level, the court can choose to drop the fee requirements.

Debtors will have to provide a great amount of information in order to complete their Chapter 7 filing and receive a discharge of debts. They have to list out each of their creditors along with the amounts they owe then and the type of claim. Debtors have to furnish a list of all property the own. They must also give the information on the amount, source, and frequency of income they have to the court.

Finally, they will be required to provide an in depth list of all monthly living expenses that includes housing, utilities, food, transportation, clothing, medicine, and taxes. This helps the court to determine if the debtor is able to set up a repayment plan instead of discharging the debts.

From 21 to 40 days after the debtor files the petition with the courts, the trustee hosts a creditors' meeting. The debtor will have to cooperate with the trustee on any requests for additional financial documents or records. At this meeting, the trustee will ask questions to make sure the debtor is fully aware of the consequences of debt discharge by the bankruptcy court. Sometimes trustees will deliver this in written form to the debtor before or at the meeting. Assuming the trustee makes the recommendation for discharge, the Federal bankruptcy court judge will discharge the debts when the process is completed.

Clearing House

A Clearing House refers to a financial intermediary that exists between sellers and buyers of financial instruments such as stocks, bonds, futures, options, and mutual funds. At the same time, it is also an agency which operates in tandem with a futures exchange. In this capacity, they handle clearing trades, settling trading accounts, collecting and maintaining monies for margin accounts, reporting trades, and regulating delivery of the relevant financial instruments. These clearing houses serve as third parties for all options and futures contracts. They are also simultaneously buyers for each seller who is a clearing member and sellers for every buyer who is a clearing member.

Another way of looking at this is that the clearing houses take on the opposite side of every trade transacted. As two investors consent to a financial transaction and its terms, the clearing house will work in the critical capacity as middle man for the two participating third parties. This involves selling and buying securities. The ultimate reason of existence for clearing houses lies in boosting the efficiency of markets and increasing the financial stability of the relevant markets.

Futures markets are most closely connected to clearing houses. The reason for this is that their financial instruments prove to be exceedingly complex. They must therefore have a stable financial intermediary backing them up. Every futures exchange maintains its own proprietary clearing house. This forces every exchange member to clear its trades via the clearing house by no later than the end of every trading session. They will have to deposit a given amount of margin money with the clearing house based on the maintained margin requirements so that they can cover any deficit member balance.

It always helps to consider a real world clear example to illuminate a challenging concept such as this one. If Godfrey's Futures, a member broker, alerts the clearing house of the commodity and futures exchange at trading day end that it net bought 30,000 bushels of May soybeans for its customer accounts, then it will subsequently be required to deposit the margin cover of six cents or each individual net bushel position. This would amount to $1,800 in total deposit to be on hand with the clearing house in question. Since every member will have to clear out all trades via the house and so has to keep enough funds to cover their debit balances, it is ultimately the clearing house that carries the responsibility to all member broker dealers to fulfill the contracts according to the appropriate terms.

Within the United States today, there exist two separate most important clearing houses. These are the NASDAQ and the NYSE New York Stock Exchange. At the NYSE, they facilitate all mutual funds, bonds, exchange traded funds, stocks, and derivatives trading and contracts. They serve as the middle man on every side of an auction trade which allows for investors and brokers to purchase and sell off securities to other third parties and customers. They do this by matching up the highest bid price with the lowest ask price.

The NYSE actually maintains an expansive physical trading floor in pursuit of this important mission and purpose. On the other hand, the NASDAQ also has to do the same functions, yet it does not have the advantage of a physical trading floor on which to do it. All NASDAQ trades they match up entirely electronically for their various broker dealers and investor customers.

Compound Annual Growth Rate (CAGR)

Compound Annual Growth Rate refers to the measurement which attempts to reduce the volatility of annual gains in growth during a set out number of years. The growth gains it considers include income, profits, customers, and more. The idea is to reduce the volatility over the years as if the growth had occurred evenly each year in the time frame under consideration. It can also be defined more technically as the average annual rate of growth for a given investment throughout a defined time period that exceeds a single year.

This means that the Compound Annual Growth Rate is not actually the real rate of return. Instead it is more like a representative figure. In other words, it is a fictitious percentage that spells out the investment return rate assuming that growth in said investment had been even and consistent over the years. In the real world, this almost never occurs. The reason to use such an artificial construct as this CAGR is to make the returns on a given investment more understandable.

Determining this Compound Annual Growth Rate is complex. It involves taking the investment value at the conclusion of the period under consideration. This must be divided by the value from the start of the period. The result has to be raised to a power of one divided by the total period length. This number that results must then be subtracted from the whole number one to get the final result for CAGR. It is a complicated formula that is difficult for most people to grasp if they are not mathematicians.

This is why looking at a tangible example makes it simpler to follow. Assume a certain corporation had three years of sales that were $300 million in the first year, $450 million in the second year, and $800 million in the third year. The growth rate was different every year. Its second year it increased by 50 percent while its third year the growth rate was almost 78 percent. Using the Compound Annual Growth Rate would smooth this out to provide a picture as if the company's rate of growth per year had been steady over the three years considered. It is the compounding part that makes the formula so complex. This also explains why investors and analysts who figure this value will use a business calculator or a program that figures out the equation for them once they plug in the appropriate numbers of starting value, end value, and number of years.

Yet the Compound Annual Growth Rate is useful to businesses, investors, and analysts in particular. It helps investors who are interested in comparing and contrasting the rates of growth (over a predetermined amount of time) for two or more funds or firms. This would not be a simple task if they instead utilized the volatile and changing year over year growth rates.

Thanks to the simplicity of this measurement, it has utility in several other cases. In its simplest form, investors or analysts can employ the CAGR to figure out the average annual growth for one investment. As an example, investments might gain in relative value each year at the varying rates of plus seven percent the first year, minus one percent the second year, then plus six percent the third year. Using this CAGR will help the investor or analyst to get a bigger picture of the three year progress made by the investment in question.

Compound Interest

Compound interest represents interest which calculates on both the original principal amount as well as the interest that was accumulated previously during the loan or investment. Economists have called this miraculous phenomenon an interest on interest. It causes loans or invested deposits to increase at a significantly faster pace than only simple interest, the opposite of compound interest. Simple interest proves to be interest that calculates on just the principal amount of money.

Compound interest accrues at an interest rate which determines how often the compounding occurs. The higher the compound interest rate turns out to be, the faster the principal will compound and the more compounding periods will occur. Consider an example of how effective compounding truly is. $100 that is compounded at a rate of 10% per year will turn out to be less than $100 which is compounded at only 5% but semi annually during the same length of time.

Compound interest is important to individuals as it is able to take a few dollars worth of savings now and transform them into significant money throughout lifetimes. Investors do not need an MBA or a Wall Street background in order to benefit from this principle. Practically all investments earn compounding interest if the owners leave these earnings in the investment account over the long term.

This form of interest cuts both ways on the receiving and paying sides. When individuals are saving and investing money, it helps them grow the amount faster. When they are borrowing and paying the same interest on the debt, it grows against them faster. Individuals who are saving wish their money to compound as often as they can. Individuals who are borrowing wish it to compound as infrequently as possible. Savers are better off if they are able to compound quarterly instead of annually while just the opposite is true for borrowers.

For people who are compounding their investments, time works on their side. Money that grows at a rate of 6% each year doubles every 12 years. This means that it increases to four times as much as the original amount in only 24 years. For individuals paying compound interest, time is similarly working against them. Credit card companies utilize this principle to keep their card owners in debt forever by encouraging them to only make minimum monthly payments on the bills.

Thanks to compounding, a smaller amount of money that a person adds to an account upfront is more valuable than a larger sum of money he or she adds decades later. This cuts both ways. By paying down principal on a credit card with an extra $5 per month, the amount of compound interest individuals pay on a 14% interest rate credit card decreases by $1,315 over ten years. This is true even though they have paid only $600 in extra payments over this amount of time.

Anyone can make the miracle of compounding work for them. The idea works the same whether individuals are investing $100 or $100 million instead. Millionaires have greater ranges of investment choices. Even relatively poor people can compound their interest to increase their original amount and double their money as often as possible.

Compounding interest means that participants have to give up using some dollars today in order to obtain a greater benefit from them in the future. The little money may be missed now, but the rewards for the more significant amounts in the future will more than make up for the little sacrifice the individual makes now. Financial planners have claimed that the difference between poverty and financial comfort in the future amounts to even a few dollars in savings each week invested now rather than later.

Compounding of Money

The compounding of money has everything to do with compound interest. Compounding of money through such compounding interest can become among the most potent of weapons in your investing arsenal. Compound interest allows your money to grow at a faster rate as a result of the way that the interest is added to your money's balance. Various types of compound interest are available for compounding your money.

Compounding your money with compound interest works through taking the interest that your money has earned over a time frame and adding it back to the initial amount of money. Then when the next period is figured up, this total dollar value is calculated in the next portion of interest that you will earn. Simply put, every time frame's interest is placed directly back in to the entire sum of money on which the interest will be earned. Every time the interest is figured up, your money will earn a greater amount of interest like this.

A variety of different forms of compound interest exist. These always relate to the time frame over which the interest and money compounds. Such time frames of compounding of money are comprised of yearly, monthly, and daily compounding interest. With yearly compounding interest, the interest rate is figured up each year. In monthly compounding of interest, this rate is applied to the new principal balance each month. Daily compounding of interest involves an every day accounting of the interest and new principal.

Compounding of money involves several factors. These are periodic rates of compound interest, which are the rates actually applied to your balance, and compounding periods, which are the amount of the time frame before such interest is literally applied on to your total balance. As an example, if you invested $10,000 in a .1% daily periodic rate money market form of account, then on the second day, your balance would be $10,010. The next day, this rate would then be applied to the new balance of $10,010. Figuring out the actual annual effective rate entails you taking the whole year's interest and dividing it by the amount of the investment that you started with at the beginning of the year, or $10,000 in this case.

Compounding of money through such compound interest proves to be an extremely potent weapon. This is because the interest earned is immediately added on to the account balance to be counted as principal for the next time period. Each time frame the interest rate applies to the greater balance. Accounts grow faster through the compounding of money as the interest is not held back.

This compounding of money effect multiplies when you use it with accounts that are tax deferred, such as municipal bond funds and annuities. As no penalties of taxes are paid in a given year, your money increases quicker and quicker since greater amounts are constantly in the account to receive interest.

An example of how effective compounding of money using compound interest can be is illuminating. If you put $10,000 into a simple interest account that does not compound but receives twelve percent interest, then it will increase to $46,000 over thirty years. The same money that is compounded annually will rise to about $300,000, and to as much as $347,000 if the money is compounded quarterly. Money that is compounded over a daily time frame would naturally earn the greatest amount of interest and highest principal over a period of time.

Congressional Budget Office (CBO)

The Congressional Budget Office was created by Congress in 1975. Since that time, it has continuously developed and published its own independent analyses for economic and budget related issues. Its goal is to support the process of making Congressional budgets. Ever year the agency puts together literally hundreds of estimates for costs of proposed legislation as well as dozens of routine reports.

The CBO is religiously non partisan so that it can engage in unbiased and objective analysis. It only hires staff based on their professional abilities and does not consider their political affiliations. CBO never engages in recommending policies. It is concerned with all of its reports and price estimates explaining its analytical methodology.

The CBO produces Baseline Budget and Economic Projections. It does this regularly to come up with predictions for economic and budget outcomes. These estimates assume that the present conditions for revenues and spending will continue. Such baseline projections extend for 10 year time frames as utilized in the process of Congressional budget making.

Long Term Budget Projections are another item that the Congressional Budget Office offers Congress. These extend well beyond the usual 10 year budget forecasts to cover the next 30 years. They reveal the impacts of economic developments, demographic trends, and increasing health care expenses for federal deficits, spending, and revenues.

With the Cost Estimate analyses, the Congressional Budget Office delivers estimates in writing for the expenses created by every bill which the committees in Congress approve. They reveal the ways the bill will impact revenues or spending for the coming five to 10 years.

The CBO also develops Analytic Reports which consider specific elements of the tax code, programs of federal spending, and economic and budget constraints. Such reports pertain to a number of elements of federal policy. This includes economic growth, health care, social insurance, taxes, income security, the environment, energy, national security, education, financial issues, infrastructure, and other areas.

Once the President submits his Presidential Budget, CBO get involved. It re-estimates the impacts of it. The office does this by using its particular methods for economic estimating and forecasting.

From time to time, the CBO comes up with a volume on Budget Options. This reference work provides a number of ways that the government could reduce its budget deficits. The options are varied and come from a number of sources. They include raising additional revenues and lowering spending.

The Congressional Budget Office also produces Sequestration Reports. They must put out estimates of funding caps on discretionary programs in every fiscal year that goes through 2021. They consider these numbers to determine if cancelling the pre-allocation of budgeted resources is necessary.

The CBO knows what it should study because of its mandates. It's responsibilities are to assist the Senate and House Budget Committees in their jurisdictional affairs. They also are directed to support various other committees of the Congress. This includes especially the Finance, Ways and Means, and Appropriations Committees as well as the leadership of Congress. They are required by law to produce many of the annual reports which they create. The best known of these remains the Budget and Economic Outlook.

Corporate Taxes

Corporate Taxes refer to the United States' based taxes on corporations. These are not the same for every business structured entity. Corporations receive completely different tax treatment from other business entity structures. In fact such corporations are the only kinds of firms in the U.S. which have to pay in their own profit-based income taxes. With LLC limited liability companies, sole proprietorships, and partnerships, these business structures do not receive business profit tax assessment. Instead, all profits literally pass through on to the owners of the businesses in question. These individuals then report their own personal losses or income via their own individual tax returns.

The reasoning for singling out corporations for special (and some would say punitive) tax treatment like this results from their being a completely separate legal entity that has no connection with its owners. Taxable profits will be those that remain after all business expenses have been deducted. Those profits which remain in the firm accounts in order to pay for expansion or cover other ongoing expenses (sometimes called retained earnings) and profits parsed out to the stake holders (or shareholders) in the form of dividends will be the taxable profits.

Corporations employ all sorts of tactics in order to reduce their amounts of taxable profits. Among these will be a dizzying array of deductions for business expenses incurred throughout the course of the operating year. Besides operating expenses, startup expenses, advertising budgets, and product outlays, such corporations may also deduct out the salaries, payroll, and bonuses plus all expenses pertaining to retirement and health care plans for all of their staff and management.

Corporations do have to file their corporate tax return and pay their applicable corporate income taxes on any and all profits utilizing the Form 1120 from the IRS. When corporations know they will owe the government taxes, the Internal Revenue Service requires them to engage in good faith estimates for the tax dollars they will owe so that they can make quarterly payments. The IRS expects to receive these each April, June, September, and January, the months following the ends of the various four quarters.

When corporations pay out dividends to their various stake holding owners, these recipients will be required to report and then pay their own personal income taxes on such sums. Corporations will similarly have to pay taxes on all money they distribute as dividends as these are not deductible from corporate taxes. It causes dividends to be double taxed, once by the corporate income tax rate and a second time by the receiving stake holders. Smaller-sized corporations do not have such problems. Since their stake holders generally are employees of the corporation, they can receive their cuts of the profits in the form of bonuses and salaries which are in fact tax deductible instead of giving them out as dividends that are taxable.

A great number of corporations will decide that they should in fact keep some of their profits as retained earnings at the conclusion of the year. They will need this money to pay for potential future growth, expansion, or even acquisition targets. Such retained earnings become taxable at the company's corporate income tax rates.

This is a strategy for owners of a smaller corporation to reduce taxes. They can keep a portion of the profits within the corporation to avoid having to pay the higher personal income tax rates, as the first $75,000 in corporate profits assess at lower rates of from 15 percent to 25 percent. This accounting trick does now work for owners of the LLCs, partnerships, and sole proprietorships whose profits are all passed through to the individual personal level every year. This happens regardless of if they choose to take out profits from the business or instead leave them.

There is a limit to the largess of the Internal Revenue Service. They will permit the majority of such corporations to keep as much as $250,000 in the firm at any point before the government begins to assess tax penalties.

Corporation Tax

Corporation Tax refers to a United Kingdom jurisdiction method of taxing companies and associations domiciled in Great Britain. For any business that is a limited company, or is a foreign firm that boasts a United Kingdom office or branch, or operates as a cooperative, club, or other type of unincorporated association, they must pay such taxes on any and all profits which they accrue from engaging in business (called trading in Britain) in the U.K. This last qualifier means that even sports clubs and community-based groups will have to pay the tax on all profits in excess of one hundred British pounds sterling (if they have any).

The United Kingdom is similar in its corporate tax collecting efforts to other jurisdictions like the United States. Their taxing authorities do not send out bills. They follow a self-reporting taxation system. Businesses must first register for the corporation tax as they begin conducting business. Those associations which are not incorporated are required to write to HMRC Her Majesty's Revenue and Customs. These companies must maintain official accounting records to prepare a company tax return. They will then figure out how much of the corporation tax they will be required to pay. Finally they pay the tax itself. If they have nothing they are required to pay to HMRC, then they must report this.

Companies in the United Kingdom receive typically nine months and a day from the conclusion of their accounting period as a deadline to pay their taxes. The returns themselves the firms must file with HMRC by the deadline that falls 12 months following the conclusion of the accounting period. Though there are exceptions, accounting periods in Great Britain are commonly the identical 12 months to the financial year which their annual accounts cover.

Not all profits will be corporation tax assessed in the U.K. Profits which companies or associations earn from investments, trading profits (i.e. doing business), or for selling assets for higher than their cost basis (called chargeable gains in the U.K.) will be tax assessed. For those firms which are headquartered within the United Kingdom, they will be required to pay the tax on corporations for their profits which they generate not only within the U.K., but also from overseas. Those firms which merely maintain a branch office in Great Britain will only pay taxes on profits earned on British soil.

Companies which fall into a dormant status will not be required to pay the corporation tax. The definition of dormant simply means that there is no income from the firm (as with investments), nor is the firm engaging in business. Those companies that are new limited companies that have not yet begun trading are also deemed dormant. Associations which are unincorporated or clubs that owe below one hundred British pounds in such tax are also considered to be dormant. Flat management companies similarly fall under the dormant definition. The definition of trading (or doing business) includes any activities that involve selling, renting, or purchasing property, employing any individuals, advertising, or obtaining interest.

Firms that have been dormant can become active again. In scenarios where this occurs, British law requires that the owners alert HM Revenue and Customs once their dormant limited or non-trading company begins trading again. The law of the land also requires that these companies in this restarting status will have to begin amassing statutory accounts so they can once again create and file Company Tax Returns at the end of year for the company. Alerting HMRC that the business has begun to trade once more simply means that the firm should re-register for the corporation tax once again.

Cost of Goods Sold (COGS)

The Cost of Goods Sold refers to those costs which directly arise from the creation of a firm's goods or services. The phrase also sometimes is summarized by its acronym COGS or by an alternative name the "cost of sales." It will cover many expenses. Among these are all of the materials the company utilizes to physically produce the goods.

It also considers the labor expenses employed to create the items. It will not include expenses that are considered to be indirect. This means that sales force and distribution expenses will not be taken into account. COGS shows up on income statements. Accountants and economists can utilize it to subtract it out from the given company's revenues in order to establish the firm's gross margin.

Every business has the ultimate goal to earn profits at the heart of what it is doing. This is why a less expensive goods production for their product or service will lead to higher profits, all else being equal. A fuller explanation of what the Cost of Goods Sold includes involves inventory, materials, labor, factory equipment for production, and even overhead. All of these factors of production directly pertain to the goods or services the company produces. The calculation also takes into consideration the freight or shipping of inputs utilized. It would never include associated costs like rent for a facility or general payrolls of a company.

Looking at an example helps to clarify the Cost of Goods Sold concept. Where an automobile manufacturer is concerned, there will be a number of material costs. Chief among these would be those parts that actually combine to produce the car, as well as the cost of labor for assembling the car. The COGS would not include the cost of the sales force personnel which actually sell the car nor the price for getting the cars out to the dealership. Both of these last ideas are post-production costs, so they are not a part of the primary COGS.

There are a number of different ways for calculating the Cost of Goods Sold. It also varies from one certain kind of business to those in another industry. Among the most simple means of figuring this number out is to start with the costs of inventory over the production period. Next they would add in the aggregate purchase amounts in the same time frame. They would likely then subtract out the inventory at the end of production point. Such a calculation will provide the literal cost of the inventory which the company produced in a given time frame.

Another example helps to make the explanation clearer. Assume that a firm begins its production phase with $15 million worth of inventory. If they make $3 million in additional purchase in this time and end the production period with $14 million of inventory, then the firm's Cost of Goods Sold is calculated by taking the $15 million and adding in the $3 million in purchases and subtracting out the final $14 million in remaining inventory. This gives a final COGS of $15M plus $3M minus $14M for a final result of $4M.

The significance to this formula and Cost of Goods Sold figure is important. The COGS reveals how effectively the firm is able to convert its inventory into revenues and profits. This is why it is critical to compare the COGS against the revenue of the period under consideration. When the company above had a revenue exceeding $4 million, then it would boast a gross profit that was positive. If the revenue of the firm in question was less than the $4 million COGS, then there would be a negative gross profit. In other words, understanding and knowing the COGS figure for a company tells investors which companies are ultimately successful and which are in financial trouble, assuming that state of (negative profit) affairs continues for long.

Cost Segregation

Cost segregation proves to be a procedure of identifying assets of personal property that commonly become lost or bunched together in the real property asset. Cost segregation involves reclassifying costs of assets to a depreciable life that is the shortest one possible.

This allows owners of real estate to optimize their tax deductions in the depreciation category, which lessens the amount of present income tax due. Any investor who is buying a building, renovating a building, or getting into a construction project can qualify for significant Federal and state tax advantages using cost segregation.

Particular assets that pertain to these types of projects may be eligible for such accelerated depreciation. This translates to you being capable of realizing bigger tax deductions now in a shorter time frame. Advantages in bigger tax deductions now include a less expensive capital cost and greater positive cash flow over the principal several years after a purchase has been made or a project completed. Cost segregation studies help you to find such chances to claim more accelerated tax purpose depreciation. These cost segregation studies show always be performed by well qualified Certified Public Accountants.

Cost segregation is able to reduce the time frame for depreciation significantly via s simple strategy. These studies go through all of the costs involved in a property that are currently being tax depreciated over the usual thirty-nine year time frame. Many of these might be reclassified to far shorter time periods of depreciation, including fifteen years, ten years, seven years, or even only five years. The shorter the time frame of depreciation, the greater the tax deductions will be in this far shorter period of time. Greater amounts of depreciation are realized immediately when this is done properly. In this way, not only are tax savings in the present and coming years maximized, but cash flow is similarly increased.

Cost segregation studies make sense for anyone who is purchasing an already existing building. They are efficient for investors who are putting up a new facility. They similarly help those who are engaging in leasehold improvements to a present building. Finally, they give tremendous advantages to businesses or individuals who are renovating, improving, or expanding a building that already exists. Even older buildings can be cost segregated for better tax deprecation purposes.

Cost segregation should not be confused with simple deprecation analysis. A great deal more is involved than simply taking line items off of construction invoices to classify them. The procedure actually involves a team of professionals who are familiar with tax laws and accounting rules, along with construction and engineering concepts. A CPA will be the center of such a team, since he or she will have to make various building components tangible to quantify them in a way that they can be estimated as costs that work with IRS rules. This team would also feature an engineer, contractor, and possibly architect much of the time.

Between them, these professionals will examine in depth electrical and mechanical plans, working drawings, and even blueprints to break segregate out the electrical, mechanical, and structural parts of the building from other components that are associated with the personal property. Even engineering and architect fees as they pertain to various parts of the project are included as soft costs.

Debt Coverage Ratio (DCR)

Debt coverage ratio has different meanings dependent on what entity is using it. In the world of corporate finance, it is the amount of cash flow that a company has to service its current debts. This ratio utilizes the net operating income divided by the debt payments due in a year or less. This includes principal, interest, lease payments, and the sinking fund.

It has a different meaning with governments and individuals. For finances of a national government, debt coverage ratio refers to the export earnings required for the country to make its yearly principal and interest payments with the external debts of the nation. With individual finance, banks and their loan officers utilize this ratio to decide on income property loans.

Debt coverage ratios must be higher than one in order for the government, company, or individual to prove enough income to satisfy its present debt obligations. With a DCR under 1, it lacks the means to do so. This ratio is determined by dividing Net Operating Income by the Total Debt Service.

The net operating income turns out to be the revenue of a company less its operating expenses. This does not cover interest payments or taxes. The NOI can also equate to the EBIT Earnings Before Interest and Tax. Investors and lenders which are evaluating the creditworthiness of corporations and companies should use criteria that is consistent when they figure out the DCR.

Total debt service is the term that concerns the present debt obligations. This will include principal, interest, lease payments, and sinking fund all owed in the next year. Balance sheets also include both the long term debt current portion and the short term debt.

When a debt coverage ratio is lower than one, it says that the entity cash flow is negative. With a DCR of .90, the company would only possess sufficient NOI to handle 90% of their yearly debt payments. With personal finance this would mean that the borrower had to access some outside funds each month in order to cover the payments. Lenders usually discourage loans with negative cash flow. They may permit them when the borrower can show a strong outside income.

Lenders almost always consider the debt coverage ratio of borrowers before they extend loans to them. They do not want to loan money to entities with lower than one. Such groups will have to draw on sources outside of their traditional income or borrow more in order to make their debt payments. When the DCR is dangerously close to one, then the borrower is considered to be vulnerable to a slowdown in income. Only a minor setback to its cash flow would mean it would not be able to service the debts. Some lenders will actually insist that the borrowers keep minimum levels of debt coverage ratios while they have a loan balance. In these cases, borrowers whose ratios decline below this minimum level are in technical default.

Lenders can be more lenient on debt coverage ratios when the economy is booming. An expanding economy means that credit is available more easily. This often causes lenders to work with companies and individuals on their lower ratios. The problem is that borrowers which are under qualified can impact the stability of the economy.

In the 2008 financial crisis, subprime borrowers received credit in the form of mortgages without proper consideration of their finances. As such borrowers defaulted in large numbers, the lenders that had made loans to them failed. The largest savings and loan institution Washington Mutual turned out to be the most egregious example of this scenario.

Debt Ratio

Debt Ratio refers to a highly favored financial ratio. This one measures the consumer or company's debt leverage. This ratio is best explained as the ratio for all of the longer-term and shorter-term debt divided by all assets of the individual or enterprise. It is then expressed out in percentage or decimal format. Another way of stating it is the proportion of a firm's assets financed by outright debt. The debt ratio is sometimes called the debt to assets ratio as well.

All else being equal, as this debt ratio is higher it means that the firm has a higher degree of leverage. This generally implies a higher amount of financial risk. Yet simultaneously it is true that such leverage is a critical tool which many corporations employ to expand. Countless firms have discovered many sustainable uses of such debt.

Naturally, acceptable and average debt ratios will range drastically from one industry to the next. Utilities and pipelines are capital-intensive firms. They will necessarily possess far greater debt ratios than do companies in such industries as technology. Consider a clear example to help understand this term better. When corporations have assets of $200 million and aggregate debts of $50 million, then the debt ratio would amount to 25 percent or .25 alternatively. This company would therefore be in a stronger financial position than a comparable one with a 35 percent debt to asset ratio, but not always.

This is because 25 percent debt to asset ratios can be excessive in an industry that boasts unstable cash flows. These businesses simply cannot assume too much debt. Such a firm that possessed an overly high debt ratio as measured up against its rivals would discover how costly additional borrowing would become. This means that it might fall into a cash crunch in shifting circumstances. The fracking industry starting in summer 2014 found itself in dire straits thanks to its huge debt levels and plunging energy prices.

At the same time, debt levels that amount to 35 percent could be easy to manage for those firms which are in an industry like utilities. The cash flows in these businesses are far stronger and more stable. Higher debt to assets ratios are not only acceptable in this business, they are expected. For those firms that find themselves with an over 100 percent debt ratio, you know that its debt levels actually exceed its amount of assets. Conversely, when firms possess a ratio under 100 percent, the firm possesses more assets than debt. Alongside other metrics for determining financial soundness, this ratio will allow investors to ascertain how high the risk level is for a given business.

Debt ratios do not take into account all money that a firm owes necessarily. While they will always count longer- and shorter-term debts, they will leave out liabilities. Some of these liabilities that do not figure into the calculations are negative goodwill, accounts payable, and "other" items.

Consider a real-world example of how this works out in practice. Starbucks possesses a debt ratio of around 22.5 percent. Morningstar considers that the typical ratio for the industry is more like 40 percent on average. This means that the Starbucks Corporation can easily borrow money on the markets. Creditors understand that its finances are solid as a rock. They anticipate receiving full repayment on time. The non-callable and fixed rate Starbucks' bonds that mature in 2045 possess coupon rates of only 4.3 percent.

Contrast this with a basic materials firm like Arch Coal Incorporated. The industry of coal mining is regarded as highly capital intensive. This is why the industry forgives utilizing leverage to operate effectively. The average debt to assets ratio proves to be 47 percent. Yet Arch Coal Inc. has a 64 percent ratio. This makes it costly for them to borrow money. In fact their non-callable, fixed rate bonds that mature in 2023 come with a painful interest coupon rate amounting to 12 percent.

Debt to Equity

Debt to Equity refers to a ratio that is extremely important and often scrutinized in the world of business. It is the amount of longer term debt on the balance sheet of a corporation as related to and divided by the company equity. Long term debt for a company means money that it will not be expected to pay back in the coming 12 months. Both are critical factors in effective balance sheet analysis.

This ratio tells an analyst or investor a great deal about a company and the amount of debt it is carrying compared to its true net worth. This is accomplished by gathering together all of the company liabilities and then dividing this amount up by the shareholder equity. The end result which comes back in dividing the total debt by the equity proves to be the percentage of the firm which is leveraged (or more accurately stated---indebted).

Over time, the acceptable and average amount of debt to equity has varied significantly in the corporate world. Today it heavily depends on both the state of the economy, the industry in which the company operates, and the all-around feelings of society concerning credit and debt. If all else is equal, any firm with a debt to equity ratio in excess of 40 percent to 50 percent should be more careful about the risk hidden within its balance sheet and books. These could lead to a liquidity crisis at some point in the future.

When analysts consider the working capital of the company and find that both it and the current ratios of the firm are dramatically low, then this is a glaring sign of significant financial weakness in a corporation. This is why an analyst or investor truly needs to adjust any current profitability numbers to the economic cycle at hand. Many investors have lost fortunes over the years because the plugged in peak earnings at the height of an economic boom as their base case scenario metric for a firm's ability to pay back its various debt obligations.

There is no good reason to fall for this age old trap after all. All that is required to avoid it is to predict that the economy may fall off a proverbial cliff at any point and time. Then consider if the cash flow would be sufficient to cover the liabilities without the corporation being hurt and hampered by a lack of money for critical daily, monthly, and yearly expenses on items such as plant, property, and equipment.

The truth is that debt and elevated debt to equity ratios is not necessarily a bad thing. Many businesses are quite adept at earning a greater return on their capital than the cost of the interest which they incur in borrowing the money. This would make it extremely profitable to borrow money in such cases. It allows such firms to boost their earnings and profitability for one thing. The real key element is that the company management clearly understands the level of debt which will represent a danger level for smart and forward thinking stewardship of their company. Leverage cuts both ways. It dramatically boosts returns when it is working well for a firm, and it similarly can even totally wipe out a company if things turn on the firm in an economic recession or even economic depression.

Investors especially need to be careful in buying corporate bonds in such environments. Bonds issued in the lower interest rate environments of today will suffer drastically when the interest rates invariably rise higher, especially if this is quick and unexpected. This will lead to less profitability for the firm when the bonds have to be financed again. If the management did not wisely prepare for such an issue well in advance, then the company will truly have been mismanaged during the golden boom days and will suffer needlessly during the inevitable bust economic times.

Deduction

Deductions refer to any expenditure or other item which becomes subtracted from individuals' total gross income. This deduction will naturally lower the aggregate total of income which must be subjected to annual income tax. Sometimes these are referred to as allowable deductions. As an example, any individuals who earn $50,000 and who are eligible to claim a $5,000 deduction would see their taxable income lowered to $45,000.

In the United States, the IRS Internal Revenue Service allows for a wide range of permissible deductions. Taxpayers may decide to either itemize their own specific personal deductions or instead claim the government provided standard deduction.

The IRS provides taxpayers with a standardized deduction amount of $6,300 for those who file as single, as of tax year 2016. Those who file as married filing jointly are entitled to a standard deduction of $12,600 instead. For those who file as head of household, the amount changes to $9,300 in that particular year. On any money earned under these income thresholds, the filers are not required to pay any income taxes. As an example, individuals who make $6,400 and who will claim the $6,300 standard deduction will only have $100 in income which is taxable.

Rather than taking these standardized deductions, those filing their taxes may instead choose to go with itemizing their own deductions. It means they take all of their permissible deductions and add them up together. They then can take this sum as the deduction instead of employing the standard deductions for use on the income tax return.

There are many popular itemized deductions. Among these are retirement account contributions, mortgage loans' interest amounts, property taxes which individuals pay, educational expenses, child daycare expenses, and numerous others. For those who opt to take the standard deduction, a few itemized deductions may also be taken in concert with it. Some of these which are permissible include moving costs and interest on student loans which are eligible ones.

Business expenses should not be confused with deductions, though they function in much the same way. Any individuals who incur costs while pursuing profits in a business endeavor may deduct these from their business income. All of the relevant business income will still have to be reported to the IRS on the appropriate business income tax forms. The business expenses can be subtracted from the overall gross revenue. What remains is the net income. This means that business expenses function much as do deductions since they are taken off of the business earnings. Yet despite this, they are still not considered to be deductions.

Credits are similar to deductions in some ways. They also reduce the dollar amount of taxes which those filing have to pay. They do work differently however. Credits are instead subtracted from the aggregate taxes individuals owe instead of from the reported income. This is a critical difference that changes the amount of taxes which individuals must pay out directly. The IRS offers both nonrefundable and refundable credits to individuals and families. While nonrefundable credits cannot lead to a tax refund, refundable ones can do so.

An example helps to clarify these somewhat confusing points. In this scenario, if individuals report their income and claim all appropriate deductions, they still owe $1,000 in income taxes. These people could be eligible for a $1,200 tax credit. Should the credit not be refundable, the tax bill would be erased, but the extra $200 would be simply lost. When the credits are refundable instead, the filers would receive $200 as a tax refund. This means that they are actually paying a negative income tax thanks to these refundable credits.

Deficit

Deficits are shortfalls in government revenues that result from them spending more money than they bring in from revenues. The deficit of a government is measurable by including or excluding the interest it pays for its debt. Primary deficit is simply the difference in all taxes and revenues less the present level of government outlays. Conversely, total deficits, usually simply referred to as the deficit, prove to be all spending along with payments on the interest of the debt less the revenues coming in from taxes.

Such fiscal deficits also expand and contract as a result of changing trends in economics. As an example, higher amounts of economic activity in a nation give greater revenues in taxes to the Federal Government. At the same time, economic downturns generally cause a government to increase its levels of expenditures in order to boost spending on unemployment benefits and other types of social insurance programs.

The amount of public debt is also impacted significantly by the amounts of social benefits funded, alterations in the tax code or tax rates, methods of enforcing tax policies, and various additional decisions made with government policies. In other countries that have tremendous energy natural resources such as oil and natural gas, including Saudi Arabia, Russia, Norway, and other nations who are a part of the OPEC, or Organization of Petroleum Exporting Countries, these incomes form the energy sources have an enormous impact on the national finances.

Another impact on the real tangible value of a government deficit, or debt, comes from the amounts of inflation in a country. Over time, inflation lowers the real currency value of such debt. The downsides to inflation result in a government having to pay greater interest rate levels on its debts. This causes public coffers borrowing to become more expensive.

Government deficits are comprised of two main parts. These are cyclical deficits and structural deficits. Cyclical deficits result from any and all extra borrowing that a government has to engage in during the low point of a business cycle. This comes from higher unemployment levels. As unemployment rises, tax receipts fall and expenditures on things like social security inversely rise. The implied definition of cyclical deficits is that they will be completely repaid in the next cyclical peak. This is because a surplus in revenues will exist as taxes rises and spending is lower.

Structural deficits instead represent deficits that are constant regardless of the economic cycle. This results from the overall government expenditure levels being unsustainable in light of the current tax rates. The overall budget deficit is then figured by adding the structural deficit to the cyclical surplus or deficit that exists. Although this is the mainstream distinction between the types of deficits, there are economists who say that the differences between the structural and cyclical deficits are impossible to determine. They contend that cyclical deficits simply can not be measured properly.

Delinquency

Delinquency refers to primarily an individual (but also conceivably an entity or business) failing to make good on what was expected of them according to their duty or the law. It often pertains to failing to affect the minimum due payment or carry out a fiduciary responsibility. An individual who practices Delinquency is called a delinquent. These persons have contractually undertaken obligations to turn in payments on loan accounts according to a pre-arranged routine deadline.

This might include minimum monthly amounts of money owed on a car payment, a credit card payment, or a mortgage payment. As the individuals do not make these payments on time, they become delinquent. When mortgage holders become delinquent, the financial institutions holding the loans are able to start working through foreclosure processes. They will do this when the mortgage account stays unpaid for a specific length of time.

There are many different types of accounts on which people fall into Delinquency. This could be retail account payments, income taxes, mortgages, lines of credit, and more. Individuals who become delinquent suffer the consequences for these financial actions. Such impacts vary with the kind of Delinquency, cause, and length of time it has continued in this unfortunate state. As individuals become late on credit card bills, they can be charged late fees. Those who do not make their required tax payments can have their wages garnered or even their bank account levied by the Internal Revenue Service.

Besides these financial Delinquencies, there are responsibilities which when they are not carried out can be labeled delinquent. By not carrying out one's fiduciary duties, professional responsibilities, or other contractual obligations as set forth by custom or the law, individuals can be called delinquents as well. Police officers who do not professionally carry out their responsibilities to protect ordinary citizens in the line of duty can be found to be delinquent.

It is important not to confuse Delinquency with default. Individuals are officially delinquent at the point when they miss making a required payment of some sort in a timely fashion. By contrast, loan defaults happen as borrowers do not pay back a loan according to the terms on which they agreed to in their original contract. Loans can stay in the delinquent stage without being treated as in default for an unspecified amount of time. The amount of time this remains delinquent rather than in default varies considerably from one creditor and financial institution to another. For example, with student loans, the United States' Federal Government permits these to be fully delinquent for as long as 270 consecutive days before they become considered to be in default.

The U.S. keeps track of its various national Delinquency rates. Per the year 2016 in the fourth quarter, such Delinquencies amounted to 4.15 percent for real estate loans on residential loans, 2.15 percent on loans for consumer credit cards, and .85 percent for real estate loans on commercial loans. The government also maintains official statistics for these rates by year of loan issued. For 2016, this amounted to 2.04 percent, which was near the historically typical average.

The devastating global financial crisis and U.S. mortgage crisis which erupted in 2007 caused the rates to spike to a high in the Great Recession years which reached fully 7.4 percent in the year 2010 in its first quarter. For residential real estate, the rate topped out at 11.26 percent for these specific types of loans. Up to the year 2008 in its second quarter these Delinquencies had not been higher than three percent all the way back to the year 1994 in its first quarter.

Depreciation

Depreciation is the means of spreading out the price of a usable physical asset during the period of its practical life. Businesses engage in this process of depreciating assets for accounting and taxing purposes. Depreciation can also be the reduction of the value of an asset that poor market conditions create.

Where accounting and taxing purposes are concerned, the process of depreciation demonstrates the portion of the value of the asset in question that has been utilized. Where taxes are concerned, the rules are stricter. The IRS sets out the regulations for taking depreciation of tangible assets.

Businesses are permitted to deduct the expenses of the asset they buy as a business expense. They simply must abide by the IRS' rules as far as when and how much of the deduction they are permitted to log. This all comes down to which category the asset falls in and the amount of time for which it is expected to last.

In accounting, businesses attempt to correlate the cost of a particular asset with the amount of income that it practically earns the company. With regards to an item of equipment that costs them $1 million, it may have a practical life expectancy of 10 years. They would depreciate this asset over the course of ten years. The company would then expense out $100,000 of the asset value each accounting year. They would match up the income that the equipment generated the company every year as well.

Accountants can use depreciation tricks to impact the company's financial bottom line. This is because with enough depreciation, the income statement, cash flow statement, balance sheet, and statement of the owners' equity will all be impacted significantly. It is true that certain depreciation assumptions can have significant impacts on both the long term asset values and the results of short term earnings.

Other assets can see their value depreciated by unfortunate circumstances or poor conditions in the market. Two standout examples of this type include real estate and currencies. In the housing crisis of 2008, many home owners living in the most severely impacted markets like Las Vegas watched helplessly as their home values depreciated by even 50% of the value. The post Brexit vote results day saw the British pound plunge by over 10% in a single day.

Generally accepted accounting principles affect depreciation figures. This is because a company might pay for a long life asset in cash, as with a tractor trailer that delivers its goods to customers. According to GAAP principles though, this expense would not be shown as a cost against income then and there. Rather than this, the expense is listed as an asset on the company balance sheet. The value of the asset is consistently and continuously reduced out during the in-service life of the asset in question. As the expense is reduced, this is a form of depreciating the asset.

This is done because GAAP principles insist that all expenses must be recorded along with the accounting time-frame as are the revenues which they generate. In the example of the tractor trailer that costs $100,000 and lasts for approximately ten years, GAAP would look to see what the salvage value would be at the end of that time. Assuming it expected the trailer to be worth $10,000 at the end of the depreciating period, than the expense would be depreciated at a rate of $9,000 for each of the ten years (using the formula of cost – salvage value/number of years depreciating).

With long term assets, the depreciating typically involves two lines. There would commonly be one that displayed the price of the assets and another that demonstrated the amount of depreciating that had been charged off against the assets' value.

Discretionary Expenses

A discretionary expense refers to those business or home costs that are not considered to be critical for the entity to function or operate effectively. This is important, since both businesses and individuals often are required to pay for discretionary expenses using discretionary income.

As an example, businesses might permit their staff to charge specific kinds of entertainment and meal expenses to the firm when they engage in these activities to build up business ties with clients, vendors, or potential customers. They might also cover meals and entertainment simply to foster better relations with their staff. A home would refer to discretionary expenses as those that they do not need, but instead want to have.

Discretionary income refers to any funds which remain after businesses or individuals pay their taxes and mandatory costs. On an individual level, those persons who do not have any money left once they pay the bills do not have any discretionary income. In order for them to pay for a discretionary expenses, they will be forced to take on debt by obtaining a loan or utilizing credit cards. An example of using debt to pay for a discretionary expense is utilizing credit cards to pay for a family vacation.

There are two kinds of expenses which consumer households incur. Some they are required to pay according to the law. This includes income and other taxes as well as health insurance (at least in tax years 2014 and 2015). Costs they have to pay out in order to make sure the family and household functions are also non-discretionary in nature. These include transportation costs, food, utilities, and rent or mortgage.

The people making the money do not have a choice of whether or not to pay these costs every month without suffering sometimes-severe consequences. The other kind of cost qualifies as a discretionary expense. This would be luxury items such as fine clothing, watches, or expensive liquor and vacation related costs. These are simply those services and goods costs which an earner may choose to pay for according to their personal discretion.

When economic conditions warrant, both businesses and households may find that they have to reduce their outlays as revenues and incomes go down. This is why it is important to have a thorough understanding of discretionary expenses before hand. When these are separately broken out on paper or a spreadsheet, then businesses and consumer decision makers can quickly and easily ascertain what expenses can be lowered or cut altogether.

A helpful technique for budgeting lies in ranking those discretionary expenses by their order of relative importance. This could be done by putting the least important at the top of the list and continuing on down to most important. When business income reduction or a cut back in hours on the job occurs causing businesses or households to slash expenses, then it is easy for the spending decision makers to choose which expenses can and should be cut first.

It is also to keep in mind that there are differences between what businesses and consumers consider to be discretionary in nature. Families which have two cars will likely have two car payments. They may think that the two cars are necessities and not discretionary. The truth is different. In an emergency, they could manage with only the one car in many cases. When times become hard and a job is lost, the family can decide the second car is actually discretionary and not essential. This way, they can sell the second vehicle to remove the second payment overhead from the family or household budget.

Distressed Securities

Distressed Securities refer to a corporation's financial instruments when the underlying companies are nearing or actually undergoing bankruptcy presently. Because such a firm is unable to cover all of its various financial responsibilities, its financial instruments will have undergone a dramatic decline in value. Yet thanks to the implied volatility that comes along with such inherent risk, the instruments actually provide investors with the very real possibilities of enormous returns. Such securities might be comprised of corporate bonds, trade claims, bank debt preferred stock, or common stock shares.

In the challenging investing climate of today, there are often many investors competing for opportunities which are bargain priced that might come with higher risk in the form of such Distressed Securities. There are scenarios where investors will carefully study up on the company plight and determine that it is not actually so serious as the market and public perceive it to be.

Because of this, they believe that their investments bought at a steep discount may increase dramatically in value as the situation of the company's finances becomes finally resolved. There are other cases where the investors agree with analysts that the firm may fall into bankruptcy. Yet they might be confident at the same time that the liquidation proceeds will be sufficient to cover the value of the securities which they obtain at a drastic discount to face value.

Individual investors should be extremely familiar with what will happen to such Distressed Securities should the company slide into either Chapter 7 or Chapter 11 bankruptcy. With the overwhelming majority of these bankruptcies, the common share equity will be completely wiped out. This means that investing in distressed stocks is highly risky. Yet many of the senior-most debt instruments like bonds, trade claims, and bank debts can provide some amount of payout after liquidation.

This is particularly the case when businesses elect to file a case of Chapter 7 bankruptcy. This halts operations and forces liquidation. The resulting funds will then be collected and dispersed out to the creditors according to their various degrees of seniority. With Chapter 11 bankruptcy, the corporation will restructure and resume its business operations. Assuming that such reorganization becomes a success, the distressed securities in the form of either corporate bonds or company stock could return incredible profit percentages as they stage a massive recovery alongside the company's improving fortunes and future prospects.

The trick is to understand at what stage such securities become Distressed Securities. Analysts will commonly label them as such when the firm that issues them cannot effectively meet a great number of its financial obligations. In the overwhelming majority of such scenarios, these securities will have been previously downgraded to junk credit rating status, as in CCC or lower by the major credit ratings arms of the debt rating agencies like Moody's Investor Services or Standard and Poor's.

Distressed securities are not necessarily always junk bonds though and should not be confused as such. Junk bonds only need to feature a credit rating of BBB or lower in order to be classified as junk. The underlying firm of the bonds is not in bankruptcy nor imminent to go there just because its bond issues carry the junk bond rating and label.

It is worth noting that the expected rate of return for distressed securities will be greater than 1,000 basis points (ten percent) over the rates of return for risk-free assets. This would include U.S. government bonds or Treasury bills' effective rates of return. It means that when the yield on five-year Treasury bonds amounts to one percent, then the Distressed Securities corporate bond should offer a rate of return of at least 11 percent.

Due Process Oversight Committee (DPOC)

Within the structure and organization of the IFRS International Financial Reporting Standards, the trustees have various bodies that help them to perform their duties. The Due Process Oversight Committee is the one that carries the responsibility to monitor the procedures for effective due process. They also do this for the IASB International Accounting Standards Board and its Interpretations Committee.

This Due Process Oversight Committee generally holds meetings four times per year on the sidelines of the usually quarterly IFRS Foundation trustees meeting. When they require additional meetings, the DPOC usually handles them via conference call. Each year, they select different international locations for their meeting places. One of their quarterly meetings is usually held in London. In May and June of 2016, the IFRC Trustees and DPOC met in Jakarta and London, respectively. The Trustees and committee met in Beijing in October of 2015, London in June of 2015, Toronto in of April 2015, and Zurich in February of 2015.

There are a number of different responsibilities that the Due Process Oversight Committee carries out for the IFRS and the IASB. These are all spelled out within the Interpretations Committee Due Process Handbook of both the IFRS and the IASB. The first of these is to review the standard setting activities in which the IASB and staff of the IFRS Foundation engage. They do this review of due process activities routinely and with expediency as their mandate requires.

The Due Process Oversight Committee is also responsible for reviewing the Due Process Handbook that governs the committee among other things. They are to suggest updates to it that are in order. These updates would pertain to developing new and reviewing old standards, their various interpretations, and the Taxonomy of the IFRS itself. They do this to make sure that the procedures of the IASB are the best practice possible.

Besides this the Due Process Committee is tasked with reviewing the consultative groups of the IASB. They check who makes up the groups to ensure that the perspectives included are well balanced. They wish to have representation from the various relevant sub-disciplines. It is the committee's aim to ensure that these consultative groups are effective in their duties.

When outside parties request information on any due process issues, this Due Process Committee is the one that has to respond to them. They work with the technical staff of the Director for Trustee Activities to cohesively do so.

The IFRS Foundation bodies are also monitored for effectiveness by the Due Process Oversight Committee. They check up on the activities that involve standard setting at both the Interpretations Committee and the IFRS Advisory Council. Other groups within the IFRS Foundation which address the setting of standards are also followed up on by this Due Process Committee.

Finally, this important oversight committee is responsible for coming up with and issuing its recommendations to the IFRS Trustees about changing the committees. When the Due Process Oversight Committee determines that the makeup of these various committees that deal with due process needs to be changed, they let the Trustees know so that the committees can be appropriately re-balanced.

The Due Process Oversight Committee issues summaries of all of its meetings. These and any other papers and reports which they author are all found on their websites which are sub-pages of the International Financial Reporting Standards and the International Accounting Standards Board.

Earned Income

Earned income comes from involvement in a business or a trade. It is comprised of salary, wages, commissions, tips, and bonuses. Earned income proves to be the opposite of unearned income.

Any money given to you for work that you have done is termed earned income. As an example of money that is not considered to be earned income, if your employer advanced you money against your upcoming pay check, this would be unearned income. This is because you have not yet performed the work that earns the income.

It is generated in one of two different ways. You might work for a person or company that pays you for the work. Alternatively, you could work as a self employed person in a business that is yours.

For taxing purposes, earned income is a broader category. It involves not only salary, wages, and tips, or alternatively self employment net earnings, in the calculations of the IRS. They also include benefits from union strikes and benefits for long term disability that are earned before a person achieves the minimum retirement age as unearned income. Combat pay for military personnel is not usually considered to be taxable earned income either.

There are various forms of income that are considered to be unearned income, or not earned. These include investment returns, such as dividends, interest, and capital gains. Social security and unemployment benefits are also unearned income. Finally, pensions, child support, and alimony are all not considered to be earned income.

It is not only used by the IRS to determine an individual's tax liability for the current year. It is also employed to determine eligibility for the Earned Income Tax Credit, more commonly referred to by its acronym the EITC. This Earned Income Tax Credit proves to be a credit against taxes for individuals who work and receive low wages for their earned income.

Tax credits such as this one commonly translate to additional numbers of earned income dollars staying in the person's pocket, or a lower tax liability for the year than would otherwise be anticipated. Not only does this decrease the amount of tax that might be owed, but it could lead to a tax refund if the adjusted gross income results in negative income tax being due.

Earned Income Tax Credit (EITC)

The Earned Income Tax Credit, also known by its acronym EITC or EIC (for Earned Income Credit), is a benefit offered by the Internal Revenue Service to working people who only have lower to moderate levels of income. In order to qualify for it, prospective taxpayers have to measure up to specific requirements in a year in which they file their tax return.

The IRS requires that they file even when they do not owe any taxes, or if they otherwise do not have to file a tax return. A key benefit of the EITC is that it not only lowers the amount in tax receipts these families owe the government, but it can also create a negative tax liability that translates into a personal income tax refund.

Among the requirements necessary to qualify for this Earned Income Tax Credit, individuals have to receive at least some income while working as an employee for a person or business. Alternatively, they are able to qualify by owning or running either a farm or a business. There are also basic additional rules that involve having a qualifying child or children who meet each of the qualifying rules as set out by the IRS.

The Earned Income Tax Credit is intended primarily to help those families who have children, though it can also apply to other couples and individuals who receive lower to moderate levels of income. The actual amount of the benefits from the EITC is based upon the specific income of the filers as well as the actual number of children they have.

For those couples and individuals who claim children which qualify, they must be able to prove age, parental relationship, and shared residency. For the tax year 2013, the income levels that met IRS requirements had to be under $37,870 on up to under $51,567, which varied based on the numbers of children considered to be dependent in the family. Those workers who have no children yet who earn under $14,340 for an individual or $19,680 for married couples were eligible to get a tiny EITC amount in benefits. Those who do not have children which qualify are able to utilize U.S. tax forms including 1040, 1040A, or 1040EZ to apply. When qualifying children are involved, the head of household filer must utilize either the 1040 or 1040A forms alongside an attached Schedule EITC.

In the tax year of 2013, the IRS had established maximum benefit levels which individuals, couple, and families with qualifying children could obtain. For those who had no children which qualified, the maximum was $487. With a single child who qualified, the maximum benefit rose to $3,250. Where there were two children, this amount grew to $5,372. Finally, with three or even more children who were qualified, the maximum amount increased to $6,044. Each year, these numbers are raised according to the inflation index. In tax year 2015, this reduced tax revenues owed to the U.S. federal government by a not-insignificant around $70 billion.

It should not come as a surprise that these Earned Income Tax Credits have been and still remain a significant item for discussion in the ongoing political conversations within the United States. The debate has centered on the question of which approach would help the poor and lower middle class most. One idea is to raise the minimum wage significantly. The other is to boost the maximum amounts of the EITC. Back in the year 2000, The American Economic Association took a random survey of 1,000 of their members to learn their perspective. Over 75 percent of American economists agreed that it made sense to increase the program of the Earned Income Tax Credit.

Electronic Funds Transfer (EFT)

EFT is the usual acronym for Electronic Funds Transfer. This program refers to the all-electronic money transfer processed out of one bank account and into another. This could be done within a single bank or over a number of different and often intermediary financial institutions. Computer systems handle these transactions entirely unaided by the intervention of human bank personnel. There are actually many different names for EFTs. Within the United States, they are often called e-checks or even electronic checks.

The phrase relates to a wide range of varying payment systems. Some of these are bank debit card or other credit card payments which a cardholding customer initiates voluntarily at a store or merchant, direct debit payments in which the firm directly debits the bank account of the consuming customers in payment for their services or goods, and payer initiated direct deposit. Other examples of this EFTs include wire transfers done utilizing the SWIFT banking international network, private currency transactions that deal with electronic money storage, and online banking electronic bill pay services that are often delivered via Electronic Funds Transfer or alternatively by using paper based checks.

Government agencies within the United States have also taken to utilizing Electronic Funds Transfers in recent years. The federal government touts them as an efficient and often practical means of collecting money and similarly paying it out electronically without having to engage in the time consuming and wasteful process of resorting to relying on paper based checks, purchasing and obtaining stamps, and generally considerable processing and mailing time lags. They encourage government agencies to adopt this payment technology if they have not already.

As the Federal Government has recently noted, EFT payments are secure, safe, and efficient. They are also less costly to utilize than any form of paper check collection or payment process. As a clear and concrete example, it helps to consider a real world case. The federal government calculates that it requires a full $1.03 in order to make a payment via a check. This represents over a dollar for a single payment transaction. Naturally this cost adds up considerably when agencies are engaging in millions of individual payments per month. Compare these costs with the government expenses for running payments via electronic formats. Every time the government enters and initiates an electronic funds transfer, it only pays the equivalent of .105 dollars (or slightly more than a single dime) per individual transaction.

In order to participate in either the government's version of EFT or any bank's version of electronic funds transfer, individuals must first sign up for the payment platform. Nowadays, all federal benefits have been switched over to and must be paid out electronically, which makes this more critical and timely to do now than ever before. For any person who receives any kind of these benefits, including SSI Supplemental Security Income, Social Security payments, civil service retirement payments, Veteran's benefits, railroad retirement payments, or military federal retirement, all benefits must be received by electronic funds transfer in order to be processed and paid out each month.

There are still other benefits which both the federal government and other private parties pay utilizing Electronic Funds Transfers. The Federal government calls its various benefit payment programs either Direct Express or Go Direct. Private parties and banks utilize a range of different labels and names for these various privately run programs.

Embezzlement

Embezzlement is a type of crime that is considered to be white collar. It is usually committed by well educated and employed individuals. In this type of economic crime, the individual takes or misallocates the assets or funds with which he or she has been entrusted.

With this kind of fraud, the perpetrator does not steal the money in the first place. The individual concerned obtains it legally and even is rightfully entitled to hold them. The crime comes when these assets or funds are utilized in a way they are not allowed or intended. This is why the crime of embezzlement is breaking the legal and financial responsibilities with which someone entrusted a person.

It is entirely possible for embezzlement to involve a large or a small amount. If a clerk in a store puts money from the register in his pocket, this is a minor case of embezzling money. The term generally refers to larger scale instances. An example of this is when major corporate executives illegally expense off even million of company dollars. They would then transfer such money into their own bank accounts. Authorities punish embezzlement on larger scales with huge fines and significant jail time.

Among the largest cases of embezzlement ever recorded was Bernie Madoff and his enormous Ponzi scheme. The man received a 150 year prison sentence for operating the biggest fraud in the history of the United States. Thousands of investors had entrusted him with billions of dollars to manage on their behalf.

He promised to make them significant outsized profits for this trust. Authorities eventually caught up with him in December of 2008. In the trial that followed, they charged the man with eleven different counts of money laundering, fraud, theft, and perjury. When authorities examined what remained of his lavish assets such as foreign homes, boats, and planes, it became clear he had used much of the funds legally entrusted to him for his own personal ends. Very few of the Madoff victims every recovered much in the way of their losses.

Madoff's particular embezzlement and Ponzi scheme allowed him to cheat his numerous investors out of $65 billion. He kept this a secret for several decades. He would take in money from newer investors and use this to pay off promised returns of his older ones or those who requested redemptions from his hedge fund. Meanwhile, he used much of the money from the older investors to fund his high flying lifestyle around the globe for decades.

Madoff's financial crime started out as a legitimate business until he began to lose control of the operation. When he took losses, he felt he had no choice but to keep older investors in the fund. He promised them greater amounts of money if they remained. His investing strategies were kept secret in order to protect the hedge fund and business. Madoff's operation produced statements of accounts showing balances that no longer existed as he continued to lose money and live large with the funds.

In his case, Madoff was able to keep the fraud going far longer than is typical of people who have embezzled funds or run a fraudulent scheme. This was because he had been a former chairman of the NASDAQ. He was also a well respected investor for years before he began his crimes. No one bothered to look into the consistent outperformance his fund claimed to have because owner and operator was Bernie Madoff.

His crimes only became clear when investors demanded $7 billion in redemption at a point when he only had $200 to $300 million in funds on hand. At this point, he confessed what he had done to one of his sons who turned him over to the police.

Enron Bankruptcy

The Enron bankruptcy turned out to be among the largest corporate failures in American history. When the company filed for protection from its creditors, it showed assets amounting to $49.8 billion and debts that equaled $31.2 billion. These debt totals left out a number of items that were not properly listed on the company's financial statements.

The Enron bankruptcy was subsequently massively eclipsed by Lehman Brothers and it's over $600 billion in assets and bad debts when it filed. At the time Enron failed, it represented the seventh largest company in America by revenues. The failure cost around 20,000 employees their jobs and made worthless the company share retirement holdings of many employees and the stock holdings of countless investors.

The Enron corporation arose in 1985 because of a merger of Houston Natural Gas and InterNorth. The two were regional American corporations that were fairly small. Before the Enron bankruptcy happened, the company grew by 2001 to become the largest energy trader in the world which stood as among the biggest natural gas, electricity, paper and pulp, and communications companies on earth. It permanently changed the way that companies bought and sold electricity, energy, and natural gas. The company's revenues for the year 2000 were almost $111 billion. Fortune had awarded the company the prestigious designation of "America's Most Innovative Company" for six years in a row.

In the end of December 2001, the ugly truth emerged. The company had sustained its existence through cleverly disguised accounting fraud. This creatively orchestrated and systemic corruption became known as the Enron scandal. One of the major five accounting firms in the U.S., Arthur Andersen, became dissolved as a result of its complicit role in auditing the company books. Enron's stock went from $90 per share to worthless in a period of under a year.

The scandal significantly rocked the business and political world. A great number of corporations around the U.S. had their business activities and accounting practices questioned as a result of the attention Enron brought to bear. It encouraged Congress to pass the Sarbanes-Oxley Act of 2002.

Before the company failed, Houston based Dynegy attempted to rescue it from imminent bankruptcy. Negotiations broke down as Dynegy backed out after uncovering the extent of the misrepresentations and deterioration of Enron. The company sued Dynegy for taking control of its largest and most lucrative natural gas pipeline when the deal collapsed. Enron also attempted to secure $1 billion in loans and the financial backstopping of JP Morgan Chase and Citibank, but this fell through as well.

The complexity of the company ensured that the Enron bankruptcy would be a long, drawn out process. Weil, Gotshal, & Manges served as bankruptcy attorneys for the company's Southern District of New York court filing at the end of 2001. The bankruptcy did not end until November of 2004, nearly three years later. The court sanctioned a reorganization plan to distribute assets to creditors.

The new board of directors altered the company's name from Enron. They changed it to Enron Creditors Recovery Corp. The main endeavors of the new outfit were restricted to regrouping and selling off assets and operations the company had held before it went into bankruptcy.

With pipelines and 12 business units, this process went on for another two years. It was not until September 7 in 2006 that the company sold its last energy business. Ashmore Energy International Limited (AEI) acquired Enron's Prisma Energy International and ended the saga of one of America's most spectacular business collapses.

Expenses

Expenses refer to costs that business undergo in order to conduct their daily business operations, expand and grow their business, and acquire additional assets, property and factories. Firms are capable of investing their cash into a few different kinds of investments. They might buy a new building or some real estate. They could similarly purchase office or computer equipment for their premises. They might update older technology for the firm or aging machinery for production so that the business gains a higher level of productivity. These companies might also acquire vehicles for their traveling staff, such as executives, sales people, or for their delivery personnel. Any of these various types of investments would be for capital assets, which would make them capital expenses (sometimes also called expenditures).

Such expenses represent payments that a firm makes to acquire or increase the performance of longer-term capital assets such as equipment, factories, and buildings. These are generally expensive and substantial purchases which companies pursue for a corporate investment. Another way of thinking about this is that such capital expenses increase the overall business value. In consequence, as the asset values gain, so too does the net worth of the owner or stake holders. Yet at the same time the expenses incurred in acquiring the asset will similarly increase the liability of the owners.

Another expense that businesses realize analysts call depreciation. This simply means that assets decline naturally in value with time. It diminishes the company's value as it inevitably occurs. Such costs of capital expenses thus can be depreciated or capitalized throughout a given amount of time. This time equates to what the business world refers to as the useful life of the asset in question.

It always helps to consider an example of difficult concepts like these. When companies acquire equipment in the office for $20,000, they can depreciate this expense amount over a period of five years. It means that they will be allowed to take their depreciation of capital expense to the tune of $4,000 per year. Sometimes, this depreciation can be accelerated so that businesses realize the expense benefits quicker. There are also accountants who choose to include such intangible assets as copyrights, trademarks, and patents in the capital expenses category. Such assets become amortized, which is not unlike the process of depreciation in many ways.

It follows that companies should be able to expense the costs to keep a given capital asset up, in service, and working properly and efficiently. While this surmise is true, it cannot be done under the capital expense categories. Instead, they are treated as operating expenses in many cases. Yet with repairing equipment, this would likely increase its value. In that instance, this would represent a capital expense. This is why tax professionals have to help firms with figuring up the appropriate categories and depreciating.

Some other types of assets cannot be depreciated at all. Land is one of these. Because real estate does not lose value, the IRS considers that it possesses an indefinite value. This means firms may not depreciate real estate like they can with capital expense and operating costs.

When all else is equal, companies would rather obtain their tax deductions for asset purchases sooner rather than later. Yet the Internal Revenue Service has something to say on the subject. They maintain the rigorous rules on what may or may not be expensed out immediately. Startup costs are a good example of this. They will certainly boost the firm's value but they are spent upfront. The IRS permits just a certain quantity of such startup costs to be expensed out during the first year of business. The rest of these have to be amortized. In 2015, the government passed new legislation that permitted for more liberal benefits of corporate depreciation for those companies that buy capital assets.

Factoring

Factoring refers to a financial transaction which is considered to be debtor finance. In such an arrangement, companies actually sell off their invoices or accounts receivable to a third party factor for a discount. There is a major reason why a company would be interested in doing this. They may require cash for immediate needs which cannot wait for the accounts receivables to be effectively paid. When exporters engage in selling off their receivables in international trade finance, this is alternatively known as Forfaiting.

Factoring itself is typically also called invoice factoring, accounts receivable factoring, and accounts receivable financing. The foremost trade association for factoring proves to be the Commercial Finance Association. It handles both factoring transactions as well as asset based lending.

It is important to differentiate between factoring and invoice discounting. With factoring, receivables are actually sold off. Invoice discounting refers to a form of borrowing that utilizes for collateral on the loan the various accounts receivable assets. This is not the case in the United Kingdom however. Discounting is a type of factoring in the British market, which merely pertains to assigning receivables. This means that in Great Britain, this activity is also not deemed to be a form of borrowing. Confidentiality proves to be the principle difference between invoice discounting and factoring in the United Kingdom.

Four main events cover the factoring transaction. Each of these must be accountant-recorded by the individual financial professional who bears the responsibility for recording the transaction in its entirety. In the first step, the factor receives its fee. Next the interest expense must be paid out to the factor for advancing money on the transaction.

In the third step, the seller must allocate a certain percentage of the fees as bad debt expense. This relates to those receivables which the seller does not have confidence in being collectible. Finally, the seller will have to arrange a merchandise returns amount in the form of a "factor's holdback receivable." This category also covers any potential other gains or losses the seller will be forced to concede to the process of the invoice collecting.

There will be times when the charges the seller pays out to the factor will cover considerations such as extra credit risk, a discount fee, and additional services rendered by the factor. The final profit for the factor will amount to the ultimate difference between the amount it paid to obtain the invoices on accounts receivable and the actual money it finally recovers from the debtors. Any money which the factor loses because of non-payment is subtracted from this profit total.

With industries like clothing and textiles, companies which are completely financially sound will factor off their accounts. This results from the particular historical means of financing production in this industry. It permits the firm to cover its current cash needs and allows companies to operate with lesser cash balances. This leaves a larger amount of cash free for investing in future growth opportunities of the firm.

This debt factoring also serves a useful purpose as a means of improving cash flow control for those firms that find themselves in the unenviable position of possessing many accounts receivable that have various terms of credit which must be actively managed. Such a firm will often sell off its invoices at the appropriate discount because it decides that it will benefit financially in utilizing the resulting proceeds to improve growth. This serves them better than in acting as a de facto bank to their various clients.

This effectively means that factoring will happen at any point in any industry where the return rate for the proceeds put into future production is higher than the costs to factor out the receivable accounts. This is why the difference in money spent to factor must be carefully evaluated to ascertain if the value of producing additional goods will be higher than the money the company pays to work with the factor. A side but still important consideration revolves around how much cash the company possesses on hand for its operations and future growth potential.

Fiduciary

A fiduciary is an organization or individual which owes its trust and good faith to another person or group. It means that one party takes on the most serious legal responsibility to the other party. Fiduciaries are ethically and legally required to carry out their activities in the best interest of the other person or organization.

This could involve another's well being, but it usually revolves around finances. People who manage another individual's assets or finances are good examples of fiduciaries. This means that a fiduciary could be a board member, banker, accountant, money manager, estate executor, or corporate officer.

The responsibilities and duties of a fiduciary turn out to be not only ethical but also legal. After a group or individual willingly takes on such duties for another, they must carry out the tasks with the very best interests of that party at heart. This means fiduciaries have to manage any assets for the benefit of those individuals instead of to benefit themselves or realize personal gain. This level of responsibility is called a prudent person standard of care that came out of court ruling in 1830. This prudent person rule means that the individual functioning in the fiduciary's role must always carry out the duties with the beneficiaries' needs foremost.

Conflicts of interest are not allowed to arise between the principal and fiduciary. Per an English High Court ruling on the case of Keech versus Sandford in 1726, fiduciaries are not allowed to profit from holding such a position of trust. Because of this, the only exceptions are when the beneficiary grants specific consent when the relationship starts. When the principal gives such approval, fiduciaries are allowed to enjoy any benefits received, whether they are monetary in nature or opportunities.

Where business relationships are concerned, there are many different kinds of fiduciary duties. The most typical of these occur between trustees and their beneficiaries. There are also a number of other kinds of relationships where this can occur. Some of these are between executors and legatees, company board of directors and shareholders, stock promoters and stock subscribers, guardians and wards, investment corporations and investors, and attorneys and clients.

As the trustee and beneficiary relationship is the most common for fiduciaries, it is important to understand. Trustees handle arrangements for estates and also implement trusts. The beneficiary is the one whom they are serving. The fiduciary in this case is the person who will be the estate trustee or the trust. The beneficiary is also the principal.

In this type of arrangement, the trustee commands legal possession of the assets and/or property. The trustee is fully empowered to manage assets in the trust's name. Because the beneficiary has equitable title of the property or asset, the trustee has to engage in best interest decisions. Such a relationship as trustee and beneficiary is critical in effective and all inclusive estate planning. This is why the trustee should be chosen with great care and thought.

Blind trusts are those where the trustee who has authority over the investment does not allow the beneficiary to be aware of the way the assets are being invested. The trustee still has the legal duty to use the prudent person conduct standard, especially because the beneficiary is unaware of what is happening. Politicians and other public figures create such blind trusts so that they can stay away from scandals involving conflicts of interest.

Finance Controller

A Finance Controller turns out to be an employee who carries the responsibility for the higher level accounting, financial activities, and managerial accounting for a given firm. Such an employee will usually report to his or her supervisor the company CFO Chief Financial Officer. In smaller corporations and companies, the two positions may be one and the same. There are many important duties for these controllers. Among them are overseeing the duties of financial reporting, preparing the de facto operating budgets, and handling all critical affairs pertaining to payroll and many times staff development and continuing education.

It is a natural fact that controller duties and jobs will be different from one firm to the next because of the complexity, nature, and size of the particular firm and its industry as well. Some firms for example call their Financial Controllers comptrollers. This tends to be more of a senior position which is most typical in not for profit organizations and government departments. Naturally small firms will expect their controllers to wear more hats, while at bigger and multinational firms; they can delegate even some of the controller functions out to a broad spectrum of finance people, such as the Treasurer and Chief Financial Officer.

Financial reporting and auditing are critical functions and duties of many Financial Controllers. They are typically the point man responsible for keeping a close eye on the day to day financial condition of the firm. This position will work closely with the company or corporation's external auditors to be sure that the correct standardized reporting is being done. Controllers also set up, monitor, and even enforce the internal controls on financial reporting aspects. With the mega publically traded firms, the controllers often receive the thankless but essential task of handling the company's all-important quarterly public filings with the SEC.

A second important duty for the Finance Controller centers on the crucial role of budgeting for a firm. He or she will be expected to prepare the budget for the corporation and then to go through the important schedules for budgeting with the various departments and members of the organization in question. This will necessarily involve the collecting, analyzing, and consolidating of all relevant financial information on the company. The controller may not be the one who is ultimately tasked with maintaining the yearly budget, yet the position certainly monitors for discrepancy, investigates unexpected deficiencies, and summarizes trends of the finances within the firm. It will be the controller tasked with reporting any meaningful variances on the annual budget or expenditures to the upper level echelons of management on the board.

Besides these important roles, many financial controllers will also be expected to monitor any changes coming out or new legislation in the offing which may materially affect the company operations and their particular tax situation. Among the jobs in this category is to look for future risks while making sure that all necessary licenses, permits, and requirements for operating are attained. This is more than just filing crucial mandatory financial reports. The controller can also expect to handle tax preparation tasks like actually filing for federal and state taxes as well as various industry duties and taxes.

Finance Controllers also handle the development of staff from time to time. This might involve hiring, recruiting, and even training of some staff. It will require the person be able to appraise a result done in a job, delegating disciplinary actions when required and leading various employees or even temporarily small departments as necessity dictates. The controller will often be responsible for the company educational programs such as continuing professional educational requirements which are offered in the form of webinars, seminars, conferences, and other training events off site.

Financial Analyst

A Financial Analyst refers to a salaried individual who handles analysis, financial planning, and projection for both corporations and smaller companies. These accounting field experts create future forecasts for expenditures and revenues in order to come up with projected costs and capital budgeting for company projects. Those analysts who are senior level have the opportunity to work with executives in the corporate team and Chief Financial Officers to help determine across the company investments, policies, and future strategies.

These Financial Analysts draw on strong backgrounds in compliance and accounting in order to evaluate historical financial information, to forecast results for the future, and to push policy and process improvements. Their daily responsibilities include many different elements. They must analyze past and current financial performances and information. They have to evaluate depreciation and current capital expenditures. They must also consider various opportunities for investments of the company. These professionals do a great deal of projections and report preparing using their analyses. They work to find trends in the financial performance of the firm and offer suggestions for improving them. The analysts also evaluate and establish profit plans. Finally, they deliver financial projections and models for the finance team and executives to review.

There are a number of other positions which are related to this important job in a corporation or company. Some of these include financial analysis manager, senior financial analyst, investment analyst, and financial reporting manager. It means there are always opportunities for advancement in such a career path.

In today's increasingly technologically interconnected world, it should not come as a surprise that technology plays a major part in the careers of today's financial analysts. The ones who will be most successful in this field will gain as much exposure to these systems, tools, and platforms which service the field as they possibly can. Among the most typical technological requirements of these positions nowadays is having a complete grasp of the ERP enterprise resource planning systems. Second most in importance proves to be a command of both big data systems and data analytical systems. This is increasingly the case because firms more often rely on data-driven decisions now instead of the old school intuition-driven ones.

This job has a bright outlook for the future, according to the authority in the careers and employment industry--- the United States Bureau of Labor Statistics. In fact this organization states that the career outlook is tremendously positive for this position. The field will increase by approximately 16 percent during the years from 2012 to 20122.This makes it a more rapidly growing job opportunity than the average of every other career path in the U.S. The reasoning behind it is that corporations have put the recession and global financial crisis in the perspective of the past and so are putting on more financial analysts who they feel will help them to increase both their overall corporate growth and profits for the coming years.

The bureau similarly finds that these positions remain among the most heavily demanded jobs in either finance or accounting. This is the case not only for senior level positions, but also even entry level financial analysts. The respected industry publication U.S. News and World Report recently listed these jobs as among the top 100 Best Jobs, at number 63 in the United States. For the category of Best Business Jobs, they award it the number 13 best position in the nation.

This helps to explain why in the year 2014, financial analysts who possessed even from no to two years of experience earned average salaries amounting to $49,459 with an average range of from $39,252 to $60,352. The variance and range depends heavily on the industry, size of firm, location, and other factors of the employer. Senior financial analysts who possess over four years of experience can count on earning an impressive average $74,265 salary each year.

Financial Forecasting

Financial Forecasting refers to the corporate or government fiscal management tool for delivering information based on estimates from past, present, and anticipated future financial conditions of a firm or national government finances. It is extremely useful in projecting future revenue streams or expenditures. These can create a longer term or short term impact on corporate or government goals, policies, spending, and other activities. Such forecasting proves to be an indispensable component in the yearly budgeting activities.

Financial Forecasting is also the implementation of historical data in order to prognosticate future financial directions and trends. Companies employ such means of forecasting so they can decide how best to allocate out their budgets in order to plan for expected expenses over a future time period. This prediction model will commonly be derived from the forecast for demand of the corporate services and goods they purvey.

Investors can also employ such forecasting techniques to their advantages. They may run scenarios to decide if corporate events, including sales or revenue expectations, will boost or lower the stock price in a given firm. It gives the companies themselves a crucial means of benchmarking, which requires a longer term perspective on company operations.

Stock market and economic analysts also utilize Financial Forecasting in order to extrapolate the way that economic trends like unemployment and GDP will alter in the future quarters or even years. The problem with this is that it is not a precise science ultimately. As a forecast is farther removed from the present, the chances for it to be inaccurate only grow with time.

Statisticians also use Financial Forecasting for those scenarios that need future predictions. Data on customer satisfaction and how it will shift when a business' hours change can be gathered and measured using it. Similarly they can quantify and predict the impact of shifting working conditions on the company staff morale.

Stock analysts deploy a range of forecasting techniques in order to decide the ways that a given stock price will fluctuate over the future. They could begin by investigating a corporate revenue stream and contrasting this with national economic indicators for the country as a whole. They would have to measure any changes to statistical or financial data in order to ascertain the interconnecting relationship of numerous variables. Such relationships can be derived from particular events or the normal passing of time. Sales model forecasts could rely on a given event which is anticipated, such as buying the business of a competitor.

Financial Forecasting also takes on data sets or problems. Economists are able to engage in assumptions that pertain to a certain situation or simulation. They will select the most relevant data set to manipulate. After analyzing the information, they come up with their prognosis. Finally, there will be a reasonable verification time frame during which the analysts will compare their forecast to the real world results. They do this so that they can create still more accurate forecasting models for the future.

There are two types of specific Financial Forecasting techniques. The first particular kind is Qualitative forecasting models. Analysts utilize these to create prognoses that have a more limited scope. Such models will be greatly dependent on the opinions of experts. They benefit most heavily any short term forecasts. There are a number of examples of qualitative forecasting models available. Some of them are polls, market research, and survey which employ the Delphi method.

On the other hand, the alternative type of Financial Forecasting is quantitative forecasting. This means of forecasting will rule out expert opinions. It employs statistical data reliant on quantitative information. These quantitative forecasting models cover such series as discounting, methods, econometric modeling, and analysis of lagging and/or leading economic indicators.

Financial Statement

Financial statements are official records of a business' or personal financial activity. With businesses, financial statements present any and all pertinent financial activity as usable information. They do this in a clear, organized, and simple to comprehend way.

Financial statements are commonly comprised of four different types of financial accounts that come with an analysis and discussion provided by the company's management. The Balance sheet is the first of these. It is known by several other names, including statement of financial condition, or statement of financial position. The balance sheet details will outline a corporation's ownership equity, liabilities, and assets on a particular date. This will give a good picture of the general strength and position of the company.

Financial statements similarly include income statements. These can also be called Profit and Loss statements too. They outline numerous important pieces of company information, such as corporate expenses, income, and profits made in a certain time period. This statement explains all of the relevant financial details to the business' operation. Sales and all associated expenses are included under this category. This section of the financial statement proves to be the nuts and bolts of the whole document. It provides a snap shot of the company's ability to generate sales and turn profits.

A statement of cash flow is also a part of a complete financial statement. As its name implies, this section will share all of the details regarding the company's activities pertaining to cash flow. The most important ones that will be outlined include operating cash flow, financing, and investing endeavors.

The last element of a financial statement includes the statement of retained earnings. This section of the document makes good on its name to detail any changes to a corporation's actual retained earnings for the period that is being reported. These four sections of a financial statement are all combined together to make the consolidated financial statement, once they are combined with the analysis and discussion of management.

With large multinational types of corporations, such financial statements are typically large and complicated, making them challenging to read and understand. To assist with readability, they may also come with a group of notes for the financial statement that also covers management's analysis and discussion. Such notes will go through all items listed on the four parts of the financial statement in more thorough detail. For many companies, these notes for financial statements have come to be deemed a critical component of good and complete financial statements.

Financial statements are used by several different groups of people who are looking at a company. Investors use them in order to determine if the company and its stocks or bonds make a sound investment with a chance of providing good returns on investments and profits in exchange for limited risks. Banks utilize these financial statements to decide if a company is a good credit risk for their loan dollars. Institutions and other groups that may be considering a cash infusion or buyout of the company use such financial statements to decide if the company is a viable investment or acquisition target.

Fiscal Year

The fiscal year refers to an accounting period which governments or companies choose to use for their own accounting and in developing financial statements. Fiscal years are not necessarily the same as the calendar years. The U.S. government employs a different starting and finishing point for its own fiscal year.

The IRS Internal Revenue Service permits companies to choose whether they will use calendar years or fiscal years in their tax computations. When individuals or companies discuss budgets, they often invoke fiscal years. They prove to be a useful reference point when contrasting corporate or government financial results over the medium to long term.

The IRS has its own definition of fiscal year. To them these are comprised of 12 contiguous months that conclude on the final day in any month besides December. This means that where tax reports are concerned, a fiscal year could run February 1st to January 31st. American taxpayers also have the opportunity to utilize either 52 or 53 weeks long fiscal years instead of a 12 month one. In the case of the weeks' version, the years will rotate back and forth between 52 and 53 weeks in length.

Because the IRS automatically uses a calendar year system, those who employ fiscal years will need to adjust their own deadlines for turning in specific forms and getting in different payments. The biggest difference concerns the tax filing deadline. For the majority of American households and businesses, this will be no later than April 15th after the year in question for which they file. Those taxpayers working with the fiscal year system instead must file no later than the 15th day in the fourth month that comes after the conclusion of their fiscal period. This means that a business choosing to have fiscal years that span from May 1st to April 30th will need to turn in all tax returns no later than August 15th.

The U.S. tax code makes it relatively easy for companies to use fiscal years in their income tax reporting efforts. All that they are required to do is to turn in on time their tax return which covers that particular fiscal period. The companies also have the right to opt back to using calendar years whenever it suits them. To make the change from fiscal back to calendar years, they need to obtain individual permission by asking the IRS. Otherwise, they will have to measure up to the criteria that they outline in their Form 1128 called the Application to Adopt, Change, or Retain a Tax Year.

These fiscal years have a particular way of being addressed. Individuals who are discussing them reference them either by the end date or alternatively the end year. This means that one would refer to the American federal government fiscal year that starts on October 1st and ends on September 30th by saying the government fiscal year which ends on September 30th, 2016. If instead they were referencing spending by the government that happened in November of 2015, they would have to call this expenditure one that occurred in the 2016 fiscal year.

Fixed Assets

Fixed Assets refers to tangible property which are longer term holdings by their very nature. Companies and corporations both own and utilize them in their normal everyday business operations to produce their revenues and profits. They do not typically become converted back to cash or consumed any quicker than in under minimally a year time frame. Many corporations refer to their collective fixed assets as "the plant." Classic examples of these types of assets include real estate, factories, office space and buildings, furniture, computer equipment, and other operating equipment.

There are longer term assets that do not typically qualify as fixed assets though. Among these are patents and trademarks. They are generally considered to be simply intangible assets on company balance sheets.

Such assets also go by the names of property, plant, and equipment (PP&E). Corporations purchase fixed assets to create and supply services and goods. They might also rent them out to third parties to generate a revenue stream. They could simply deploy them within the company's own internal organization as well. These often include such tangible assets as office equipment, computers, and laptops, as well as manufacturing equipment and factories. Copyrights, goodwill, patents, and trademark could fall into either the fixed or intangible assets categories, depending on the accounting method favored by the firm.

There are many different types of equipment that fall under the classification of fixed assets. Among these are office buildings and plants, software and computer equipment, land, furniture, vehicles, and machinery. It often helps to consider a real tangible example when discussing difficult concepts like this one. Think about the company Amazing Fruits and Vegetables. They sell and even deliver fresh produce. This makes their delivery vehicles a fixed asset. The firm's distribution center would also be such a fixed type of asset. Even the parking lot where customers park while they shop the fruits and vegetables stand would be considered a fixed asset.

There are several reasons why it is helpful (and often times even essential) to have reliable information on the assets of a given company. The most important is that it leads to concise and precise financial reporting, as well as a better valuation of a going concern via financial analysis. Investors rely on such reports in order to ascertain the true financial health and real value of a given company. It enables them to make well- informed choices as to whether they should trust the firm enough to loan it money or instead invest in the equity of the corporation. One thing that makes it more confusing for investors is that firms have a choice of acceptable means of recording, depreciating, and disposing of their own assets. It requires qualified analysts who are willing to read the fine print and notes on the financial statements of the company in question in order to accurately determine on what basis the numbers were compiled.

It is an inevitable fact of life that fixed assets will gradually decline in value terminally as they grow older. They do offer long term income generation, which explains why they become expensed differently than do other company items. While tangible assets become subjected to occasional depreciation, intangible assets are subjected instead to amortization. A specific portion of the costs for the asset will be expensed out yearly. The value of the asset will correspondingly diminish alongside the amount of depreciation on the balance sheet of the corporation. The firm is then allowed to match up the cost of the asset in question with the longer term value of the item.

The method that a given firm utilizes to depreciate its assets will change the book value of the firm which is based on the amount they paid for the asset. This will make the equity book value different from the current market value of the asset in question. An exception to all of this depreciation and book value discussion concerns raw real estate. Land cannot be depreciated since it does not become depleted. The exception is when it is natural resource land, as with oil land, gold or silver mining land, or timber lands. These resources are finite and become expended over time and culling.

Fraud

Fraud turns out to be an intentional misstating or misrepresentation that leads businesses or individuals to encounter harm. These damages are frequently reflected as monetary loss. Several elements must be involved for acts to be considered fraudulent. A number of different kinds of fraudulent activities exist. They range from insurance fraud to identity theft to supplying false tax information to offering false statements. In some cases, this type of deception is only one part of a larger crime. It is typically handled in criminal court, though it may be tried in a civil court case as well.

Not every jurisdiction or country has the same definition of what constitutes fraudulent activity. The United States judges it to include a number of different components. A fact or statement has to be misrepresented or untrue. This statement must be relevant or important. The person making the statement must be aware that it is a false declaration. He or she must also mean for the listener to rely on the statement. The hearer can not be aware that the declaration is untrue. This listener must be relying on the veracity of the declaration in order to make a choice. The hearer also can not have a reason to believe the statement could be untrue. Most importantly, the hearer has to experience some form of damages for it to be considered fraud.

In other words, the persons speaking have to supply a lie which they know is untrue while intending the hearer to believe it to be true. The hearer can not know it is a lie or believe the lie might be false. The hearer also has to rely on the lie in a decision making process. The listener must suffer damages from believing the lie to be the truth.

There are numerous different kinds of fraudulent activity. These can mostly be arranged according to three categories of employee, government, and consumer. Employee fraud means that workers defraud the company or individual who employs them. This could be done by intentionally falsifying expense reports or by embezzling corporate funds.

Government fraud revolves around activities that are done intentionally to trick a government agency or some types of businesses protected by law. Insurance and tax frauds are components of this group.

Consumer fraudulent actions revolve around scams and cons. They are designed to cheat individuals out of money or personal information, like with scams that involve investments, telemarketing, or gathering sensitive components of personal identity.

Some cases of fraudulent activity are committed by white collar criminals and pertain to complex financial deals. To be considered white collar crime, the fraudulent activity must involve business professionals who harbor criminal intentions and who possess specific knowledge. Crooked financial advisors might attempt to trick clients into buying shares of precious metal repositories.

They have credibility from their reputation as a professional investment advisor that makes them trustworthy to clients. Individuals who feel this is a legitimate business opportunity could invest large sums and obtain realistic looking share certificates from the advisor. When the advisor is well aware that there are no repositories like these and accepts payments for the false share certificates, he has defrauded the customers who contributed funds to the investment venture.

Generally Accepted Accounting Principles (GAAP)

Generally Accepted Accounting Principles, more commonly referred to by their acronym GAAP, are the mostly American used set of accounting principles, procedures, and standards. These are utilized by companies to put together their corporate financial statements. Such GAAP proves to be a blend of the most accepted means of reporting and recording accounting data in the United States combined with the American policy board set standards.

Companies must use GAAP in order for their investors to have some common standard of consistency with financial statements they compare when considering the various companies in which to invest their money. These standards include such areas as balance sheet items classification, revenue recognition, and measurements of outstanding shares of stock.

Regulators expect that companies will obey these generally accepted accounting principles rules as they release their financial statements to routinely report their financial information. American investors should be leery of company financial statements that are not properly developed utilizing these guiding principles.

Despite this fact, these accounting procedures are merely a cohesive group of guidelines and standards. Crooked accountants are still able to distort and misrepresent the numbers while using these generally accepted procedures. Although a company may utilize the generally accepted procedures, investors should still carefully go through their financial statements with a healthy degree of skepticism.

The competing accounting standards that most of the rest of the world employs is known as the IFRS International Financial Reporting Standards. There has been a recent move to harmonize the two sets of standards in past years. Because of the global financial crisis and economic collapse of 2008 and its terrible aftermath, globalization, the SEC agreeing to accept international standards, and the Sarbanes-Oxley Act, countries like the United States have been severely pressured to close the gap between GAAP and the IFRS.

Doing so would have major ramifications on accounting throughout the U.S. It also would affect investors, corporate management teams, accountants, national accounting standard makers, and American stock markets. Bringing these two sets of standards together is impacting CFO and CPA attitudes regarding international accounting. This influences the International Accounting Standards quality as well as the various endeavors that professionals are making on converging the two sets of standards.

There are some problematic inconsistencies with international financial reporting because the financial reporting standards and rules are somewhat different from one country to another. This dilemma has become more of a challenge for those international investors who are attempting to figure out the various differences in global accounting and reporting. As they are thinking about offering substantial investments to overseas companies which are earnestly seeking capital in good faith, it makes it more challenging since companies report according to the standards of the country where they do business.

The IASB International Accounting Standards Board has been sincerely looking for a practical solution to this international complication, confusion, and conflict that inconsistency in accounting standards for financial reporting has created and continues to encourage. The principle difference with GAAP and the IFRS methods lies in the totally different approaches that either one uses regarding the standards.

Generally Accepted Accounting Practices prove to be based on a set of rules. It employs a complicated group of guidelines that set criteria and rules in any given scenario. The International Financial Reporting Standards alternatively utilizes a method based on principles. The IFRS instead starts with the goal of good financial reporting and gives guidance on the particular needs and challenges of a given scenario.

Good Debt

Good debt is debt that benefits a person or business to carry. Such good debts demonstrate both the creditworthiness and the responsibility of a borrower. They also create a good base to build on in the future. There are many examples of good debt, which stands in contrast to bad debt.

Good debts are typically those debts that are taken on to acquire an item or investment that only grows in value with time. Examples of this include things like real estate loans, schooling loans, home mortgages, business debt, and passive income investments. Each of these items could provide a significant and real advantage with time. Real estate could increase in value and be resold for profits.

Higher education commonly leads to greater amounts of earnings. Loans on homes are commonly wonderful for building credit and provide properties that serve as excellent collateral. Loans for businesses may result in profits earned from trade and sales. It is important to note that cars and other items are not included in these lists. This is simply because they lose value the moment that they are purchased and driven away.

Bad debts in contrast are those that result in higher interest rates and considerable deprecation of the items purchased with time. Goods that are for short time frame use and bought on credit are commonly considered to be bad debts. Since the item's life span will only decline with time, and the interest rates are typically high, no benefit is derived from purchasing these things with debt. A great number of such purchases rapidly decline in value, even after one use.

A significant benefit to good debts lies in the increase in cash flow that they commonly create. Properly structured good debts lead to tax advantages, to the ability to invest in still more assets that can produce cash, and to higher credit scores as well. Good debts that are paid on time furthermore build up a good financial base for the future. Good debts create cash flow, which stands in contrast to bad debts that do not.

Investments that produce passive income are among the best good debts. For example, purchasing an apartment building using debt will result in both income revenue and substantial tax deductions. This proves to be good debt, since although you are borrowing money, you are receiving passive income and gaining the ability to depreciate assets that can actually appreciate with time. On top of this, you are allowed to live there while you accrue all of these other benefits.

When considering a good debt, you should make certain that the income that the investment will provide is high enough to make the investment and the accompanying debt worth while. A number of experts offer advice on this. They suggest that not tying up in excess of twenty percent of your overall value in debt is a better practice. Higher debt levels than this can sound off warning bells with banks and other lenders.

Gross Development Cost (GDC)

Gross Development Cost (GDC) refers to the aggregate costs of a given company project. It could also be called the sum of all means of finance which a company employs on a particular project. This is similarly the total costs which a firm incurs from the conception of to the final implementation of a certain project. Any costs that occur after the project's completion will be treated as operational expenses. Some analysts refer to the GDC as the expenses associated with developing either improved or new products.

Two main project cost estimate categories exist in the world of business. These are project planning estimates and project design estimates. The former will be deployed in justifying and receiving approval for a given project, analyzing alternative projects, programming the sequence of project events, and receiving the final project go ahead. The latter sum up the projected project costs pertaining to sourced materials and contracted work.

One thing about such cost estimates is that they never become complete until a given project is final. In fact, insightful companies will constantly review their estimates in an effort to ensure they remain current and accurate as possible. Project engineers carry the burden for making sure the projected cost stays updated all during the project development process. At the same time, the responsible project manager carries the responsibility for both reviewing and ultimately signing off on every estimate for the costs of the project.

Current project cost estimates prove to be the ones which are the most current estimates on file in the design and planning phases. Alternatively, project planning cost estimates will be the ones compiled before a project becomes fully approved. Project planning costs estimates can be categorized according to several different breakdowns. These include project feasibility, project initiation, draft estimate project report, and project report.

Projects rarely begin without a company coming up with a project initiation cost estimate. This is an expanded version of the estimates on project feasibility in greater detail. This estimate is the one that ultimately underlies the program project costs. This is why a highly reliable estimate is critical at this juncture. It proves to be the initial benchmark against any other and future estimates.

Next in the natural progression of a potential project comes the draft project report. This estimate utilizes the identical format to the project initiation cost estimates but naturally comes with far greater detail. In such an estimate, every competing project alternative option has to be compiled with current data derived from units actually involved with the project in question. This includes elements like structure design, materials, labor unit costs, hydraulics, right of way, etc.

The next project estimate in the progression of a project will be the Project Report Cost Estimate. Once again, this stays with the identical format as with the previous project planning cost estimates. The estimate for project costs should be more conclusive at this stage. Finally, once a project is fully approved will come the project design cost estimates.

The Project Manager will update such estimates during the project development. The Project Design Cost estimates can be labeled as either final or preliminary. Such design cost estimates concentrate on the project's construction costs. These estimates should be the most detailed, up to date, and accurate of the various planning cost estimates. They should cover everything from upfront project evaluation to construction design data and costs as available. Such data permits the project manager to develop the most detailed cost estimate possible in the ongoing progress of the project in question.

Gross Margin

Gross Margin is also known as gross profit margin. This concept represents a business formula that companies compute. It is best expressed as the firm's total revenue less its cots of goods sold which is then divided by the total revenue. This provides the answer as a percentage. In other words, Gross Margins are the percentage of revenues the corporations keep after paying their direct expenses of creating both their services and goods. Higher percentages mean a company keeps a larger amount of every dollar worth of sales. This greater amount of retained income provides it with more money for servicing debt, making new investments, retained earnings, and paying out dividends to shareholders.

Gross margin equates to the amount from every sales dollar that the firm is able to keep for their gross profits. Consider a concrete and tangible real world example to better understand this idea. If HSBC Bank has a gross margin in a quarter of 30 percent, then this means it keeps 30 cents from every dollar in revenue it creates. The other 70 cents would go into the Cost of Goods Sold (COGS) category. Since all of the bank's COGS are already considered, the other 30 cents per dollar in revenue may be applied to general overhead, paying down any debt, expenses on interest, and shareholder dividend distributions.

Corporations utilize this gross margin in order to ascertain how their costs of production are measuring up against their revenues. When a corporation's gross margin is declining, it will try to find ways to reduce its costs of suppliers and labor costs. The supplier costs can be slashed by finding alternative suppliers who will supply the goods at lower prices. The other solution is to try to raise the prices on the company goods and services so as to increase the value of the corporate sales revenues.

Another effective use of gross margins lies in predicting the amount of money which they will retain towards general operating costs. Companies with 45 percent gross margins know they will have to work with 45 cents on each dollar of revenue they collect in order cover their remaining administrative and operating costs. The measure also allows for firms to measure up their efficiency as a company. Investors and analysts are able to compare and contrast two or more corporations of varying sizes against one another with the metric as well.

Gross margin should never be erroneously confused with net profit margin. Gross margin simply considers the connection between the cost of goods sold and the sales revenue. On the other hand, net profit margin covers every expense a corporation has. Calculating up the net profit margins requires firms to start with their revenues and subtract out their cost of goods sold and other expenses. This includes sales rep wages, distribution of product costs, taxes, and various operating costs.

Another way of looking at the differences between the two related but still different concepts is that the gross profit margin allows firms to determine the level of their manufacturing operations' profitability. Alternatively the net profit margin assists firms in considering their level of all around profitability.

Consider another example for calculating up gross profit margin. If a company brings in two million dollars in sales revenue, it might spend $800,000 on its labor expenses and another $200,000 on the manufacturing inputs. Once these costs of goods sold of one million dollars are subtracted out, a full million dollars remains in total gross profits. When individuals take the gross profits and divide it by the total revenue, the result is 0.5. Turned into a percentage, this equals a gross profit margin of 50 percent.

Hedge Account

A hedge account is an account established with a hedge fund. There are several reasons why a person or business would be interested in setting up a hedge account. These mostly center on the desire for investments that commonly produce higher profits or the wish to hedge, or protect, a business' operations from certain unpredictable and undesirable swings in market prices. Businesses can open up their own hedge accounts in various futures and commodities markets to protect themselves from these business impacting price movements in important related commodities.

A person who is interested in opening a hedge account will have to make application to a hedge fund. Hedge funds are typically restrictive in the types of funds that they will accept from an investor. The investor will have to prove certain income levels or asset base holdings that demonstrate that they are capable of bearing the substantial losses that could result from trades in a hedge account. They must also have liquid cash that they can tie up for long periods of time, since most hedge funds do not allow immediate on demand withdrawals.

Funds that are invested with them could be tied up for a year or longer, and minimum waiting periods apply. Because of all of these reasons, hedge funds are typically looking for people as investors who have in excess of a million dollars of liquid net worth.

Hedge accounts can also be accounts that businesses use to offset the changes in commodities' prices. A company's products may be heavily dependent on prices such as sugar and cocoa if they are a chocolate company, oil and other energy prices if they use energy intensive processes or are shipping companies, or even industrial metals such as copper if they produce wires or cables. Gold and silver mining companies, along with oil producers, routinely hedge their quantities of precious metals and energies that they expect to produce to protect against anticipated declining prices. By locking in the present price for these goods and commodities that they require or will produce later on in the year, they can insulate themselves from price swings that move against them.

This can mean the difference between having to raise prices and risk losing market share or selling goods at a much lower profit margin. Because of this, many major multinational companies around the world routinely protect themselves and their operations through the use of hedge accounts. Some of them even have individuals or departments that oversee these operations.

For a business to set up such a hedge account is not difficult. They only have to open a commodities account with one of the major commodities exchanges, such as the Chicago Mercantile Exchange, the Chicago Board of Trade, New York Mercantile Exchange, or the New York Board of Trade. These accounts can be used by companies for speculating on the price movements of underlying commodities as well, and not only for hedging their operations. In this case, care has to be taken, as the leverage provided by hedge accounts, such as commodities accounts, is enough to bring down a company overnight if they are irresponsible with the trades in the account.

Income Statement

An Income Statement refers to a corporate financial statement that relays the performance of the company for a specific accounting time frame. Analysts measure such performance through reading the summary of the business revenues and expenditures in its non-operating and operating endeavors together. This statement reveals the net loss or net profit which the business experienced in the particular accounting time period. These documents are also referred to as statements of revenues or profit and loss statements.

As one of three important financial statements, these become contained within the yearly 10-K and corporate annual reports. The other two critical documents are the statement of cash flows and the balance sheet. Every publically traded firm is required by law to deliver such legal documents to the investing public via the SEC Securities and Exchange Commission. These three combined statements relay all of the critical information on the firm's financial affairs. Yet the income statement is special in that it alone reveals the company's net income and overall sales' overviews.

Income statements are different from the balance sheet in at least one critical way. Balance sheets provide a single moment in time snap shot of corporate performance. Income statements on the other hand deliver useful information on an entire time frame or period. They start with the company sales figures and conclude with the total net income and appropriate EPS earnings per share figures.

These income statements become sub-divided into two sections. The first is operating. The second proves to be non-operating. Operating sections of the statements on income reveal all of the pertinent data on expenses and revenues which result directly from the normal principal daily operations of the business. It helps to look at a real world example to better understand the concept. If a company makes computer equipment, then it will mostly earn its revenues through manufacturing and selling such computer equipment.

In the non-operating segment of the income statement, investors learn about the expenses and revenues associated with extraordinary operations of the firm. Continuing on with the prior example, the computer equipment firm may also sell some investments and real estate properties. Any and all gains it realizes on the sales would be included under the non-operating items portion of the statement.

Analysts find a number of important uses for these income statements. Among the key ones is figuring up critical financial ratios like ROA return on assets, ROE return on equity, gross and operating profits, EVIT earnings before interest and taxes, and EBITDA earnings before interest, taxes, and amortization. As such, these statements will commonly be portrayed in a standardized format that lays out every line item as a percentage of the sales. This method allows for analysts and investors alike to quickly and easily determine the expenses that comprise the greatest amount of the sales.

These statements may similarly compare and contrast both the QOQ quarter over quarter performance and the YOY year over year performance. This is why the income statement commonly delivers at least two and often three years of comparable historical data for analysts to consider. There are also two methods for presenting the income statements. They might be offered in a multi-step format. Accountants for the company could also portray them in a single step format. Each of the two methods is consistent with the important GAAP standards. They also both provide the identical net income final numbers. In fact their figures are formulated in more or less the same way. It is only their compilation and format which proves to be different from one another.

Income Tax

Income tax refers to the tax on income which governments mandate for all personal and business entities and organizations which reside or are based in their jurisdiction. The law states that both individuals and businesses have to file their income tax returns once each year. Such filing demonstrates if they owe the government taxes or are instead able to claim a tax refund. This makes the tax on income a critical source of funding for governments. They employ it to pay for their various activities, goods, and services which they provide to the citizens and residents of their home country.

Income tax systems are usually progressive in nature. This is because national governments tend to understand that higher income earners have the broadest shoulders to bear the heaviest burdens of higher tax rates. The lower income earning individuals (and businesses) can not pay so much of their gross incomes.

The United States first imposed an income tax on its citizens in the time of the War of 1812. The goal for this tax was only to help repay the still-fledgling nation's $100 million worth of debt. They ran this up in the expenses related to the costly war on both land and sea. The government actually made good on its promise to repeal this tax on income after the conclusion of the war and repayment of the national war debt.

Despite this fact, income tax in America became a permanent fixture in the country in the early years of the twentieth century. The United States' entry into the First World War especially ran up enormous costs and debts for the nation. The tax never again disappeared in the U.S. The story is similar in many Western economically developed nations such as Great Britain, Canada, and others.

Within the U.S. today, it is the IRS Internal Revenue Service which carries the responsibility of enforcing tax laws and collecting these income taxes. They utilize a complicated and bureaucratic system of regulations and rules on incomes that have to be reported. They also monitor and decide which credits and deductions those filing individuals and businesses may claim. This agency collects the taxes from any type of income including wages, commissions, salaries, bonuses, investment earnings, and business income.

Individual income tax is one of the largest revenue generators for the Federal government of the United States today. The majority of citizens and residents within the country do not have to pay taxes on the entirety of their full earnings. Instead, the government utilizes a system of deductions on many different items to reduce the people's taxable income. Among these important deductions are dental and medical bills, interest on a mortgage, and educational expenses.

Taxpayers are allowed to minus these from their gross income in order to decide how much of their income is actually taxable. Should a taxpayer make $120,000 income and receive $20,000 worth of deductions, then the IRS will only impose taxes on the remainder of $100,000. After this, the tax agency will apply credits against the taxes which individuals owe. This means that an individual who owed $25,000 worth of taxes and received $5,000 in credits will only have to pay $20,000 total taxes.

Besides federal income taxes, a great number of the fifty states within the U.S. also collect their own state income taxes. Only seven states did not levy such taxes on their residents as of 2016. These lucky state residents lived in Wyoming, Washington state, Texas, South Dakota, Nevada, Florida, and Alaska. The two states of Tennessee and New Hampshire only levy such income taxes on any earnings realized from investments and dividends.

Businesses and corporations must also pay taxes on their earnings. The IRS deems any type of partnerships, corporations, small businesses, and even self-employed contractors to be businesses. Such groups must first report all of their business income and then subtract out their capital and operating expenses. What remains is called taxable business income.

Insolvency

Insolvency refers to the point where an individual, business, or even governmental organization is not able to cover its various financial obligations any longer. This means that it is unable to settle debts with its creditors and lenders as they are due. Many times, before such an indebted individual, company, or government becomes embroiled in any type of insolvency or bankruptcy procedures, they will try to enter into informal negotiations with creditors. This could involve setting up other payment schedules and arrangements.

Insolvency can happen for a variety of reasons. Among these is a decrease in cash flow and profitability forecasts, poor management of cash resources, or a rapid expansion in costs and expenses. Where businesses are concerned, this type of insolvency is classified according to one of two separate categories. The first of these is Cash Flow insolvency. This happens as a corporation or company simply can not pay the business debts as they become due. The second form is Balance Sheet insolvency. This type results from a company reaching the point where it possesses a negative net asset position. It simply means that the corporation's aggregate debts are greater than its total assets.

It is entirely possible for firms to be solvent by balance sheet figures but at the same time be insolvent by cash flow. The opposite scenario could also occur. If a company is bankrupt according to its balance sheet while still solvent by cash flow, it simply means its incoming revenues permit it to cover its current financial obligations. There are numerous companies which possess longer term debt obligations that continuously operate in this balance sheet-bankrupt status.

Technically, insolvency and bankruptcy are not exactly the same thing. The former is a condition of being in financial trouble or at least difficulties. Bankruptcy is instead a court order. It describes the ways in which a debtor which is no longer solvent will continue to meet its obligations or instead have its assets sold off to settle with the creditors.

This means that it is entirely possible for a company, individual, or government entity to be no longer solvent but not yet be officially bankrupt.

This could result from a temporary or sometimes fixable problem. The reverse is never the case. An entity can not be bankrupt yet still be solvent. Such a lack of solvency often translates into an eventual bankrupt state when the debtors are not able to improve their financial conditions.

Corporations and firms that have become insolvent are able to improve their financial state. They might slash costs, borrow money, sell their assets, renegotiate the terms of their debts, or seek out a bigger corporation to acquire them. The buyer could settle their debts as part of the assumption of their services, products, technology, and proprietary trademarks.

Several unfortunate events can lead to a company becoming insolvent. If they do not have enough management in human resources or accounting departments, this could contribute to the problem. A lack of qualified accounting staff could cause a company's budget to be either ignored or misappropriated.

There might also be sharply increasing vendor prices which the company is powerless to stop. Higher prices for their goods and services mean that companies will have to raise their prices in an effort to pass these along to the consumer. The problem arises when customers then shop another company or product to get a better price. Lost clientele nearly always translates into a drop in cash flow. This means that they no longer have the cash coming in to cover the bills due to the company creditors.

There could also be lawsuits brought by employees or customers that break a company's finances. The firm could be forced to pay enormous bills for both defense and in settlement damages which make it impossible for them to continue ongoing operations. As operations cease and revenue naturally drops, the ability to pay bills disappears quickly.

A final reason centers on the lack of evolution in a company product line. It might be customers simply change their needs and therefore purchasing habits. This could lead them to rival firms which offer a broader product range or line. The company which could not or did not adapt its products will find its revenues and profits decreasing to the point where they are unable to cover their expenses with their remaining income.

Intangible Assets

Intangible assets refer to the possessions of a company that are not physical. They are difficult to quantify for several reasons. These types of assets can not be physically measured. They also represent an unknown or undetermined cash value to a company. Several criteria for intangible assets are that they are invisible and can not be touched. Despite this interesting characteristic they are intrinsically valuable. These assets prove to be critical to the overall success of any business.

Intangible assets are typically classed in two categories. These are legal assets and competitive assets. Legal assets are easier to understand than are competitive assets. Legal assets include the wide varieties of intellectual and creative property. In this category are such important holdings as patents, copyrights, brand names, trade secrets, and trademarks.

Each of these can be owned and has value, though it is not easy to assign a value to these elements. Patents are the rights to inventions. Copyrights give ownership of writings and similar creative property. Brand names are a company's physical name or product, such as Coca Cola, McDonald's, or Big Mac.

Trade secrets refer to a company's ways of making things that are not known to rivals and competitors. The formula for Coca Cola is a well-known example of a trade secret. Trademarks are the ownership of popular company or product slogans or phrases as used in advertising.

The second category of intangible assets is the competitive intangible assets. These are more abstract and difficult to grasp. Competitive assets refer to reputation and the knowledge of how to do things for the business. Such assets as these can be obtained with experience mostly. These types of assets include human capital, know how, leveraging, reputation, and collaboration. Naming such ideas is hard enough, but assigning them values is a matter of conjecture.

There are reasons why coming up with values on such intangible assets is so incredibly hard. Valuing properties means that an analyst must gaze into a company's future to determine the ways that these assets will impact its bottom line in the coming years. In the process they take the assets' cost and allocate it through the expected life of the asset. Some intangible assets are valued in legal terms. An intangible asset will never be given a longer life span than forty years. When the analysts and accountants do this allocation, it is referred to as amortizing the intangible assets.

Another division of intangible assets is the category of either definite or indefinite assets. With definite assets, individuals are referring to those that will endure for a specific amount of time. Contract agreements are good examples of these types.

Indefinite assets can last for an indefinite time span. A well-known example of this is a company's brand name. Such an asset will endure so long as the enterprise keeps making the products.

Intangible assets may be hard to value, but they are still valuable for a company. Clearly an intangible asset can not have the same easily assessable value that a physical plant or other equipment would. Such intangible assets are often of great value to the company though.

There are many cases of such a property being instrumental in the company's eventual success or failure. McDonald's is so wildly successful because of the tremendous value it gains from consumer recognition of its brand name. This recognition can not be physically touched or seen.

The results of its impact on the company profits are unquestionably valuable to McDonald's. The strength of their global brand pushes sales around the world on every year. These intangible assets like brands are so powerful precisely because they make an impact on customers' choices. This allows companies to charge higher prices for their products.

Internal Rate of Return (IRR)

The IRR is the acronym for internal rate of return. This IRR proves to be the capital budget rate of return that is utilized in order to determine and compare and contrast various investments' profitability. It is sometimes known as the discounted cash flow rate of return alternatively, or even the ROR, or rate of return. Where banks are concerned, the IRR is also known as the effective interest rate. The word internal is used to specify that such calculation does not involve facts that are part of the external environment, such as inflation or the interest rate.

More precisely, the internal rate of return for any investment proves to be the interest rate level where the negative cash flow, or net present value of costs, from the investment is equal to the positive cash flow, or net present value of benefits, for the investment. In other words, this IRR will yield a discount rate that causes the net current values of both positive and negative cash flows of a specific investment to cancel out at zero.

These Internal Rates of Return are generally utilized to consider projects and investments and their ultimate desirability. Naturally, a project will be more appealing to engage in or purchase if it comes with a greater internal rate of return. Given a number of projects from which to choose, and assuming that all project benefits prove to be the same generally, the project that contains the greatest Internal Rate of Return will be considered the most attractive. It should be selected with the highest priority of being pursued first.

The assumed theory for companies is that they will be interested in eventually pursuing any investment or project that comes with an IRR that is greater than the expense of the money put into the project as capital. The number of projects or investments that can be run at a time are limited in the real world though. A firm may have a restricted capability of overseeing a large number of projects at once, or they may lack the necessary funds to engage in all of them at a time.

The internal rate of return is actually a number expressed as a percent. It details the yield, efficacy, and efficiency of a given investment or project. This should not be confused with the net present value that instead tells the particular investment's actual value.

In general, a given investment or project is deemed to be worthwhile assuming that its internal rate of return proves to be higher than either the expense of the capital involved, or alternatively, than a pre set minimally accepted rate of return. For companies that possess share holders, the minimum IRR is always a factor of the investment capital's cost. This is easily decided by ascertaining the cost of capital, which is risk adjusted, for alternative types of investments. In this way, share holders will approve of a project or investment, so long as its Internal Rate of Return is greater than the cost of the capital to be used and this project or investment creates economic value that is viable for the company in question.

International Accounting Standards Board (IASB)

The International Accounting Standards Board is an independent and private entity which arose back in 2001. The group was originally created to replace the former International Accounting Standards Committee. The IFRS Foundation maintains all oversight of the IASB.

Under their auspices, the IASB creates, publishes, and approves the International Financial Reporting Standards for the global accounting community. There are presently 14 members of the IASB. The IASB group is headquartered in London, Great Britain.

The constitution of the IFRS foundation gives the IASB full control over all technical and operating issues. This includes pursuing and developing the technical agenda after consulting with the public and the appropriate trustees of the foundation. They also approve and deliver interpretations that the IFRS Interpretations Committee recommends. Finally, they prepare and publish the International Financial Reporting Standards and all accompanying related drafts as laid out in the constitution of the IFRC Foundation.

The IASB itself was originally organized under the auspices of the IFRS Foundation. The foundation itself proves to be a non profit company incorporated in Delaware in the United States on March 8, 2001. The IFRS Foundation oversees all of the tasks that the IASB pursues as well as its strategy and structure. At the same time, the IFRS maintains the responsibility for fund raising for the IASB.

Another governing agency within the IFRS Foundation is the DPOC Due Process Oversight Committee. This trustee committee bears responsibility for the function of overseeing the IASB, as per the foundation's constitution. The last governing board is the Monitoring Board. It monitors the trustees of the IFRS foundation. It also participates in nominating the Trustees as well as approving all final appointments that the board makes to the Trustees.

There are several technical groups within the framework of the organization of the IFRS Foundation. The International Accounting Standards Board itself is among these. It bears the sole responsibility for setting all International Financial Reporting Standards since 2001.

There is also the IFRS Interpretations Committee. Their job is to create interpretations that the IASB actually approves. It also engages in tasks as requested by the IASB since 2001. Finally there are the various working groups. These different task forces are for particular projects that meet a necessary agenda of the group.

There are also numerous advisory groups within the IFRS Foundation that carry out important functions for the IASB. The ASAF Accounting Standards Advisory Forum gives advice regarding the activities for setting technical standards by the IASB. The IFRS Advisory Council provides advice to both the IFRS foundation and the IASB.

There are also a variety of specific policy committees that serve advisory roles to the IASB and the IFRS foundation. These include the Capital Markets Advisory Committee from 2003, the Effects Analyses Consultative Group of 2012, the Emerging Economies Group from 2011, the Financial Crisis Advisory Group that merged with FASB in 2008, the Global Preparers Forum, the IFRS Taxonomy Consultative Group from 2014, the Joint Transition Resource Group for Revenue Recognition of 2014, and the SME Implementation Group from 2010.

One of the important tasks of the IASB has been to help with the project to converge the differing GAAP and IFRS standards. In order to simplify the understanding of different countries' accounting and financial statements, the group is trying to bring the standards into some sort of harmony. This will especially help out investors who must read and compare the financial statements and reports of various international companies.

International Financial Reporting Standards (IFRS)

The International Financial Reporting Standards prove to be the principally used set of accounting regulations in the world. Their main rival is the United States' based GAAP Generally Accepted Accounting Procedures. These IFRS turn out to be a single collection of accounting standards. They were created and are maintained still by the IASB International Accounting Standards Board based in London.

The IASB developed these IFRS standards with the goal of them being effectively utilized on a consistent basis throughout the globe. They were written with developed, developing, and emerging market economies and nations all in mind. These standards provide both investors and other consumers of business financial statements with the necessary tools to make like comparisons between various companies. Thanks to the IFRS, investors can effectively compare and contrast the financial performances of various publicly traded corporations on a consistent basis against their global peers.

This is a high standard for the IFRS. It of course requires more and more countries sign on to these accounting standards in order for the objective to be effectively and eventually met. This vision of a single set of worldwide accounting standards is well supported by numerous globally active organizations. Among these are the International Monetary Fund, the World Bank, the G20, the Basel Committee, the IFAC, and the IOSCO.

Thanks to the tireless efforts of the IASB and the IFRS foundation along with the support of these other active international organizations, the IFRS account standards have now been made law in over 100 countries. These include all of the 27 core countries in the European Union plus Great Britain as well as over two thirds of the member nations comprising the G20. This makes sense as the G20 and other critical worldwide bodies have always encouraged the important task of the IASB and its goals of achieving a universally recognized set of international accounting standards that everyone can rely on and understand.

Since the year 2001, the International Accounting Standards Board has created and continued to improve and promote the International Financial Reporting Standards. The IASB turns out to be the body that sets the standards for the IFRS Foundation. This foundation is an organization that serves the public good. It has been well recognized for the award winning examples of its organizational transparency as well as the participation of all of its stakeholders and other participants.

The 150 members strong staff based in London hail from around 30 individual countries. The IASB operates under the auspices of a 14 member Board of Directors that is appointed and monitored by 22 different trustees coming from around the globe. These trustees themselves are further accountable to a public authority monitoring board. This way all of the various members of the leadership at the IASB are accountable to someone else.

The work of the IASB via the IFRS allows international accountants to more consistently deliver a standard means of detailing the financial performances of companies and other financial entities. This benefits investors, companies, and regulators. The standards of accounting that the IASB creates and the IFRS represents give the preparers of financial statements a complete set of principles and rules to follow when they are compiling the financial accounts of these organizations. This makes for an international standardization throughout the global markets.

It all works because the various corporations traded on public stock exchanges are required by law to prepare and produce financial statements that follow the appropriate IFRS accounting standards as do their business rivals and peers. The IFRS foundation maintains an online database of profiles on 143 countries and jurisdictions to show whether or not they accept and utilize these standards.

International Monetary Unit

International Monetary Unit can refer to two different things. It could be the U.S. dollar, which is the world's primary reserve currency. The International Monetary Unit is also the Special Drawing Rights, which are the currency units that the International Monetary Fund issues.

Special drawing rights are not an actual unique currency per se. They are units that are made up of a special basket of currencies. These days, these are comprised of U.S. Dollars, British Pounds, Japanese Yen, and Euros. The Special Drawing Rights, also known as SDR's, can be said to be International Monetary Units since they prove to be reserve assets for international foreign exchange. The International Monetary Fund actually allocates them to different countries. These SDR's offer the ability to get foreign currencies when a country needs hard cash for emergencies and other financial crises.

Although they are still expressed in units against U.S. dollars, the Special Drawing Rights remain the International Monetary Fund's only unit of account. They have their own currency code, XDR. They may be only little used now for an International Monetary Unit, but their utilization is growing, particularly at the insistence of Russia, China, and the United Nations.

Since the end of the Second World War, the U.S. dollar has proven to be the world's main reserve asset for foreign exchange. This makes it a primary candidate for the world's International Monetary Unit. As over sixty percent of central bank reserves are still held in dollars, it is unarguably the world's reserve currency even though many nations would like to see this changed and its share of reserves has been dropping consistently for some time now. Countries ranging from China and Russia, to Iran and Venezuela, to France have all called for a new International Monetary Unit to be established, particularly in the wake of the Financial Crisis of 2007 to 2010.

A new international monetary unit may arise to replace the dollar, but it does not look to happen any time too soon. This is mainly because no suitable replacement for it has been found yet. Euros are not yet widely enough held, though they are gaining in share of reserves each and every year. Neither Japanese Yen, nor British Pounds, nor Swiss Francs are significantly representative enough of economic spheres of influence to be a viable challenger. The special drawing rights are one possible replacement for the dollar, as would be a gold backed International Monetary Unit. Gold served this purposes for several hundred years during the gold standard era of the 1700's to 1971.

Gold is a last candidate for a new International Monetary Unit. As it has universal appeal and acceptance, it does offer a strong challenge to the dollar. Gold is a hard international monetary unit to argue with because it does not bear the liabilities of any single nation. It can not be manipulated by any single government or corporation. This makes it a likely choice as at least part of a new International Monetary Unit in the coming century, if not the sole one.

Inventory

Inventory refers to a collection of items that are an important part of any firms' assets. These finished goods, products which are being built, and even raw materials constitute items that the company will sell. As such, analysts often consider inventory to be among the most crucial assets of companies since it is the sale of such goods that constitutes the main revenue generating sources. This leads to the corporate earnings which ultimately accrue for the good of the company stake holders.

Such inventories can be in a range of stages of completion, so long as the corporation keeps them on its company premises. It is also possible to have this on consignment. Consignment refers to a deal where the firm holds its goods at locations that are third party owned and operated. The company still maintains the ownership all the way to the point where it sells the goods.

Corporations report their inventories on their balance sheets. They do this beneath the category of current assets. Inventories are the intermediary stage standing in between order fulfillment and manufacturing. As these inventories become sold off, their carrying cost moves under the category for cost of goods sold found on the income statement.

Three different parts of inventories are broken out beneath this account on the statement. These are finished goods, works in progress, and raw materials. The finished goods prove to be those final products which have completed production processes. The business can put them up for sale. There are so many examples of this type of goods. Finished trains, boxed up electronics, and available to ship airlines are some of them. When retailers purchase such goods to resell them, they utilize the name of merchandise. Merchandise covers countless items which stores sell such as jewelry, clothing, and electronics that the retailers decide to stock.

Under the category of works in progress are a range of goods. These would still be under the manufacturing process to change them into soon to be completed goods. Examples of this include a ship under construction, sweaters which are half knit, and cars that are partially assembled.

Raw materials are those items which become a component in the production process. They are the source materials of the finished goods. Airline manufacturers would purchase steel, refineries would buy crude oil, and chocolate companies would buy sugar and cocoa.
There are also three different ways to value inventories as accountants measure them. FIFO First In, First Out means that their cost basis for the goods relies on the materials which the firm bought first. The last inventory would have carrying costs that relied on the last bought materials for its basis. There is also a LIFO last in, first out method. This does just the opposite. Goods' costs depend on the pricing of the materials bought last, with other inventory having earliest purchased materials as the cost basis. The last methodology utilizes a weighted average for cost basis. Goods' cost sold and inventory alike become based on the materials purchased average cost for the entire period.

Inventory management is a critical concept for any business that wishes to be profitable. Those companies which hold a great quantity of inventory will run afoul of expensive storage costs, spoilage possibilities, and their goods gradually becoming outdated. It is similarly a problem to not have sufficient inventories of goods. Companies can miss sales and possible market share gains when they do not possess enough goods to sell. This is why the near-science of inventory management attempts to predict and strategize so that these costs can be minimized and goods may be constructed and obtained as they are required. One of these effective management process systems is called the JIT just in time inventory system.

Itemized Deductions

Itemized Deductions refer to an amount of money that is subtracted off of an individual American's adjusted gross income. These deductions are comprised of money the individuals spend on some services and goods that officially qualify during the tax year in question. It is the American IRS Internal Revenue Service which decides what deductions specifically will be permitted as outlined in their codes. These include certain expenses like charitable gifts, local and state taxes, mortgage interest, and medical costs.

Most of the time, such itemized deductions will be restricted to only a particular percentage of the adjusted gross income. Itemized deductions in fact are alternatives to the IRS-granted standard deduction. The itemized variations mandate that taxpayers who employ them must keep careful track of all expenses that could reduce adjusted gross income during the tax year in question. This takes time, work, and effort.

Those persons who have no choice but to often spend huge amounts of money on mortgage interest, local and state taxes, medical care, and other deductible expenses will often save more from their annual tax bill by itemizing. Yet the U.S. tax laws are not so favorable to this type of deducting, as they establish certain spending minimums which the individuals have to surpass before they are able to take and apply the deductions in question.

It often helps to consider an example to demystify difficult concepts like this. Look at the medical category. Only those costs that are higher than 7.5 percent of the filer's adjusted gross income will be deductible at all. If individuals do not spend that minimum amount, then sadly not any of their medical expenses will be allowed to be deducted.

These tax reductions are crucially important come tax time as they actually reduce individuals' taxable income. Lower taxable income equates to a lower tax bill in the end. Taxpayers have the choice of deploying the itemized deductions or opting instead for the standard deduction which the IRS sets out each year. Ultimately it is taxpayers' personal and family circumstances which will determine which of the two methods are more advantageous though.

According to the Internal Revenue Service, the majority of taxpayers in America opt for the standard deduction. What makes this more confusing is that the so-called standard deduction is not one single, simple to grasp number. Instead it varies for every filing status every year. It becomes higher for retirement aged people over 64 and for blind taxpayers than for normal situation individuals. The amounts are also a moving target ultimately as the IRS adjusts them for inflation most every year.

As an example, married couples filing jointly will get significantly higher standardized deductions than will only an individual or even head of household filer. In fact married couples who filed jointly have seen their standard deduction amounts rise significantly over the last few filing years. This is because of the final elimination of the marriage penalty which became permanently set into federal statutes, along with help from inflation adjustments over the last few years.

It means that today's standard deduction is often even more appealing to a larger group of taxpayers than ever before. In those frequent cases when adding up all of the allowable expense receipts from the past year yields a smaller itemized deduction than the standard deduction amount, the best move is to simply throw them out. Why waste time filling in additional time-consuming and complicated forms to save less on taxes after all?

Yet for those individuals who do spend huge amounts of money on their mortgage interest, medical costs, local and state taxes, and charitable giving, the itemized deductions will often save more money from the dreaded tax bill.

Land Law

Land law represents the type of law discipline that pertains to the various inherent rights of individuals to utilize (or restrict others from) owned land. There are many jurisdictions of the world that employ the words real property or real estate to describe such privately, corporately, or government owned land. Land utilization agreements such as renting prove to be a critical intersecting point where land law and contract law meet.

Water rights and mineral rights to a piece of property are closely connected to and interrelated with land law. Such land rights turn out to be so important that this form of law always develops one way or another, regardless of whether or not a country, kingdom, or empire exists to enforce it. A classic example of this phenomenon is the American West and its claim clubs. These institutions came about on their own as a means for land owners to enforce the rules which surrounded staking claims and mines' ownership.

When people occupy land without owning it, this is called squatting. This problem was not limited to the old American West, but is in fact universally practiced by the poor or disenfranchised throughout the world. Practically all nations and territories of the world maintain some form of a system for land registration. With this system there is also a process for land claims utilized in order to work out any disputes surrounding land ownership and access.

International land law recognizes the territorial land rights of indigenous peoples. Besides this, country's legal systems also acknowledge such land rights, calling them aboriginal title in many regions. In societies which still utilize customary law, land ownership is primarily exercised by customary land holding traditions.

Land rights also pertain to the inalienable abilities for individuals to freely purchase, use, and hold land according to their wishes. Naturally this assumes that their various endeavors on the property do not interfere with the rights of other members of society.

This should never be confused with the concepts of land access. Land access means that individuals have the rights to use a piece of property economically, as with farming or mining activities. Such access is considered to be far less secure than ownership of the land itself, since a person only using the property can be evicted from it at the whim of the land owner.

Land law also deals with the statutes which a nation sets out regarding the ownership of land. This can be difficult to reconcile in some countries as they have the more traditional customary land ideas such as group or individual land rights as part of their culture instead of legal understandings. This is why the various laws between land rights and land ownership have to be harmonious to prevent bitter disputes, fighting, and indigenous territorial standoffs.

Around the world, a growing focus on such land rights and the way these intersect with traditional laws on the land has emerged. Land ownership represents an important and often necessary for survival (in many cultures) source for food, water, resources, shelter, financial security, and even capital. This is why the United Nations Global Land Tool organization links landlessness in rural areas with both poverty and malnutrition.

It led to the Millennium Development Goal 7D which works to better the lives and livelihoods of around 100 million individual slum dwellers. This project is working to promote land rights and land ownership for poor people the world over in hopes that this will finally lead them to a higher quality of life and more stable and secure existence.

Ledger

A Ledger is also often called a general ledger. It refers to a firm's set of (numbered) accounts that it maintains for its corporate accounting records. With such a record, the firm has a full history of all its financial transactions it has entered into throughout the entire existence of the firm. In this master set of company books, the firm keeps all of the necessary information it must have to compile its financial statements. The data will always cover such useful facts and figures as liabilities, assets, cash flow and positions, revenues, expenses, profits, and owners' equity.

Accountants work with these general ledgers as part of their book keeping system for drawing up the company financial statements. All transactions must be included in the master document. Accountants will first pursue creating a trial balance. This represents a report of all account balances and the corresponding accounts. It is this adjusted trial balance which will be employed to create all relevant corporate financial statements.

These general ledgers are employed continuously by those firms which utilize the method of book keeping known as the double entry system. In such a methodology of accounting, every financial transaction will impact minimally two different ledgers and accounts. It also signifies that every entry will have an equal and opposite credit and debit transaction. Such double entries will be arrayed in two separate columns. Generally the debit postings will be to the left while the credit entries will be posted to the right column. It is imperative that all credit and debit entries balance out all the time.

It helps to look at a concrete example to better understand this challenging concept. When a customer pays a $300 invoice, the cash account will rise. The accountant will book a $300 credit to cash. At the same time, he or she will then log a $300 debit on the other column for the accounts receivable. In this way, both the credits and debits will equal out.

There are four key financial statements which accountants can produce from these general ledgers. The balance sheet is one of them. Under balance sheets there are sub divisions including accounts receivable and cash accounts reports. The formula for any balance sheet proves to be assets minus liabilities equals equity. The one cash account in the example above gains by $300 while the accounts receivable category becomes reduced by the amount of $300. Thanks to this simultaneous increasing and decreasing of the balance sheet equation left side, the equation will stay in perfect balance.

A second critical financial report which is impacted by the general ledgers proves to be the income statement. It also has a formula, which amounts to revenue minus expenses equals net income (also called profit). It is crucial that this formula similarly remains balanced for the financial statements to be correct. A single given transaction might also affect both the income statement and the balance sheet. Consider another example. Firms might bill their clients $750. They would note a $750 debit on to the accounts receivable category. At the same time, they would put up a $750 credit on to the revenue (or cash) categories. Both the credits and debits grow by $750 this way. The two totals remain in balance.

This double entry accounting contrasts with single entry accounting methods. In either methodology of book keeping, the common element will be the accountant or book keeper working with a general ledger of some type.

Levied Taxes

Levied taxes are taxes that are forcefully collected from an individual, business, or other entity. Among the many taxes most frequently collected these days are income taxes. These taxes could be said to be levied, since the law requires that an individual's income tax is levied for the government by the company where they work.

Three main types of tax systems are in effect in the world today where income is concerned. These include progressive, proportional, and regressive tax systems. Progressive taxes levied are those that employ progressively greater rates of tax as earnings are higher. As an example, the first $10,000 that an individual makes might be taxed at only five percent, while the next $10,000 is possibly taxed at a rate of ten percent, and income above this could be taxed at a twenty percent rate.

Proportional taxes use a pre set flat rate of tax. This applies to all earnings, no matter how high or low they are. With a ten percent flat rate, everyone will pay their ten percent of income as taxes levied, regardless of what amount of money they actually make.

Regressive taxes are said to hurt the poor by shifting the tax burden to lower income earners. This type of tax levy only taxes income to a certain dollar level, such as the first $80,000. Any money made above this amount would simply not be taxed. In reality, most tax systems employ the various kinds of tax levying methods to address various forms of income.

Levied taxes also apply to corporations and businesses. The income of a company is taxed in what is known as a corporate tax. This is sometimes alternatively referred to as a profit tax or corporate income tax. With corporate taxes levied, the net income is generally the figure that is taxed. Net income refers to the difference of gross income and expenses and other allowable write offs.

With individuals, the total income for a family or individual is commonly taxed. Some deductions are usually allowed before the taxes to be levied are determined. Income may be reduced by a certain amount as a result of how many children a family has to support, as an example.

There are many other forms of taxes levied in modern capitalist countries such as Great Britain and the United States. More than two hundred different types of taxes can be identified in the U.S. alone. These include such various taxes levied as income tax, sales tax, property tax, estate tax, capital gains tax, dividends tax, gasoline taxes, leisure taxes, luxury items taxes, and so called sin taxes on items such as cigarettes and alcohol. The United States has been called the most heavily taxed society in all of world history.

Liabilities

Where a business is concerned, liabilities prove to be amounts of money that are owed by the company at any given point. These liabilities are displayed on the firm's balance sheet. They are commonly listed as items payable, or simply as payables.

There are two types of liabilities. These are longer term liabilities and shorter term liabilities. Long term liabilities turn out to be business obligations that last for greater than the period of a single year. Mortgages payable and loans payable are included in this category.

Short term liabilities represent business obligations that will be paid in less than a year. There are many different kinds of short term liabilities. They include all of the items detailed below.

Payroll taxes payable are one of these. They represent sums automatically collected from the employees and put to the side by the employer. They have to be given to the IRS and any state taxing agencies at the pre determined time.

Sales taxes payable are another short term liability. The business collects them from its customers when sales are made. They hold them until it is time to give them to the proper revenue collecting department within the state.

Mortgages and loans payable are another short term liability. These represent payments made every month on mortgages and loans. They are not large single payments or the total amount of a loan that is eventually owed, but instead represent recurring monthly obligations.

Liabilities for individuals are another type of liabilities altogether. They also represent money that has to be paid out. For people, they are debts owed, as well as monthly cash flow that goes out of the individual's accounts.

Liabilities and assets are the opposites of each other, yet people often get them confused. While assets are things that contribute positive cash flow to a person's finances, liabilities are those that create negative cash flow, or money that leaves an individual's accounts every month. For example, a house that an individual owes money on and makes monthly payments on is a liability, not an asset. The house takes money from the person in the form of monthly mortgage payments each month. For a house to be an asset, it would have to be completely paid off. Even still, if monthly taxes and insurance payments are being made, then technically it would still be a liability. Houses can only be assets really and truly when they are rented out and the rental income that a person receives is greater than all of the expenses associated with the house every month, including any mortgage payments, taxes, insurance, upkeep, and property management fees. When the net result of a property is money coming in, then it is an asset and not a liability.

Limited Liability Company (LLC)

A limited liability company is often referred to by its acronym LLC. These business setups combine the best in both worlds of proprietorships and corporations. They offer the sole proprietorship or partnerships' advantages of pass through taxation. At the same time, an LLC provides the same limited liability for the owners which a corporation receives.

With a limited liability company, the owners will file their business losses or profits with their individual tax returns. This is because an LLC is not considered to be its own taxable structure. When lawsuits against the company are involved, it is only business assets that are at risk of seizure.

Creditors and lawsuit parties are not usually able to get to the LLC owners' personal assets, like cars or houses. This is not absolute protection. If the owners of the LLC engage in unethical, illegal, or irresponsible behavior, then they can forfeit this level of security.

Setting up a limited liability company is harder than establishing either a sole proprietorship or partnership. Once this hurdle is cleared, it is much easier to run the LLC than it is a corporation. Officers of corporations are not completely protected from actions they undertake in the business.

LLC owners must be careful not to behave like the entity is a mere extension of their own individual activities. Should the owners not act as if the LLC is its own separate business concern, then courts can determine that the business LLC does not really exist. In these cases, the judge could decide that individuals are masquerading their business affairs and conducing business as a personal venture. They can became liable then for these actions if this determination is made.

Taxes are another major reason that individuals opt to set up a limited liability company. As pass through entities, the income from their business passes on through the entity directly to the members of the LLC. This means that they must report all financial gains or losses from the enterprise directly on their own tax returns. They do not have to file separate business tax returns. The IRS does require that LLC owners make an estimated quarterly tax payment four times per year.

LLCs which are owned by more than one individual do have to file the informational return Form 1065 every year with the IRS. This form clearly states every owner's share of the limited liability company profits or losses. The IRS goes over these to be certain that the owners are all appropriately reporting their share of the earnings.

Limited liability company management is specific in how it has to be conducted. There are two forms of this. Member management involves an equal participation of the owners in the operating of the business. This is the way that the majority of smaller LLC owners run them.

The alternative form of management is called manager management. In this type of business operation, the collective owners of the LLC must choose someone to handle the daily responsibilities of managing the company. This could be an owner or several of the owners. It could also be someone who is not a part of the LLC ownership who professionally manages the business on their behalf. In this arrangement, the owners who are not managing are only tasked with sharing in the profits or losses of the business. This is often the case with family members or friends who invest in a limited liability company.

Liquidation

The meaning of liquidation depends on the use of the word. In financial terms, there are three different definitions of it. In economics or finance it refers to a failed company. A company that is insolvent is unable to pay its bills when they are owed. Liquidation is the process of winding up the company. The operations of the company cease at this point. The assets would then be divided up among its creditors and stock holders. This is done based on whose claims have priority.

Insolvent companies that choose to go into liquidation generally do so under U.S. bankruptcy code Chapter 7. This legal statute gives the rules on liquidation of companies. Companies that are still solvent but are in trouble may also file a Chapter 7 bankruptcy. This is less common. There are also bankruptcies for companies that do not force liquidation. One such provision that covers this scenario is Chapter 11. In a Chapter 11 filing the trustee saves the company and restructures its debts.

When the process of liquidation occurs, the company halts all operations. All of its assets are tallied up and then distributed to the various claimants. After this is finished, the trustee finally dissolves the business. The debts actually have not been discharged in this process. They still exist to the point where the statute of limitations on the debts expires. There is no debtor in existence to pay off these debts. Creditors simply write them off in practice.

The assets in this liquidation process are handled in a certain methodical way. The Department of Justice appoints a trustee. This individual supervises the process. Assets are distributed to those who have claims based on their priority. Secured creditors are first in line. This is because their loans are backed up by collateral.

The lenders are allowed to seize this collateral and then to sell it. Many times they receive far less than the actual asset value because there are limited time frames. Sometimes the assets are not enough to cover their debt. These creditors are compensated from any other liquid assets in this case.

Unsecured creditors come next in the process. In this category are holders of bonds, the IRS, and employees. Bond holders are a form of unsecured creditors. The company may owe the IRS taxes. Employees may be waiting on payroll or other money they are due. The last category to receive compensation is shareholders. If any assets are left they receive them. Preferred stock investors receive priority before the common stock holders. Usually there is nothing left for either class by the time the creditors are paid.

Another definition of liquidation surrounds huge sales. Sometimes a company needs to close out a great deal of inventory. They would do this by liquidating their inventory at deep discounts. Any company can do this. They do not have to file for bankruptcy in order to sell off inventory.

A third definition of liquidation involves closing out an investment. This generally occurs when an investors sells their holdings in exchange for cash. An individual might also liquidate out of a one position and into an opposite one. If he or she held long shares in a stock, they could instead take on the identical number of short shares.

Brokers can force liquidate trader positions in certain cases. Traders who have acted or traded recklessly with risk can have this happen. If traders' account values drop below the minimum margin requirements they can suffer from forced liquidation as well.

Liquidation Value

Liquidation Value represents the full value of a corporation's complete range of physical assets if and when it declares bankruptcy or actually goes out of business. This value is compiled when every asset on the company books and balance sheet becomes tallied up. This value then includes real estate, equipment, factories, fixtures, and inventory. Those assets that are intangible would never be a part of the firm's final liquidating value.

This is one of four key types of value assigned to a corporation or company's various assets. These include book value, market value, salvage value, and liquidation value. With every category of value, this delivers an alternative view point for both analysts and accountants alike to classify the total value of all assets. For individuals and investors who engage in workouts and bankruptcies, this Liquidating Value is absolutely essential to know.

Book value and market value generally vie for the crown of largest assets' category valuation. In cases where any group of assets' market value has deteriorated because of decreasing market demand instead of the business using it up, this proves to be true. With book value, the asset value equates to the one declared upon the corporate balance sheet. Since the company balance sheet declares these assets for their historical price and cost, this means that the book value could equate to more or less than the relevant market prices which apply on a given day. When the all around economy is growing and prices in general are rising, then this book value is traditionally less than the relevant market value.

With liquidation value, the sum represents the anticipated price for the asset after it has been sold, generally for a loss as compared the original price. Salvage value refers to the one assigned to the assets once they reach the conclusion of their natural and useful life. This then would represent the scrap value of assets. Liquidation value typically proves to be less than the book and market values yet still higher than basic salvage value. Liquidating assets are still valuable, they just sell for less than they otherwise should and would because of the proverbial fire sale in a shortened time frame. It causes them to be sold for losses versus their listed book value.

There are reasons why such liquidation values never include any intangible asset prices. Such intangible assets comprise the goodwill, intellectual property, and brand recognition of the company or corporation. When firms are sold off instead of being liquidated, the firm's value will include both intangible assets' value and liquidation value. This is why traditional value investors will consider and contemplate the variances between the ongoing concern value and the market cap value. They are able to decide this way whether or not the stock of the corporation represents a good value.

It is always useful to consider an example in order to clarify the concept of liquidation value. A given corporation the Snappy Pop Company has $550,000 in liabilities. They also possess book valued assets of $1 million on their company balance sheet. The auction value of these assets might be $750,000, which represents three-quarters of their fair value. At the same time, the salvage value is $75,000. To determine the liquidation value, analysts simply subtract out any liabilities (in this case $550,000) off of the auction value (in this case $750,000). This gives a value of $750,000 minus $550,000 for a grand total of $200,000 liquidating value.

Loan to Cost Ratio

Loan to Cost Ratio, or LTC, proves to be a measurement utilized by finance companies in extending loans for commercial real estate projects. It is employed ultimately to make comparisons of the offered financing for a given building project versus the expenses of completing said project. With the LTC ratio, lenders of commercial real estate loans are able to decide on the risks involved in backing a particular construction project via loans. The LTC ratio is similar to the LTV loan to value ratio. They both compare the amount of the construction loan to the value in fair market terms of the project in question.

Lenders work with the Loan to Cost Ratio in order to decide what loan percentage or dollar amount the financier is agreeable to finance. They do this with a basis on the firm costs stated in the construction project budget. After construction completes, these projects then possess a new and often times significantly higher value. Future values can often be double what the construction costs prove to be. This means that on a loan for $200,000 in construction, the future value of the project is likely to be $400,000 once it is fully concluded.

Consider how LTC will look in this example. With $200,000 in construction costs, and an 80% LTC ratio, the lender would be willing to loan out $160,000 on the total project. Using a similar 80% LTV ratio metric instead would significantly change the amount of money the lender is wiling to extend to $400,000 x 80% for $320,000.

Lenders never completely finance 100% of construction costs. This is because they feel that the builders also need to have significant exposure to the project in order to guarantee they will give their all to see them succeed. This is what is meant by the colloquial expression "skin in the game." It prevents a builder from simply getting up and walking away from a project gone bad. It is why the majority of lenders will require a builder to kick in minimally 10% to 20% of the construction costs to secure a financing deal.

Loan to value ratios are not the same as the Loan to Cost Ratio, though they have much in common up to a point. LTV evaluates the loan issued versus the project value once it will be fully completed. Since most banks assume that construction projects will double in value once they are finished, this is why an identical LTV percentage to the LTC ratio will yield twice the loan amount.

Lenders hold firmly to the LTC ratio. It helps them to clearly express the levels of risk in a given financing project for commercial construction. In the end, using a greater Loan to Cost Ratio will entail a significantly riskier project from the lender's perspective. This is why the overwhelming majority of reputable mainstream lenders will not surpass a pre-determined percentage when they consider any given project. They usually limit this amount strictly to a maximum of 80% of the project's LTV or LTC. When lenders are willing to become involved at a higher percentage and ratio, they will most always insist on a substantially greater project and loan interest rate to compensate them for the additional level of risk to which they are consenting.

Lenders will also have to consider other information and circumstances beyond simply Loan to Cost Ratio and Loan to value ratios when extending such financing. They take into consideration the value of the property and its location for where the project will be constructed. They also contemplate how much creditworthiness and experience the commercial builders in the application possess. Finally, they consult both the borrowers' loan payment histories on other loans and their credit record as demonstrated in their company credit report.

Market Value

With regards to real estate, market value is the price which a real property seller can anticipate obtaining from the property purchaser in normal open and fair market negotiations. In general, appraisers value a home or other piece of real estate property utilizing a number of critical factors. When markets are volatile, such prices will vary significantly. Real estate agents may place one value on a home or other piece of real estate, yet in the end, the true property value is only what an able and willing buyer will actually pay to acquire it.

It is crucial to be aware of the market value of a piece of property individuals or businesses are selling as this ultimately sets the asking price of the real estate in question. Those sellers who are not intimately aware of this will either overprice their houses or under price them. Either of these actions will often lead to poor financial results. Not being aware of a property's true value can cause homeowners to become victims to practices of predatory lending. In this unscrupulous lending behavior, the bank or other lending financial institution will prevail upon a borrower to take out a greater amount of money than their property is really worth.

It is real estate agents or better still professional appraisers who determine most accurately the market value of a house or piece of real estate through measuring it up to other properties in the area or neighborhood which share similarities with the one in question. Real estate agents and appraisers call such recently sold area properties "comparables." They will always seek to find houses which are as alike in style, size, and location to the one they are appraising as possible.

Such properties must have sold within the prior six months to a year. According to this strategy, the professionals will similarly discern what the typical price per square foot of the houses in the area actually is. This practice by itself will not set the market price of a house, but it will give the professionals a good starting point from which to set a reasonable and viable asking price for the property.

There are also various other factors which influence a property's market value. These include the condition of the property in question as well as any improvements which the seller makes. Where a home is concerned, bathroom and kitchen renovations and updates are the main ones which will boost the selling price. Other more cosmetic appearance improvements like new carpet, fresh paint, updated light fixtures, and special window treatments will help a house to show better and perhaps sell faster, yet they will not increase the all around value of the home.

Yet it is absolutely true that the overall condition of any piece of real estate will impact its total value. Houses that boast more current and better maintained appliances and systems, roofs, windows, and even entry doors will realize a significantly better final selling price than those which offer flawed structures or outdated appliances, systems, entry doors, and mechanics.

In corporations and investments, market value is the price for which a given asset will sell in the open market. This measure of value can often be applied to the market capitalization of any company which is publically traded. Determining the market cap value is a matter of multiplying out the current price per share by the quantity of total outstanding shares.

This measure of market value is simplest to calculate for those instruments which are traded on exchanges, like futures and stocks. This is because their market prices are readily available and commonly disseminated. With over the counter securities such as fixed income securities, it can be far harder to ascertain. Yet the most difficult to determine market values are those commonly associated with less liquid assets such as businesses and real estate. This is why business valuation experts and real estate appraisers determine the market values for such assets as these.

Net Asset Value

The Net Asset Value refers to a mutual fund and its per share value. It is also known by its acronym NAV. Exchange traded funds, or ETFs, can also be referenced by the NAV. These values which the companies themselves compute for investors only provide a snap shot of the NAV at a particular time and date. In either security type, the fund's per share dollar value arises from the aggregate value of every security within its portfolio minus any liabilities the fund may owe. Finally this is expressed over the total number of outstanding shares in order to arrive at the shares' ultimate NAV.

Where mutual funds are concerned, the Net Asset Value is derived one time every trading day. They utilize the closing market prices for every security within the fund's holdings in order to determine this. Once this is done, the fund is able to settle all sell and buy orders which are outstanding on the shares. These prices will be set by the NAV of the mutual fund in question for the value per the trade date. Investors will always be required to wait to the next day in order to obtain their actual trade-in or trade-out price.

Because mutual funds do pay out nearly all their capital gains and income, such NAV changes are never the optimal gauge for the performance of the given fund. Instead these are better determined by looking at the yearly aggregate return, or total return.

With ETFs, these are actually closed end types of funds. This means that they actually trade more like stocks do. The shares of these Exchange Traded Funds therefore constantly trade at the market value. It might be a literal value which is higher than the NAV. This would be trading at a premium to the Net Asset Value. It could similarly trade under the NAV. This would mean the prices were trading at a discount to the NAV.

With these ETFs, the Net Asset Value becomes computed once at the markets' close so that the fund can correctly report the ETF values. During the day however, these are figured differently than the mutual fund computations. This is because the ETFs will compile the during-the-day NAV in real time at numerous points in every minute of the trading day.

It is helpful to consider an example of how the mutual funds compute their Net Asset Value calculations. The formula is actually very straightforward. It is simply that the NAV is equal to the mutual fund's assets less its liabilities with the difference divided by the total number of shares outstanding. The assets in the case of mutual funds include cash equivalents and cash, accrued income, and receivables. The main portion of their assets commonly are their investments, which will be priced per the end of the day closing values. Liabilities equate to the complete longer-term and shorter-term money owed, along with each accrued expense. Among these expenses will be utilities, salaries of the staff of the fund, and various operational costs for running such a fund.

Consider that the fictitious Diamond Stocks Mutual Fund counted $200 million in investments, figured utilizing the end of day closing prices of all their assets. Besides this, it has $14 million in cash equivalents and cash and another $8 million in receivables in total. The daily accrued income amounts to $150,000. Besides this, Diamond Stocks owes $26 million in its shorter-term liabilities and has $4 million of longer-term liabilities. The daily accrued expenses amount to $20,000. With 10 million outstanding shares, the net asset value would equate to $19.21 in the case of the Diamond Stocks Mutual Fund.

Net Operating Income

Net Operating Income can refer to two different concepts. It may be used in regards to companies and corporations, or to properties and their annual incomes. Where companies are concerned, Net Operating Income, also known by its acronym NOI, is the income after deducting the company's operating expenses. It is figured up in advance of taking off interest and income tax deductions.

When this number proves to be a positive number, it is called net operating income. If the number turns out to be a negative value, then it is referred to as a Net Operating Loss, also known by the acronym of NOL. Many analysts like to look at the Net Operating Income as a realistic picture of how a company is performing. They feel that this number is more difficult for management to manipulate than are other numbers in the income statements of a company.

Pertaining to properties, Net Operating Income equals the annual gross income minus the expenses for operating. In this respect, the gross income is comprised of real income from rentals as well as other incomes like laundry receipts, vending receipts, parking charges, and every type of income that is related to properties. Operating expenses prove to be the expenses that are encountered in the typical maintenance and operating of the property in question. Among these expenses are insurance, maintenance, repairs, utilities, management fees, property taxes, and supplies. Some costs are not deemed to be operating expenses, such as capital expenditures, interest and principal payments, income taxes, depreciation, or amortization of the points on a loan. So, calculating the Net Operating Income on a property involves first taking the various forms of annual gross income and adding them all up. Then the operating expenses should be taken and added up. Finally, the operating expense total is subtracted from the operating income total to achieve the Net Operating Income figure.

In real estate, Net Operating Income is utilized within two critical real estate ratios. The Capitalization Rate, also know as the Cap Rate, is employed to come up with an estimate of the actual value of properties that produce income. For example, maybe a property being considered for purchase possesses a market capitalization value of ten. Coming up with the market cap rate is achieved by considering the financial information from the sales of properties that produce income and are similar in a particular market.

The other important real estate ratio that relies on Net Operating Income is the Debt Coverage Ratio, also know as the DCR. The Net Operating Income proves to be a critical component of this DCR ratio. Investors and lenders alike utilize the debt coverage ratio to determine if a property has the capability of covering both its mortgage payments and operating expenses together. A result of one is deemed to be the break even point. The majority of lenders want at least a 1.1 to 1.3 ratio in order to contemplate making a commercial loan to a given property. The higher this debt coverage ratio works out to be in a banks' opinion, the safer the loan will ultimately be.

Net Operating Profit After Tax (NOPAT)

Net operating profit after tax is also called by its acronym of NOPAT. This refers to the potential earnings (in cash) of a corporation working under the pretense that it has no debt. This NOPAT metric is often utilized in so-called EVA economic valued added calculations. The formula for determining NOPAT is as follows: the operating income times the result of one minus the tax rate. For companies which are debt leveraged, this NOPAT proves to be a more precise and exact way of examining their operating efficiencies. As such it does not factor in the tax advantages which a number of corporations enjoy from their debt load.

Analysts and accountants consider a number of varying performance metrics when they are evaluating a corporation in which to invest. The two most frequent performance measures turn out to be sales (or revenue) and net income growth. With the revenue/sales figures, this delivers a top line performance metric. It does not say anything about the company's operating efficiency value though. Similarly the net income does include the operating expenses of a firm, yet it also factors in the net tax benefits and savings from the company's particular debt leverage.

This is where the Net operating profit after tax comes in as a useful hybrid form of alternative calculation. It permits the analysts to compare and contrast a company's performance against past metrics and other companies by removing the effects of debt leverage from the equation. This allows analysts to truly fairly measure one company against another, regardless of the two firms' net debt positions.

It always helps to consider a real world, concrete example with these complex terms. If a company's EBIT Earnings Before Interest and Taxes was $12,000 and their tax rate was 25 percent, then the calculation for NOPAT would translate to $12,000 times the result of one minus .25,(or .75). This equals $9,000 as a NOPAT. It is an after tax cash flow estimate that does not include the tax benefits of debt. For those companies without debt, Net operating profit after tax equals the same amount as does the net income after tax.

It is worth noting that analysts prefer to compare and contrast firms within the same industry when utilizing the NOPAT metric. This is because every industry has its own normal range of operating costs. Some industries' typical expenses turn out to be dramatically lower or higher than others' do.

For example, cable utilities would have extremely high operating costs associated with initially putting in, continuously upgrading, and maintaining their technology and physical hard-wired distribution networks. Soft drink businesses like Dr. Pepper/Snapple Group (DPS) have relatively low costs since they generally license out their products to other companies which produce and distribute them on their behalf.

Net operating profit after tax has other uses besides the helpful view of a company without its debt leverage being considered. Those analysts who follow and predict mergers and acquisitions utilize this NOPAT value all the time. It helps them to figure up the FCFF free cash flow to firm. This is equal to the NOPAT less any changes to working capital. It also equates to the net operating profit of the firm after taxes less the firm's capital.

These two metrics NOPAT and FCFF are commonly utilized by those types of analysts who hunt down targets for acquisition. The reason for this is that the financing of the acquiring firm will then substitute in for the present financing arrangement (their corporate debt).

Net Present Value (NPV)

Net Present Value refers to a principal profitability measure that companies utilize in their corporate budget planning process. It helps them to analyze the possible ROI return on investment for a particular proposed or working project. Thanks to the involvement of time value and its depreciating effect on dollars, the NPV is forced to consider a discount rate and its compounding effect throughout the term of the entire project.

The actual Net Present Value in an investment or business project considers the point where revenue (or cash inflow) is equal to or greater than the total investment capital that funds the project or asset in the first place. This is particularly useful for businesses when they are comparing and contrasting a number of different projects or potential projects. It allows them to draw a valuable comparison of their comparative profitability levels to make sure that they only spend their limited resources, time, and management skills on the most valuable ventures. The higher the NPV proves to be, the more profitable it is as an investment, property, or project in the end.

Another way of thinking about the Net Present Value is as a measurement of how well an investment is meeting a targeted yield considering the upfront investment that the firm made. Using this NPV, companies can also determine precisely what adjustment they need in the initial investment in order to reach the hoped for yield. This assumes that all else remains constant.

Net Present Value can also be utilized to effectively visualize and quantify investments in real estate and other asset purchases in a simple formulaic expression. This is that the NPV is equal to the Current value minus the cost. In this iteration of the NPV, the current value of all anticipated future cash flow is discounted to today utilizing the relevant discount rate minus the cost of acquiring said cash flow. This makes NPV essentially the value of the project less the cost. When analysts or corporate accountants examine the NPV in this light, it becomes easy to understand how the value explains if the item being purchased (or project being funded) is more or less valuable than the cost of it in the first place.

Only three total categories of NPV ultimate values are possible for any property purchase or project funding. NPV could be a positive Net Present Value. This means that the buyers will pay less than the true value of the asset. The NPV might also be a Zero NPV. This simply means that the buyer or project funder is paying precisely the value of the asset or project worth. With a negative NPV in the final categorization, the buyer will be paying too much for the asset technically. This will be more than the asset is actually worth. There are cases where companies or buyers might be willing to pursue a project or acquire an asset with a negative NPV when other factors come into play.

For example, they might be interested in purchasing a property for a new corporate headquarters whose NPV is negative. The reasoning behind such a decision could be the unquantifiable and intangible value of the location of the property either for visibility purposes or because it is next to the present company headquarter premises.

It is always helpful to look at a concrete example to de-mystify difficult concepts like Net Present Value. Consider a corporation that wishes to fully analyze the anticipated profits in a project. This given project might need an upfront $10,000 investment to get it off the ground. In three years time, the project is forecast to create revenues amounting to $2,000, $8,000, and $12,000. This means that the project is expected to provide $22,000 on the initial $10,000 outlay.

It would appear that the return will amount to 120 percent for a gain greater than the initial investment. There is a reason why this is not the case though. The discount rate for the time value of money has to be factored in, and this means a percentage of several points per year at least. The figure of 4.5 percent is often utilized on a three year project like this. This takes into consideration the fact that dollars earned three years from now will not be so valuable as today's earned dollars. This is why the corporate accountants will use business calculators in order to plug in the discount time value rates to figure the true NPV. Discounting by the 4.5 percent means that the project actually will return somewhere near $21,000 in terms of today's dollar value.

Net Profit

Net Profit refers to the remaining sales dollars which are left over after a firm pays for all of its operating costs, interest on debt, preferred stock dividends, and taxes. Common stock dividends are not included in the amounts deducted from the firm's aggregate sales revenue. Sometimes analysts call this type of profit the net income, the bottom line, and/or the net earnings.

A simplistic (but useful) way of thinking about this form of profit is that it is all of the money which remains after all of the expenses of the going concern are paid in full. Calculating the net income is done when aggregate expenses are subtracted from total revenue. Because these net earnings traditionally occur on the final line in an income statement, companies often refer to it as their "bottom line."

It remains true that this Net Profit is still among the most closely watched business indicators in the world of finance. Because of this, it has a substantial part in the computations of financial statement analysis and ratio analysis. Stake holders in the corporations also scrutinize this bottom line carefully since it ultimately proves to be the way they become compensated as shareholders in the firm. When corporations are unable to realize enough profits to pay their shareholders, stock prices plunge. On the other hand, when corporations are growing and in solid financial health, the more available profits become reflected in greater stock prices.

A common mistake that many individuals make is in their understanding of what net profits actually represent. Net profit is never the metric for the total cash earnings a firm realized in a certain period. The reason for this confusing fact is that income statements also showcase a range of expenses that are not cash-based. Some of these are amortization and depreciation. In order to understand the true amount of cash which corporations actually generate, investors and analysts must carefully review the cash flow statement.

In fact any changes to net profit will be constantly and thoroughly reviewed, examined, and discussed. When firms' net profits are negative or even lower than anticipated, there are a host of issues that could be causing it. It might be that the customers' experience is negative. Sales could be decreasing for one or more reasons. Expenses at the company could be out of control or simply poorly managed and monitored. New management teams may not be performing at the anticipated or promised levels.

In the end, the Net Profit will range wildly from one firm to the next and according to which industry they represent. One industry's profits will likely be substantially different from another industry's. It is not a useful comparison to make between one corporation and another since these profits are quantified in dollars (Euros, pounds, Swiss francs, or yen). It is also a fact that no two corporations will be exactly the same size by either revenues or assets.

This is why many analysts prefer to make comparisons between corporations and industries by utilizing what they call profit margin. This is the net profit of a company as a percentage amount of its total sales. Sometimes analysts and investors will also look at the P/E Price to Earnings Ratio alternatively. This widely cherished ratio reveals to considering investors what the price is (in the form of stock price) for every dollar of net profit the corporation actually generates.

Analysts still like the metric of net profit despite these limitations. A survey conducted querying around 200 marketing managers who were senior level revealed that an incredible 91 percent agreed that they believe this measurement to be very useful.

Net Worth

Net worth is a figure that represents a business, an individual, or another group's difference between the assets that they have and the liabilities that they owe. Figuring up this net worth is done by first taking all of the entity's debts and obligations and then subtracting that number from the entire sum of assets. If the total of all of these assets is greater than the sum of all of the debts and obligations, then a positive net worth results. Otherwise, when the debts are greater than the assets, then the entity has a negative net worth.

When you sit down to determine the net worth figure, every asset should be totaled in the operation. There are many different kinds of assets. These are comprised of cash in the bank, holdings of stocks, real estate, bonds, and other types of investments, and major possessions like vehicles. Correctly figuring out the different assets' values is done with the use of the up to date fair market value, not the cost paid for the item when it is purchased.

You must also correctly add up the total of debts and obligations when you are attempting to get a correct net worth value. Liabilities cover many different obligations, like a car payment, mortgage, total of credit card debt outstanding, and any other forms of loans that have balances left on them. Both every asset and liability must be measured in order to come up with an accurate net worth.

Knowing your present net worth is very useful and meaningful. If you are able to cover all of your outstanding debt obligations simply by selling of all of your assets, then you have a financial condition that is fairly stable and in order. If your assets are more than sufficient to cover all of your obligations, then your finances are in greater shape. Most businesses and people seek to reach a point that they have actual positive net worth.

There are a few benefits from having a correct understanding of your net worth. It is essential that your present assets' value is greater than your present debt load. A person who owes more money than they actually own presents a profile of a person who is not an especially good credit risk. Without a positive net worth, many lending institutions like banks will think twice about providing you with the most advantageous loan rates offered. This is because they feel that you present more of a risk to lend money.

It is also good to know where your net worth stands because it is a helpful beginning point for your general financial planning. Should you discover that you hardly have sufficient assets with which to cover your present amount of debts, then this is a good sign that you should not engage in any other purchases until later, after you have eliminated several of your debts. This means that if you occasionally figure up your net worth, then you will comprehend not only where you stand now, but also when you will be in a better position to purchase a new car.

Non Performing Asset (NPA)

A Non Performing Asset is also known by its acronym NPA. This pertains to a certain way of categorizing loans on a banks' balance sheet. Such NPA loans are those which are in arrears on their regular payments or are otherwise in outright default. In the majority of instances, loans become categorized as nonperforming as the payments on the loans are not received consecutively over 90 days. It is possible for the time lapse to be less or more than the typical 90 days in order for NPA classification to occur. It all comes down to the individual conditions and terms which each loan spells out in the documents and the policies of the bank in question.

Following 90 days of non-payment, most banks will commonly reclassify the loans as Non Performing Assets or loans. This might happen during the term for the loan or as a failure ultimately to pay off the balance principal of the loan which becomes due upon maturity. It always helps to consider a real world example in order to better understand a somewhat complicated topic.

Consider a firm that takes out a $20 million loan with associated payments that are interest-only in nature for a $100,000 payment amount each month. If the borrower misses payments for three months in a row, the bank which originally made the loan could be forced to classify the loan as a Non Performing Asset in order to comply with its government-mandated regulatory requirements. It is also possible for loans to finally become nonperforming if the borrower pays out all of its interest payments but is unable or alternatively fails to pay back the final principal that becomes due at maturity date.

Banks which carry such Non Performing Assets on their books and balance sheets create three separate drags for themselves. The cash flow of the bank lender in question becomes reduced as principal and/or interest payments do not become made. This can reduce earnings or even upset budgets. Provisions for loan losses must be set aside in order to compensate for possible defaults. These provisions actually lower the amount of total capital with which the bank can issue additional loans. After the realized losses are booked, the bank or financial institution will have to write them off versus their earnings.

There are as many as four different means for lenders to recover all or part of their losses that arise because of Non Performing Assets. Smart lending institutions will be willing to restructure loans in order to keep cash flow incoming. It also permits them to keep the loan from becoming categorized as a nonperforming asset. Banks might also seize the underlying collateral of the loans. They can then sell this off in order to reduce their losses as much as the market value of the assets will allow.

Thirdly, financial institutions might also choose to convert their NPA loans into equity. This could grow back all the way to full value over time. As bonds become converted to new equity shares, the original stakes' value typically disappears. Finally, banks might sell off their bad debts for substantial discounts to such firms as specialize in collections on loans. Lenders will tend to sell off their NPA loans which do not come collateral-secured. This is particularly the case when the other methods of recouping their losses do not prove to be especially cost effective for the bank or other lending institution.

Open Market Operations (OMO)

Open Market Operations are also called by their acronym OMO. These describe both the purchasing and selling of open market-based government securities. The Federal Reserve central bank of the United States has a committee which engages in these transactions with the goal of expanding or contracting the total quantity of money flowing through the banking system.

When the Fed buys up instruments, it forces money into the banking system to stimulate growth. When it sells its various securities, this has the opposite effect and contracts the economy. The idea behind the Federal Reserve's thinking with this technique is to tweak through manipulating the federal funds rate. This rate represents the price for which the banks will loan money to each other.

This Open Market Operation proves to be the most frequently deployed and highly flexible tool from the toolkit of the Federal Reserve. It permits them to both control and implement their monetary policy for America. They also work with the reserve requirements for the banks and the discount rate. While they have all three tools at their disposal, the buying and selling of government securities proves to be their favorite and also most often deployed tool. This permits them to precisely control the amount of bank reserve balances. It assists the Federal Reserve in decreasing or increasing the short-term interest rates as they deem to be appropriate for any given time.

The Federal Reserve committee which determines the monetary policy is called the FOMC Federal Open Market Committee. They carry out this monetary policy through actually setting the target for the federal funds interest rate and also by implementing their Open Market Operations, along with manipulating the reserve requirement and discount rate strategies to get the federal funds rate to their desired levels. This fed funds rate turns out to be incredibly important for them to finely control since it impacts practically every other interest rate found in the United States today. Among these are the prime rate, car loan rates, and home loan mortgage rates. Only the London-based LIBOR is more important today.

When the FOMC is attempting to attain a desired federal funds rate, they first fall back on the Open Market Operations. They carry out either the contractionary or expansionary monetary policy to achieve their desired movement and ultimate ends.

When the Fed sets its sites on expanding the economy this way, they want an expansionary policy. They need to reduce the fed funds rate in order to facilitate this goal. They will buy government securities off of private bond dealers to deposit funds into the accounts for the financial institutions, entities, and investors who sold them the government bonds. These deposits then became a component of the commercial bank held-cash on account with the Federal Reserve. It grows the money supply available to commercial banks for their various lending operations. It is these commercial banks which seek to loan out their cash reserves. To do this, they will lower their interest rates to bring in more customers.

The Fed also occasionally has moments when it seeks to cool off an overheating economy in the U.S.A. To do this they will begin their contractionary monetary policy and seek to boost the federal funds rate. In practice, this involves them selling off their seemingly limitless supply of government securities to the financial institutions and banks. It reduces the amount of money the commercial banks have left to loan out. This makes the cost of money more expensive and so boosts the associated interest rates, including the federal funds rate too.

Operating Cash Flow (OCF)

Operating Cash Flow is also known by its abbreviated acronym OCF. It refers to a metric for the quantity of cash which a corporation or company's typical daily business operations produce. As such, it provides a good insight into a firm's ability to generate enough cash flow in order to either grow or at the very least maintain its existing operations. It might also prove that a going concern requires outside financing in order to fund its expansion plans.

Publically traded firms must calculate their Operating Cash Flows through employing an indirect method of calculation. This GAAP Generally Accepted Accounting Principles mandate means that they have to adjust their net income into a cash basis. They do this by making alterations to their accounts that are not cash. This includes accounts receivable, depreciation categories, and inventory changes.

In fact the Operating Cash Flow is a true representation of the cash portion of the firm's net income. This will also take into account other non-cash items thanks to the requirements which the GAAP sets out for net incomes to be done as accrual-based reporting. This means that amortization, compensation which is based upon stock shares, and incurred but as of yet not paid for expenses would be included in the calculations.

Besides this the actual net income has to be adjusted to reflect changes to working capital kinds of accounts in the balance sheet of the corporation. Especially important is the fact that any accounts receivable increases actually equate to booked revenues for which no collections have been completed. Because of this, these increases have to be taken off of the net income figure. This is partially offset at least by any reported accounts payable increases that are due but as of yet not paid, since this remains in the net income number.

Analysts have opined that such Operating Cash Flow represents the most accurate and basic form of outflows and inflows of cash as a company engages in its normal operations of the daily business. Where the health of a firm is concerned, this represents among the most crucial of metrics. Yet it most appropriately and usefully works for those corporations that are not overly complex.

The Operating Cash Flows focus on the both outflows and inflows which a corporation's principal business activities involve. This includes buying and selling inventory, paying employee salaries, and delivering services. It is important to remember that all financing and investing activities will not be included in the Operating Cash Flow. These become reportable separately. A part of these excluded activities would be purchasing equipment and factories, borrowing money, and engaging in share holder dividend payouts. Finding this cash flow number is easy by looking at the corporation's cash flows statement. This statement will break out the numbers into several categories including cash flows from operations, from financing, and from investing.

Operating Cash Flow is a very important number on a company balance sheet. Many financial analysts and investors would rather consider such cash flow measures since they reduce the impacts of confusing and opaque accounting tricks. It also delivers a better, sharper big picture for the business operations' health and reality.

Consider the following examples. When a firm concludes a big sale, this delivers a major increase to its revenues. This is irrelevant though if the firm can not collect on the money owed. It does not represent a real gain for the corporation. At the same time, firms could be producing elevated operating cash flow numbers. Despite this, they might have an abysmally low net income number if they employ an accelerated depreciation calculation or possess many fixed assets.

Operating Expenses

In the world of business and corporations, operating expenses is the term that pertains to the continuous costs of running a business. This makes operating expenses the expenses for everything happening behind the scenes. Such operating costs include any expenses incurred for the literal operation of the business.

You occasionally see the words operating expenses written as OPEX. This is especially true in internal memos and documentation that are relevant to the earnings of a company. The most frequent operating expenses are those having to do with employee benefits and salaries. These commonly make up the biggest individual expenses for a corporation. Other operating costs could be office supplies, marketing budgets, licensing and legal fees, raw material expenses, costs of research and development, accounting fees, and office utilities.

Another key operating expense is depreciation. Depreciation proves to be the quantity of value that diminishes in an asset over a period of time. This means that accounts can take equipment, vehicles, and other assets and subtract out the lower value off of the initial value to come up with depreciation as assets gradually lose value. This depreciation can be counted as an operating expense so long as the asset is still employed by the business in its operations.

Some expenses are deemed to be capital expenses instead of operating expenses. This is generally the case for single event expenses, like buying replacement equipment for completely depreciated existing equipment. This division of costs allows both the firm and its investors to have a more realistic snap shot of for what the money is used before it is able to be put to profits. When you are self employed, then you may count both CAPEX and OPEX as business expenses.

Operating expenses have to be included in the annual reports of both not for profit outfits and corporations that are publicly traded. This kind of information commonly comes with charts that compare the operating expenses of several years. In this way, a reader is able to obtain a good understanding of how the expenses are progressing with time.

By tracking operating expenses in an ongoing fashion all year long, the information is easily at hand for a company to include it in their reports. Accountants, or alternatively programs that do financial management, are generally used to help with operating expense tracking and calculation. When operating expenses go up and down every year, investors will want to know why this is the case. Detailed records provide good explanations for the final numbers to satisfy the questioning parties. Corporate treasurers are generally responsible for answering these queries and coming up with answers.

Oversight

Oversight is a critical regulatory concept. Thanks to the Congressional act the Sarbanes-Oxley Act of 2002, independent oversight became a major new requirement for occupations pertaining to accounting at public companies. This act and trend in government regulating led to the creation of the PCAOB. PCAOB stands for the Public Company Accounting Oversight Board.

This organization proves to be a not for profit entity which oversees the auditors at publicly traded corporations. The aim of the board lies in safeguarding both stakeholders and investors in public firms. They do this by making certain that the company financial statements and auditor statements follow a rigorous set of guidelines.

The PCAOB also has borne the responsibility since 2010 of overseeing broker-dealer audits. This means that any compliance reports which auditors file according to the requirements of the federal securities laws must foster protection of investors. It is up to the United States SEC Securities and Exchange Commission to approve all standards and rules of this particular regulatory entity. This organization has brought about the historical first time oversight (via both independent and external means) of American public company auditors. Before this Sarbanes-Oxley Act passed in 2002, the profession and industry was self-regulated from within its own ranks.

There are four main functions of the Public Company Accounting Oversight Board. These include overseeing auditors in the specific capacities of standard setting, inspection, registration, and enforcement. They do this to ensure that there will be accurate, highly informative, and completely independent audit reports prepared for the good of the investing and buying public.

Today's Public Company Accounting Oversight Board counts five members on its continuously standing board. The Chairman is the head of this governing and steering body. They receive appointments for five year terms of service which are staggered for continuity in and stability of the board composition. It is the SEC Securities and Exchange Commission who appoints the board members. They do this after consulting with the Secretary of the U.S. Treasury and the Board of Governors for the Federal Reserve System's Chairperson. Besides approving the composition of the board members for the PCAOB, the SEC has other important functions. They must also sign off on the board's budget as well as their standards and rules.

The PCAOB activities are paid for through means provided in the Dodd-Frank Wall Street Reform and Consumer Protection Act. This provided a means of funding for all of their functions. The money mostly is derived from annually assessed accounting support fees. Public companies are required to pay these fees. The amounts are set by the size of their average monthly market capitalization relative to other publicly traded firms. Broker dealers are also now assessed fees (since 2010) that go to the PCAOB's support. These are determined by the firms' average quarterly tentative net capital on a relative basis to the other broker-dealers in the industry.

The vision for this Public Company Accounting Oversight Board is to establish itself in the tradition of a model organization for regulation. They do this by employing cost-effective means and tools which are innovative. They seek to better the quality of audits overall and to lessen the dangers of auditing failures for the United States' public markets. They are also working towards improving public trust surrounding the auditing profession in particular and the process of financial reporting in general.

This Public Company Accounting Oversight Board arose because of a constantly increasing series of restatements from the accounting filings of American public firms during the 1990s. There were especially a number of embarrassing and highly damaging accounting scandals that decade which led to horrific and record-making bankruptcies of huge public firms. Among these were the two major scandal examples of Enron and WorldCom. Arthur Andersen was the big five accounting firm that was incriminated in helping to make these scandals possible. They became complicit in signing off on the financial statements and filings of the two companies in question.

Before the PCAOB became founded, it was up to the AICPA American Institute of Certified Public Accountants to self-regulate the industry. The board became dissolved officially on March 31st of 2002. SEC Chairman

Harvey Pitt appointed William H. Webster as official first chair of the PCAOB.

Paper Assets

Paper assets have three different meanings depending on whether you are discussing business, investments, or fiat currencies. Where business is concerned, paper assets are assets that you can not easily use or change in to cash. These paper assets possess extremely low liquidity, meaning that they are difficult to sell too. The term in this case literally arises from assets that are valuable on paper, or that have a paper only value.

In investments, paper assets mean something entirely different. They refer to assets that are representations of something. Paper assets in investments literally are pieces of paper that define ownership of an asset. Classic examples of investing paper assets prove to be stocks, currencies, bonds, money market accounts, and similar types of investments. For paper assets to have a tangible value, there must be a working financial system in order to back them up and exchange them. In the cases where a financial system collapses, paper assets commonly sharply decline along with it. The majority of Americans have placed an overwhelming percentage of their money in paper assets, and as the Financial Crisis of 2007-2010 showed, this makes them extremely vulnerable to economic calamities.

Paper assets stand apart in contrast to hard assets. Hard assets contain actual value in the nature of the item itself. There are many forms of hard assets, but among the most popular are gold, silver, diamonds, oil, platinum, land, and other such physical holdings. While financial collapses can cause a set back for the value of hard assets, these types of assets almost always hold up far better than do paper assets.

Many people are shocked by the fact that the U.S. dollar is also a paper asset, as are all Fiat currencies in the world except for the Swiss Franc. These paper currencies are no longer backed up by the long running gold standard. Instead, they only have value because their respective issuing governments, as well as the underlying currency users, say that they do. The Swiss Franc is a lonely exception. The Swiss constitution requires that for every four paper or electronic currency Swiss Francs in existence, there must be one Swiss Franc worth of gold in the Swiss National Bank vaults. Since the Swiss only value their gold holdings at around $250 per ounce, and gold has been trading between $1,300 and $1,400 per ounce for some time now, the Swiss actually have a greater gold backing to their currency than one hundred percent.

Paper Investments

Paper investments can be several things. Where businesses are concerned, paper investments turn out to be investments in commercial paper. Commercial paper investments prove to actually be money market instruments that companies and banks sell to raise money. There are many large issuers with good credit who offer these types of paper investments to interested investors. They represent inexpensive other sources of short term funding as opposed to standard bank loans.

Commercial paper investments come with a fixed maturity of from one day to two hundred and seventy days. These types of paper investments are generally regarded as extremely secure, although they are unsecured loans. The companies that take advantage of them are commonly utilizing these short term operating funds for working capital or inventory purchases.

Corporations like to utilize commercial paper because they are able to quickly and effectively raise significant sums of money without having to get involved with costly SEC registration through selling paper investments. This can be done through working with independent dealers, or on their own efforts directly to investors. Institutional buyers commonly prove to be significant buyers of these types of paper investments.

Such notes come with amounts and maturity dates that can be specifically crafted to meet particular needs. The key features of these types of paper investments are that they are of short term maturity, commonly ranging from only three to six months of time. They liquidate on their own, with no action being required by the investing party in question. There is little to no speculation involved in their intended use as well. This gives them an appeal of clarity.

Offering this type of paper investments offers several advantages for the issuer as well. The issuer is able to access cash at rates that are lower than those offered at the bank. Companies taking advantage of commercial paper are able to leave open reserves of borrowing power at their area banks. Finally, they are capable of getting cash on hand which will allow them to benefit from trade creditors who offer special discounts for those who pay for supplies and other needs with cash.

Where traditional investments are concerned, paper investments also prove to be investments whose value is stated on and represented by paper. A number of different kinds of popular investments in the United States qualify as paper investments. These include stocks, bonds, mutual funds, certificates of deposits, and money market accounts. Shares of stock are pieces of paper that relate a certain percentage of ownership in a publicly traded company.

Most any type of investment that does not have a physical component of the investment associated with it is considered a paper investment. Commodities, as well as futures and options on futures that permit you to take delivery of the underlying commodities if you wish, represent examples of investments that are not only paper investments. These types of investments, along with real estate holdings, are considered to be physical, or hard, investments.

Payroll Tax

Payroll tax refers to the specific withholding tax that employers take from their employees' checks. They do this for their employees so that they can pay it to the national (and sometimes also state or provincial and local) government. These tax amounts are deducted based upon the salaries or wages of the employees in question. In the majority of nations such as the U.S., the federal government (and many provincial or state governments as well) levy some kind of a payroll tax.

Such governing bodies deploy the revenues they gain from their payroll taxes in order to pay for specific government services and programs such as health care, retirement benefits (like Social Security income), workers compensation, and more. Besides these large scale national programs, local governments sometimes also levy smaller payroll taxes so that they can improve and maintain in good condition the area specific programs and infrastructure. This would includes such vital services and programs as road maintenance, first responders' emergency services, and parks and recreation programs, among others.

A payroll tax which is deducted is generally itemized out for the employees on their payroll stub. On such an specific breakdown as this, it usually denotes the amounts which Social Security and Medicare programs took from their pay, along with the municipal and/or state taxes held.

The Federal payroll taxes within the U.S. include contributions for Medicare and Social Security. In the year 2016, employers were required by law to hold back 6.2 percent of all employee earnings as a payroll tax. Besides this, the employers themselves are required to match these amounts from all employee payrolls and then turn in the two amounts to the IRS Internal Revenue Service.

As an example, for those employers who pay their workers $2,000, they will be required to hold back $124 in the federal component of payroll taxes. The employing company also must match this dollar amount. They send in an aggregate amount of $248 for the employee in this case directly to the IRS.

Employers only had to do withholding on payroll taxes for the initial $118,500 of employee earnings as of 2015. On income amounts higher than this, they withhold another .9 percent of all net earnings. This is a special extra Medicare tax. Employers are not mandated to do their matching portion of this additional tax on employee income.

With all those who are self employed, the procedure is different. Self-employed individuals such as small business owners and independent contractors have no employer who can withhold and turn in their payroll tax for them. This means that they will have to be their own accountants and pay these taxes directly. These are known as self-employment taxes, even though they are basically the same as payroll taxes.

Because the self employed do not have any counter-party to match their payroll deductions, they have to pay a punishing 12.4 percent of all earnings to the Social Security Trust Fund and another 2.9 percent to the Medicare Trust Fund, as of 2015. These taxes are levied by the IRS on all earning up to $118,500. Beyond this dollar amount, the extra .9 percent Medicare tax still applies, as with the payroll taxes.

Payroll taxes should not be confused with income taxes. The main difference is that such payroll taxes cover particular programs. They are kept separate from the government primary revenues collected through the national income taxes that go instead into the government's general coffers. All employees have to pay their flat payroll tax, even though this is regressive. Income taxes are instead progressive, meaning that the rates increase along with higher earnings. Income taxes are never matched by employers either. Self-employed people will not pay higher income taxes than their employed counterparts as they must with the payroll tax.

PEG Ratio

The PEG Ratio refers to the stock PE price to earnings ratio divided up by the earnings growth rate over a certain fixed time frame. This ratio itself is popularly utilized to ascertain the real value of a stock taking into account the firm's earnings growth. Many analysts consider it to be a better big picture view of the company and its progress than simply using the standard PE ratio.

The misleading fact is that a lower PE ratio tends to make any stock seem like a screaming buy. When one considers the growth rate of the company along with this in the form of the PEG Ratio, it may reveal that a stock is even more undervalued considering the performance of its corporate earnings. It is also true that the amount of a PEG ratio valuation and how it indicates an underpriced or overpriced stock ranges by the type of the firm and the industry in which it is. A good set of guidelines is that any PEG ratio under the number one is beneficial.

Besides this, analysts know that any PEG ratio's accuracy will ultimately depend on the quality of the information which is initially inputted. For example, if one deploys historical growth rates, this could deliver an unreliable PEG ratio, especially if the growth rates in the future are anticipated to be lower than the company growth rates have proven to be historically. This is why accountants and company analysts will often differentiate between the various primary methods of calculating the PEG Ratio according to whether they are relying on historical growth or anticipated future growth. To this effect, they will use the terms Trailing PEG or forward PEG to distinguish between the main two methods.

Figuring up the actual PEG Ratio is not difficult. Analysts and investors are able to do this by first computing the PE ratio of the firm under consideration. This PE ratio can be calculated out by taking the stock price of the firm and dividing it by the EPS earnings per share. After the PE has been compiled, it is easy to configure the PEG formula. One simply takes the PE Ratio and divides it out by the rate of earnings growth, whether he is using the trailing PEG or forward looking PEG.

This is a difficult enough concept that it makes good sense to consider a real world example to better understand the ideas involved. If Vodafone has a share price of $46 per share while its earnings per share for the year are $2.09, then last year's earnings per share might have been $1.74. At the same time, Telefonica Espana has a share price of $80 with earnings per share for this year of $2.67 and an EPS from last year of $1.78. Utilizing this data, the information on each of the two companies can be calculated. The Vodafone PE ratio is 22 while the Telefonica PE ratio is 30. Yet despite this fact, the growth rate of Vodafone is 20 percent to Telefonica's 50 percent. It means that Vodafone's resulting PEG would then be 1.1 while Telefonica would have a significantly superior .6 PEG.

Now the fact is that numerous investors would look at Vodafone superficially and say that it seems to be more appealing because it has the lower PE of the two cell phone operating firms in question. After further investigation though, Telefonica has the higher growth rate for its PE than does Vodafone.

This means that Telefonica stock prices trades at an effective discount to its company growth rate. In the end, those investors buying Telefonica corporate stock are coming out of pocket less money per unit of earnings growth in the company. All else being equal, it makes the Telefonica stock a better valued buy than the Vodafone one in this particular example.

Pension Entitlements

Pension entitlements are the monies that have been promised to employees who are guaranteed a pension by the company for which they work. The majority of newly issued pensions anymore come from Federal, state, and local government employees. Some companies still offer pension entitlements to their employees who serve a minimum number of years with the firm, such as from twenty to thirty years.

These companies are becoming fewer and farther between as more and more corporations switch over to matching 401K retirement plans that cost them far less money and entail significantly lesser liabilities every year. This is because with pre set limit matches to 401K contributions, companies can know for certain how much money they will have to come out of pocket, whereas with pensions, it has much to do with how long the retirees live.

Pension entitlements are at risk as they become larger every year. Many companies are struggling to keep up with their pension entitlements as their retiring employees live longer and longer. Because of the danger to failing pensions that many retirees count on, the PBGC was set up. This entity acronym stands for Pension Benefit Guarantee Corporation.

The government created this entity in the Employee Retirement Income Security Act in 1974. Today, it safe guards in excess of forty-four million American retirees and workers pensions, covering the pension entitlements against default from the companies underlying them. These are held in greater than twenty-nine thousand multi employer and private single employer defined benefit pension plans.

The PBGC does not derive money from the general tax revenues in protecting the pension entitlements. Insurance premiums that Congress sets are paid by the sponsors of defined benefit plans, assets from pension plans that PBGC trustees, investment income of the PBGC, and recoveries made from companies who are no longer handling their own plans.

As a result of the financial crisis of 2007-2010, many private pension funds have suffered disastrous losses. In 2008 alone, this amounted to tangible losses of in excess of twenty-six percent. Even though the markets recovered somewhat, many pension funds had locked in their losses by selling the underwater investments. As a result of these terrible financial events, even more pension entitlements in the United States are now under funded.

In order to help make up for these, businesses will have to make substantially larger contributions in the future. It remains to be seen if the Pension Benefit Guarantee Corporation will be able to keep up with and cover all of the unfunded pension entitlements that have been promised to retirees and workers. Some experts have speculated that the PBGC itself will require bailouts in the hundreds of billions of dollars in the near future.

Per Capita

Per Capita refers to a Latin language Roman phrase. It comes from per which means by or by means of, and capita which means head. Thus the full phrase signifies "for each head" or "by heads." This translates to per person or per individual. The popular phrase finds use in a great range of both statistical research and social sciences deployments. This includes economic indicators, government statistics, and studies of build environments.

The Per Capita is typically utilized by the study of statistics. Wills also utilize it to provide the context that all specified beneficiaries must obtain (either through bequest or devise) equal shares of the deceased individual's estate. The alternative arrangement is called a per stirpes division. In such an arrangement, every branch of the family inheriting receives a comparable share from the estate.

Beyond these meanings of the phrase, Per Capita finds use in any type of population description, such as with GDP or GNP. Despite this, it most commonly finds its place in situations that have to do with economic reporting and data releases. The reasons economists report using per capita is so it can be compared against other countries and jurisdictions. Coming up with this formula is easy. All one has to do is to divide the whole number which is referenced by the total individuals involved.

It is always helpful to look at a tangible real world example to better understand a difficult concept. Consider the United States Per Capita GDP. In the year 2011, the population of America was 313.4 million individuals. At the same time, the country's Gross Domestic Product proved to be $15.09 trillion. This means that the national average income per person amounted to $15.09 trillion divided by 313.4 million, or around $48,000.

Economists enjoy deploying this type of statistic whenever they are comparing, contrasting, or discussing a nation and its purchasing power of the residents. Their three favorite uses of the measurement come in the form of per capita gross national income (GNI), Gross National Product (GNP), and Gross Domestic Product (GDP). The two metrics of GNP and GDP each sum up the national economic value of all services and good produced by market value. Their main difference lies in defining national economies differently. It is the GNP that considers the citizens living abroad and their economic activities along with direct foreign investment and economic production of all overseas operations for companies domiciled in the home country. GDP only considers the economic activities which transpire inside of a country's own national boundaries. The third metric GNI is much like GNP.

The problem with utilizing such Per Capita measurements as GNP, GDP, or GNI to describe income per individual in nations has to do with the vast inclusiveness of the metrics. They are in fact describing the average income for all citizens and residents of the given jurisdiction. The problem is that they are counting all individuals including retirees, babies, and children in the measurement, even though these people do not technically work or earn income. There are also some statistical outliers that the metrics do not take into account.

This is why more economists find median income statistics to be more useful than the GNP, GDP, or GNI figures. Median income actually describes the average income which those who reside in a given nation will probably earn. It is the exact middle income for the entire list of income earners. This means that precisely half of the individuals looked at will earn less than this figure, while the other half will earn more. In the calculation of this median income, the United States Census Bureau never considers any children who are less than 15 years old. Median income measurements can also be done per capita, per family, and per household.

Ponzi Scheme

Ponzi Schemes prove to be frauds surrounding investments that are related to the pay out of returns to investors in the scheme that are covered using contributions from new investors. The individuals who run Ponzi schemes are able to attract newer investors through boasting of tremendous opportunities that will guarantee terrific investment returns, typically with little to no risk.

With a great number of these Ponzi Schemes, the managers of the scheme concentrate their efforts on constantly bringing in new sums of money in order to be capable of giving out the payments that they promised investors from earlier time periods. Besides this, they utilize the new money for their own personal expenses. Rarely does any energy actually go into real investment opportunities and strategies.

Ponzi schemes always fail at some point in time. This eventually happens since there are no real earnings to distribute. Because of this problem, Ponzi schemes need constant money flowing into them from newer investors in order to survive. As attracting newer investors becomes more challenging, or if a great number of currently involved investors request their money back, then the Ponzi Scheme will likely fall apart.

Ponzi Schemes actually earned their name from a famed early con artist Charles Ponzi. He became famous after he tricked literally thousands of well to do New Englanders into pouring their money into his speculation in postage stamps in the 1920's. The allure of his scheme proved to be hard to resist, since bank accounts were paying only five percent annual returns while he offered investors incredible returns of fifty percent in only ninety days. In the early days, Charles Ponzi really did purchase a small quantity of international mail coupons to support his investment scheme. Before long, he decided to employ the money that came in to cash out earlier investors.

The most successful Ponzi Scheme of all time proved to be the one run by Bernie Madoff. Madoff ran an over thirty year, over thirty billion dollar investment scheme that tricked thousands of investors out of their money. Madoff proved to have a different angle on his Ponzi scheme in that he did not offer his investors who were short term amazing returns. Rather than this, he sent out fake account statements that constantly demonstrated moderate but always positive gains, no matter how turbulent the market proved to be.

Bernie Madoff is presently undergoing a one hundred and fifty year sentence in federal prison for his activities. His investment advisory company began back in 1960 and did not come down until the end of 2008. All during the years that his scheme ran, he served as Vice Chairman of the National Association of Securities Dealers, and even as a member of the board of governors and chairman for the NASDAQ stock market.

The Securities Exchange Commission is ultimately responsible for discovering and prosecuting Ponzi Schemes. They typically utilize emergency actions to freeze assets while they break up the schemes. In 2009 as an example, the SEC actually pursued sixty different Ponzi schemes, the highest profile one of which turned out to be Robert Allen Stanford's $8 billion Ponzi scheme.

Portfolio Income

Portfolio income proves to be money that is actually brought in from a group of investments. The portfolio commonly includes all of the various types of investments that an investor owns. These include bonds, stocks, mutual funds, and certificates of deposit. These various financial instruments earn a variety of different types of passive income, such as dividends, interest income, and capital gain distributions. Such portfolio income returns are generated by the holdings of the various investment products in the portfolio.

Portfolio income varies with the types of investments that an investor picks. You as an investor will commonly look at two different factors when assembling a portfolio for portfolio income. These turn out to be the money that the investment itself will produce, which is also known as an investment's return, and the investment's risk level that it contains.

As an example, stocks are frequently deemed to be investments with considerable risk, yet the other side of the risk return equation is that they provide income from a company's dividends, or distribution earnings returned to the shareholders, as well as an increase in the stock price as the stock value gains with time. Certificates of deposit and bonds create interest income that is paid out on the investment that you hold. Still different kinds of investments produce other types of income, although this depends on the characteristics of the investment in question.

To maximize the portfolio income while reducing the amount of risk involved, individuals commonly choose to invest in numerous different kinds of investments. This is known as diversifying your portfolio and portfolio income. This way, you can combine both safer investments that provide lower real returns with riskier investments that offer greater investment returns. Your total collection of investments is the portfolio that makes your portfolio income for you.

This portfolio income is also classified as passive income, or income that does not require you to perform any work in order to make the money. The upfront investment actually creates the income without you having to be actively involved in the money making process. This stands in contrast to incomes that are earned through active involvement, or active income that you must expend both energy and time to create.

The ultimate goal for you with your portfolio income will probably be to build up enough of it that you are capable of living off of only the income that the portfolio generates. Once this point is reached, you would be able to not receive a payroll check any longer. Instead, you would support yourself in retirement from the dividends, interest, and capital gains created by the investments in the form of portfolio income. The best and safest way to do this is to only draw on the portfolio income itself, without drawing down the original principal.

By not touching the investment principal, you allow your portfolio and resulting portfolio income to build up over time. If you do not take out the portfolio income, then the total value of the portfolio will grow faster with time, allowing you to compound your investments for retirement. It is critical to have enough money saved for retirement that you do not need to take out this principal to support yourself. Sufficient portfolio income should be generated to cover the monthly retirement expenses. In this way, you will not be reducing your principal and risking the very real danger of your portfolio running out of money while you are still alive to need it.

Portfolio Manager

Portfolio managers are individuals who invest the assets of a fund. They generally handle either an ETF exchange traded fund, a mutual fund, or a closed end fund. Their responsibility is to carry out the daily trading of the portfolio and to put into practice the fund's investment strategy.

When investors are considering different funds in which to invest, among the most critical elements to think about is the name, reputation, and track record of the portfolio manger. This is especially true if they are involved in active portfolio management as opposed to passive management. Though there are numerous active fund managers in the markets, the track records of historical performances are not encouraging. Only a small minority of them are successful in beating the main market indices.

These managers engage in portfolio management as part of their daily routines. This is the science of making difficult decisions regarding the funds objectives. They must weigh investment mix against objectives, carefully balance the fund risk versus performance, and allocate the assets for the funds customers.

The management of a given portfolio revolves around opportunities, risks, weaknesses and strengths of various categories. These include deciding between equity investments as opposed to debt instruments, international versus domestic securities, and safety as compared to growth. There are numerous trade offs involved in this type of management as a manager makes tough choices in an effort to increase returns to the optimal point for the risk the investors are willing to take.

Passive management is the form of managing a portfolio where the holdings of a fund track an index in the markets. This is most often known as index investing or indexing. Active management is the opposite form. It requires that either one manager, a few managers working together, or even a management team strive to try to outperform the market's return. They try to do this by managing the portfolio actively. They make choices and investment decisions utilizing research on individual securities and positions. Among the different actively managed funds are closed end funds and many mutual funds.

In passive management, the style is to have the holdings of the fund identically reflect the benchmark index. This is the direct opposite of an active style of management where the managers are buying and selling securities in the portfolio according to different investment strategies.

Passive managers and the followers of this particular management type hold with the efficient market hypothesis. This idea says that the markets always reflect and factor in all relevant information all of the time. It believes that picking stocks out individually is a waste of time. Followers of this premise believe that the best method for investing is to put investment funds into index funds. History shows that these funds have performed better than most of the funds which are actively managed.

Active management still has a significant following. It utilizes the human efforts of the management team, co managers, or single portfolio manager to manage the funds portfolio on a daily, weekly, and monthly basis. These active managers work with forecasts, analytical research, and their own personal experiences and judgments to engage in the buying, selling, and holding decisions of the various securities.

The sponsors of these actively managed funds and their investment companies hold that a really good manager can beat the market. This is why they employ professional fund managers to actively handle the portfolio funds. Their goal is to beat those returns of their benchmark. For a large cap stock fund this would mean outperforming the S&P 500 index. Despite the best efforts of a considerable majority of active fund managers, they have not been able to do this successfully.

Public Company Accounting Oversight Board (PCAOB)

The Public Company Accounting Oversight Board turns out to be another regulatory group that Congress established to provide oversight on the auditing of public companies. This not for profit corporation is not a government agency. It does provide protection to the public and investors who are interested in the independent, accurate, and revealing audit reports that this group encourages. Besides this, the PCAOB oversees dealers and brokers' audits in order to foster protection for investors. This includes oversight of compliance reports that federal security laws require from public corporations.

This accounting oversight board arose as a result of the Sabanes-Oxley Act of 2002. It mandated that the firms which audit public companies in the United States endure independent and external oversight for the first time ever. Before Congress passed this 2002 regulatory law, auditors were completely self regulating.

The PCAOB Board and chairman of this board are made up of five members who receive appointments to five year terms each from the SEC Securities and Exchange Commission. They select these individuals after consulting first with both the Secretary of the U.S. Treasury and the Federal Reserve System Chairman of the Board of Governors. Given this SEC appointing role, it is not surprising that the SEC also maintains oversight responsibilities for the PCAOB. As part of this oversight, they must approve the Board's various standards, budget, and rules before they become final.

The SOX Act became amended by the Dodd-Frank Act. It created the necessary funding for all PCAOB pursued activities. This money mostly comes from the accounting support fees assessed annually on all publicly traded companies. These fees are actually figured from their average monthly market capitalization. Brokers and dealers are instead levied fees which are dependent on their quarterly average tentative net capital.

The mission of the PCAOB lies in providing oversight of public companies' audits. This ensures that they prepare and deliver reliable, honest, and unbiased audit reports for the benefit of both the interested investors and members of the public. Along with this oversight role, the PCAOB monitors the broker dealers and their audits to encourage protecting investors from fraud. This includes monitoring their federal securities law required compliance reports filing.

PCAOB has a particular vision they seek to fulfill. Their overriding goal is to prove themselves a model for regulatory organizations everywhere. They seek to reduce the numbers of audit failures throughout the public securities markets in the United States, to improve the overall quality of audits, and to foster the public's trust of auditing as a profession and the process of financial reporting itself. They aim to do this while utilizing cost efficient and cutting edged tools.

The PCAOB maintains two special advisory groups as part of its mandate. The first of these is the PCAOB Investor Advisor Group, also known by its acronym IAG. It presents advice and viewpoints to the general board pertaining to investor concerns and regarding work related matters and important policy issues. The board is able to count on the IAG to deliver it expert and quality insight and advice for carrying out its important mandate to safeguard investors as outlined in the Sarbanes-Oxley Act.

The board also relies on its Standing Advisory Group, refereed to by its acronym SAG. The SAG advises the board regarding standards of professional practice and continuing developments within the world of auditing. Among the members of the Standing Advisory Group are investors, auditors, executives of publicly traded companies, and other individuals. This SAG group holds meetings between two and three times each year. They are chaired by the Chief Auditor and Director of Professional Standards of the PCAOB.

Quantitative Risk Management (QRM)

Quantitative Risk Management represents the discipline which deals with the ability of an organization to quantify and manage its risk. This scientific approach to business is becoming increasingly critical in today's world as organizations need to satisfy stakeholders who demand it.

Government regulators similarly insist on clarity within organizations now, especially regarding the amount of capital financial institutions are holding. The firm executives are hunting for the best allocation of capital. Corporations and their boards are seeking justification to control expenditures. Project managers need to be assured they will make their timelines and meet budgets. All of these individuals and entities are looking for effective QRM nowadays.

These QRM capabilities give decision makers the facilities to both analyze their applicable risk data as well as to forecast the likely positive and negative effects in the future. It provides the organization with enormous advantages. Analyses that are more dependable and finely detailed will deliver information which management requires to make superior decisions that are ultimately better informed. As the Quantitative Risk Management process yields higher quality information and becomes more easily accessible to the relevant organizational members, the decision makers are able to more effectively utilize the techniques of QRM to decrease the amount of guesswork involved in the daily decisions of their business operations.

This allows them to obtain valuable insights into possible risks, so they can estimate their overall exposure to them and discern any weaknesses in their oversight controls. It also permits them to determine how practical new services and products will be and to consider the opportunities for up selling and also cross selling of company goods, information, and services. Finally, organization leaders will be able to evaluate any degrees of variance in their company cash flow so that they can streamline and better their ultimate operations.

Quantitative Risk Management is important as every one of those activities just mentioned contains at least some degree of risk. By quantifying and considering them all using a combination of techniques such as trending, modeling, stress tests, and metric evaluations, company decision makers can create faster and more effective responses. This allows them to benefit from any uncovered opportunities and simultaneously to deal with any possible negative effects before they actually materialize and cause significant damage.

There are numerous examples of the uses of and needs for Quantitative Risk Management in business organizations. Cash flow at risk, or CFaR, represents one of the most significant drivers of business. Company leaders require effective prognoses of their future cash flow in order to firm up important decisions for the business. These include confirming or pushing off investments, reducing expenses, reinvesting capital in the business model, or choosing to reengineer their critical operations. Correctly extrapolating cash flow involves proper understanding of such underlying factors as currency changes, sales, pricing of products and services, vendor viability, and operational costs.

Value at Risk, or VaR, is another critical measurement in an organization that benefits from Quantitative Risk Management. Bigger, international, and more complicated financial institutions such as JP Morgan Chase, Citigroup, HSBC, Standard Chartered Bank, BNP Paribas, and Banco Santander have to constantly evaluate where their risk exposures are in order to appropriately allocate the correct capital amounts to be capable of absorbing losses which they do not anticipate.

Project risk management is another area where this Quantitative Risk Management can save the day. So many projects exceed their allocated budgets, deadlines, and milestone markers simply because there is not a sufficient evaluation of the variables, uncertainty, and risk involved with the project itself. This is where the process of QRM can save enormous amounts of time, frustration, and ultimately resources by delivering on deadlines and budgets.

Rate of Return

In the worlds of finance and business, the rate of return, also known by its acronym ROR, proves to be the ratio of money lost or gained pertaining to an investment and the sum of money that is originally invested in it. This rate of return is also called the rate of profit or more commonly the return on investment, or ROI.

The sum of money that is lost or gained could be called the loss or profit, interest, or even net loss or net income. Regarding the money that is actually invested, it is sometimes called the capital, asset, or principle. It is also referred to as the cost basis of an investment. Rate of return or Return on Investment is commonly stated as a percentage and not a fraction.

This rate of return is one measurement of how much cash is made or lost as a direct result of the investment in question. It quantifies the amount of income stream or cash flow that moves from the investment itself to the investor as a percentage of the original amount that the investor put into the investment. Such cash flow that accrues to the investor comes in a number of forms. It might be interest, profit, capital gains and losses, or dividends received. These capital gains and losses happen as the investment's sale price is greater or less than its initial purchase price. The use of the term cash flow includes everything except for the return of the original invested money.

Rates of return can be figured up as averages covering a number of different time periods. They may also be determined for only one time frame. When these calculations are being made, it is important not to mix up annualized and annual rates of return. Annualized rates of return prove to be geometric average returns figured up over several or even numerous periods. Annualized returns might be the investment return on a period less than or greater than a year, for example for six months or three years. The rates of return are then multiplied out or divided in order to come up with a one year rate of return that can be compared against other annual rates of return. As an example, if an investment possessed a one percent rate of return per month, then this might be more appropriately expressed as an annualized rate of return of twelve percent. Or, if you had a three year rate of return amounting to fifteen percent, then you could say that this is a five percent annualized rate of return.

Annual rates of return are instead returns figured up for single time frame periods. These time frames are commonly one year periods running from the first of January to the last day of December. Alternatively, they could cover any year long period, regardless of what month and day they started and ended.

Reconciliation

Reconciliation refers to an accounting process. Its chief defining characteristic is that is employs two different records in order to make sure that the figures it portrays are both identical and accurate. This critical process ensures that money going out of an account measures accurately against the amount actually spent. In other words, it assures accountants that the two values will be in balance once the recording period concludes.

While no universally accepted standard exists for Reconciliation accounting, the GAAP generally accepted accounting principles prefer account conversion and double entry accounting for the primary best methods of reconciling. Individuals or companies may elect to reconcile their important records on an annual, monthly, or daily basis with either methodology.

It always helps to demystify a complex topic with real world examples. Julian like many consumers opts to reconcile his check book and credit card accounts at the conclusion of each month. He does this by comparing debit card receipts, cancelled checks, and credit card receipts along with the statements from the bank and credit card companies. It allows for Julian to determine if money is being withdrawn fraudulently or illegally. Besides this, it provides him with confidence that no bank errors have been made on any of his accounts at the various financial institutions. Julian finally benefits from a big picture view of his spending habits and patterns each month this way.

As accounts become reconciled, the ending balance should match up exactly with the transactions as noted on the statements for the month and also with the records of Julian or other account holders. Where checking accounts are involved, individuals must also be concerned with outstanding checks or pending deposits and the impact these will create on the real world balance as well as the statement balance.

Companies are also critically concerned with the processes of Reconciliation of their accounts. Corporations have to reconcile all accounts in order to make sure there are no errors on the balance sheets or that no fraud has occurred within the company at large. Larger firms and smaller ones alike will generally deploy one of several good accounting programs to take care of these internal processes. This is because there will be no computational errors when utilizing these programs. They prevent mistakes that can create major consequences for companies which are publically traded.

As an example of the usefulness of such Reconciliation, auditors will commonly do a final review of corporations' financial statements as the Sarbanes-Oxley Act and other federal regulations require. They might come across a significant error in this review. The firm would then be forced to publicly disclose this failure of internal controls. Otherwise it might have to declare it a material weakness or material misstatement. This is all critical since corporations cannot be expected to engage in intelligent decision making processes if they cannot rely on their own internal financial information.

With double entry accounting, the accountants will post each and every financial transaction according to a two-column entry on the balance sheet of the firm. When companies draw on a $50,000 longer-term loan, their accountants will credit the longer term debt category and also notate the payable columns with the $50,000 amount. They will simultaneously debit the cash column by the identical amount. The important rule is that as the amounts are all tallied together, they must reconcile to an even zero final amount.

If businesses acquire an invoice for repainting of their office building, they will then credit the invoice amount under the column for accounts payable while debiting the column for painting and other office expenses by the identical amount. As the firm pays its bill, the accountants will then debit the accounts payable while simultaneously crediting the column for office painting.

Regulatory Compliance

Regulatory Compliance refers to companies choosing to incorporate standards that meet certain government requirements. It could also be thought of as the specific set of regulations which a firm has to observe when it meets the given requirements. Because of the ever growing burdens of regulations, companies are increasingly finding they must become more transparent operationally.

This is why they find the need to adopt a universal set of controls for compliance. The idea is to measure up to all government mandated requirements while avoiding any wasted resources or duplicated activities in the process. Even when done effectively and efficiently, this level of compliance is often both costly and burdensome for businesses and other organizations to meet.

There are a number of organizations that produce a set of standards to make such Regulatory Compliance simpler. ISO is the International Organization for Standardization. They create such internationally observed standards as the ISO/IEC 27002. Another group which develops the electro-technology arena international standards is the IEC International Electro-technical Commission. There are other specialized compliance issuers in various countries and industries. One of these is the ASME American Society of Mechanical Engineers. The SEC Securities Exchange Commission issues and enforces standards of regulation compliance for publically traded stock companies. The CFTC Commodities and Futures Trading Commission handle the compliance for the commodities trading industry.

There have been numerous triggers for greater amounts of Regulatory Compliance over the past several decades. Many of these revolved around corporate failures and scandals which could have been easily prevented had more regulation been part of their various industries. A classic example of this is the Enron failure from 2001. Thanks to this and the WorldCom scandal, the United States Congress enacted the Sarbanes-Oxley Act for setting standards for greater compliance and regulation for upper level corporate management reporting accurate and truthful financial statements. The Consumer Protection Act and Dodd-Frank Wall Street Reform Act also followed after a need for still more regulation compliance became evident in events like the Global Financial Crisis and subprime mortgage meltdown from 2007-2009.

In the United States, Regulatory Compliance generally revolves around regulations and laws. Such legal statutes come with civil and/or criminal penalties for violating the relevant regulations. There are a number of agencies within the United States government which handle and enforce the issues of regulation compliance. Among these are the OFAC Office of Foreign Assets Control, the U.S. Small Business Administration, and the OSHA Department of Labor, Occupational Health and Safety Administration.

OFAC is the agency which deals with Regulatory Compliance for trade and economic sanctions. They operate under the Department of the Treasury's Terrorism and Financial Intelligence division. The goal of this regulatory agency is to handle and enforce U.S. foreign policy- and national security policy-based trade sanctions and economic embargoes. They target foreign organizations, countries, and individuals who are on the Treasury Department list.

The U.S. government maintains many Regulatory Compliance statues pertaining to businesses. The Small Business Administration offers its services to help small companies with information and access to various government services under its Business.USA.gov website.

The United States OSHA is a congressionally created agency for enforcing healthy and safe working conditions for all people in the country. They erect and enforce various standards pertaining to education, outreach, training, and assistance. This agency is responsible for Regulatory Compliance in the areas of recordkeeping, agriculture, maritime law, and construction.

Such laws are not the same in every country however. As an example, the United Kingdom has its own laws for Regulatory Compliance. These are among the most similar to the United States' own laws in many ways. Among the compliance acts and frameworks for organizations and businesses in Great Britain are those created by the Data Protection Act of 1998 and the Freedom of Information Act 2000. Their FRC Financial Reporting Council lays out standards for appropriate practices of company leadership pertaining to accountability and effectiveness for the shareholders. They issue the UK Corporate Governance Code, which is most like the United States Sarbanes-Oxley Act.

Retained Earnings

Retained earnings are a component of the earnings categories of corporations. They describe the portion of a company's net earnings that they do not give out to shareholders as dividends. Instead these earnings are kept by the firm so that they can pay down debt or reinvest in their core operations and business model. Balance sheets note earnings which are retained as part of the shareholder's equity column.

There is a formula for figuring out retained earnings. It adds the initial earnings with net income or subtracts net losses from it. Dividends must then be subtracted out from these earnings as they are paid out to stockholders.

Corporations have their reasons to keep a portion of their earnings. In the majority of scenarios, they wish to invest them into segments of the market where the firm is able to build opportunities or growth. This could be by spending money for additional research and development or in purchasing new plants, equipment, or machinery. Companies can also use these earnings to purchase other firms. Such acquisitions allow them to expand their market share or product offerings in this method of non organic growth.

It is possible for such earnings to become negative. This happens when the firm's net loss is larger than the initial retained earnings. Such a case creates a deficit. The general ledger for these earnings becomes adjusted each time an entry is placed for the expense or revenue accounts.

At the conclusion of the company's accounting period, such earnings that are retained become reported. This could be in the quarterly report or the annual report. They will either continue to be accumulated and be positive, or they can shift into negative territory and be recorded as a deficit. These changes in earnings from one accounting period to the next are not directly noted. It is easy to infer them by looking at the totals of ending and beginning retained earnings for the accounting period. Increases or decreases to the accumulated totals happen because of dividend payouts and net losses or net incomes for the period.

Every period, a firm's revenues and expenses must be closed out. This is done into an income summary that shows the total net income or loss. Finally these are closed out into the retained earnings column. Net income directly boosts or decreases these earnings this way.

Dividends are the other major item that decreases the retained earnings number. Such dividends can be paid out as stock or cash. Either type reduces the earnings which are retained. This is because cash dividends come out of the net income ultimately. The greater amount of dividends that a company distributes, the lower amount of earnings it will retain. Dividend accounts are also temporary in nature and are closed out to the earnings which are retained at the end of the accounting period.

Though newly issued shares given out as dividends do not reduce the net income, they must be reconciled on the balance sheet. This is done in the accounts for additional paid in capital on the balance sheet. The earnings which are retained category decreases by the identical amount as this paid in capital column.

Return on Assets (ROA)

Return on Assets is also known by its acronym ROA. It is also sometimes called return on investment. This proves to be an indicator of a company's profitability compared to its aggregate asset base. With ROA, investors and analysts can learn about the big picture of the efficiency of an organization's management compared to the deployment of their company assets which produces earnings.

This is figured up relatively easily. To calculate the ROA, simply take the corporation's annual earnings (or income) and divide these by the firm's total assets. The final answer is the percentage amount of ROA. Other investors will do a slight variation on the formula by adding back in the corporate interest costs to the net income. This allows them to employ operating returns before the net cost of debt.

Thanks to Return on Assets, analysts and investors can learn the amount of earnings that the invested capital or assets produced. Such a figure ranges dramatically from one publically traded company to the next. Every industry's ROA varies substantially. For this reason, analysts prefer to compare and contrast the ROA primarily against the company's own prior figures or alternatively versus another company which is both similar and in the same industry.

Company assets are made up of equity and debt together. The two kinds of financing will jointly fund most corporations' various operations and projects. Because of this Return on Assets number, investors are able to discern the efficiency with which the firm converts its investable money into actual net income. Higher ROA numbers are always considered to be superior. They mean that the corporations can bring in larger revenues and earnings on a smaller amount of investment.

Consider a real world example for clarification. If Imperial Legends Strategy Games produces a net income of $2 million on aggregate underlying assets of $6 million, then it has a Return on Assets of 33.3 percent. Another company Joy Beverages may enjoy the same earnings but against a full asset base of $12 million. Joy Beverages would have an ROA of only 16.7 percent in this scenario. This means that ILSG does twice the job of converting its all around investments into profits as does Joy Beverages. This matters because it speaks volumes of the quality of management. There are not too many managers who are able to turn over significant profits utilizing small investments.

The Return on Assets provides observers with a snapshot and analysis of a business that is distinctive from the usual return on equity formula. Consider that certain industries need to pay more careful attention to the ROA figure than other ones do. In banking, some firms managed to avoid the various banking crises of the last few decades. The ones that sidestepped the problems better than others had something in common. It was that they were more conservative based on the ROA they deployed. The more successful banks did not allow their return on assets numbers to become too unnaturally high. They did this by contemplating the underlying fine details in the loan book. Too many loans that yielded too high a return indicated that management was taking excessive risks. Yet in the business of software development firms, these enterprises are not leveraged, so this ROA comparison is less important.

An important difference separates asset turnover from Return on Assets. Asset turnover specifies that companies have sales which amount to a certain amount per asset dollar on the corporate balance sheet. Conversely, the ROA explains to investors the amount of post tax profit that a firm creates for every $1 of assets it has. This is to say that the ROA compares all of the company earnings relating to the entire resource base the company claims, including both long-term debt and the capital from shareholders. This makes the relevant ROA a strict test of shareholder returns. When companies possess no debt, then their two figures of ROA and ROE Return On Equity will be identical.

Return on Equity (ROE)

Return on equity proves to be a useful measurement for investors considering a given company. This is because it takes into account three important elements of a company's management. This includes profitability, financial leverage, and asset management. Looking at the effectiveness of the management team in handling the three factors gives you as an investor a good picture of the kind of return on equity that you can expect from an investment in such a company.

Return on equity is very easy to calculate. You can figure it up by collecting two pieces of information. You will need the company earnings for a year and the value of the average share holder equity for the same year. Getting the earnings' figure is as simple as looking up the firm's Consolidated Statement of Earnings that they filed with the Securities and Exchange Commission. Alternatively, you might look up the earnings of each of the last four quarters and add them up.

Determining share holder equity is easiest by looking at the company's balance sheet. Share holder equity, which proves to be the difference of total liabilities and total assets, will be listed for you there. Share holder equity is a useful accounting construct that reveals the business assets that they have created. This share holder equity is most commonly listed under book value, or the quantity of the share holders' equities for each share. This is also an accounting book value of a corporation that is more than simply its market value.

To come up with the return on equity, you simply divide the full year's earnings by the average equity for that year. This gives you the return on equity. Companies that produce significant amounts of share holder equity turn out to be solid investments, since initial investors are paid off using the money that the business operations generate. Companies that create substantial returns as compared to the share holder equity reward their stake holders generously by building up significant amounts of assets for each dollar that is invested into the firm. Such enterprises commonly prove to be able to fund their own operations internally, which means that they do not have to issue more diluting shares of stock or take on extra debt to continue operating.

The return on equity can also be utilized to determine if a corporation is a cash generating machine or a cash consuming entity. The return on equity will simply show you this when you compare their actual earnings to the share holder equity. You can learn at almost a glance how much money the company's present assets are producing. As an example, with a twenty percent return on equity, every original dollar put into the company is creating twenty cents of real assets. This is also useful in comparing subsequent cash investments in the company, since the return on equity percentage will demonstrate to you if these extra invested dollars match up to the earlier investments for effectiveness and efficiency.

Return on Investment (ROI)

ROI is the acronym for return on investment. This return on investment is among the most often utilized methods of determining the financial results that will arise from business decisions, investments, and actions. ROI analysis is used to compare and contrast both the timing and amount of investment gains directly with the timing and amount of investment costs. Higher returns on investment signify that the results from investments are positive when you compare them against the costs of such investments.

Over the past couple of decades, this return on investment number has evolved into one of the main measurements in the decision making process of what types of assets and equipment to buy. This includes everything from factory equipment, to service vehicles, to computers. ROI is similarly utilized to determine which budget items, programs, and projects should be both approved and allocated funds. These cover every type of activity from recruiting, to training, to marketing. Finally, return on investment is often employed in choosing which financial investments are performing up to expectations, as with venture capital investments and stock investment portfolios.

Return on investment analysis is actually used for ranking investment returns against their costs. This is done by setting up a percentage or ratio number. With the vast majority of return on investment calculation methods, ROI's that are higher than zero signify that the returns on the investment are higher than the associated expenses with it. As a greater number of investments and business decisions compete for funding anymore, hard choices are increasingly made using the comparison of higher returns on investment. Many companies believe that this yields the better business decision in the end.

There is a downside to relying too heavily on the return on investment as the only consideration for making such business and investment decisions. Return on investment does not tell you anything regarding the anticipated costs and returns and if they will actually work out as forecast. Used alone, return on investment also does not explain the potential elements of risk for a given investment. All that it does is demonstrate how the investment or project returns will compare against the costs, assuming that the investment or project delivers the results that are anticipated or expected. This limitation is not unique to return on investment, but similarly plagues other financial measurements. Because this is the case, intelligent investment and business analysis also relies on the likely results of other return on investment eventualities. Other measurements should also be used along side the return on investment to help measure the risks that accompany the project or investment.

Wise decision makers will demand more from return on investment figures than simply a number. They will require effective suggestions from the person making the return on investment analysis. Among these inputs that they will desire are the means of increasing an ROI's gains, or alternatively the means for improving the ROI through decreasing costs.

Revenue

Revenue refers to the amount of money which firms generate in receivables within a certain time frame. It includes deductions for merchandise which is returned as well as any applicable discounts. This is also known as the gross income or sometimes the "top line" amount. Net income can be figured out by subtracting the costs from the revenue.

Analysts and accountants determine the amount of revenue simply by taking the price for which services and goods sell and multiplying this by the quantity of units or the actual amount which the firm sells. Sometimes revenue is referred to as "REVs."

There are a number of other definitions and synonyms for revenues. Some call it sales in layman's terms. Whatever name businesses and individuals refer to it by, revenue proves to be the total amount of cash which a company garners through its aggregate business activities. The price to sales ratio is one measurement in business that relies on revenues for the denominator. This contrasts with the competing measurement of price to earnings ratio, which utilizes the profits instead for its denominator.

Revenue can be figured up by several different means. It is really up to the method of accounting which companies and corporations choose to employ. With accrual accounting, sales which the firm makes using credit also count among the revenues so long as the customers have taken delivery of the services or goods. This is why investors and analysts must review the company's cash flow statement in order to evaluate how effectively a firm actually collects on the money which its customers owe it.

The other primary form of determining a company's revenues is through cash accounting. This form of accounting utilizes only sales for the revenues' quotient once the money a customer owes has been collected by the firm in question. When a customer gives the money to a corporation or company, the firm recognizes it as a receipt instead of the general category of revenues. Companies can actually have receipts that do not include revenues. This is possible if a customer were to pay for a service in advance of receiving it or for purchased goods which they have not yet received.

Revenue can also be called "top line" since income statements display them first on the report. Analysts then take revenues and deduct the expenses so that they can come up with the "bottom line," which is also called simply profit or alternatively net income.

Many times investors evaluate both a firm's net income and revenues independently of one another so that they can ascertain how strong a business' health really turns out to be. The reason for this is that net income can increase while revenues remain flat. Cost cutting can actually cause this phenomenon. This scenario is not a positive sign for the longer term growth potential for a firm.

Analysts and investors often further subdivide the revenues from a given company or corporation according to the groups which generate the money. Company accountants can also divide up the receipts of the firm into several categories of operating revenues, the core business of the firm's sales, and non-operating revenues that come from secondary sources. Such non-operating variants are typically not recurring or can not be forecast successfully. This is why these are sometimes known as one-time gains or events. Examples of this could be money gained through lawsuits, investment windfalls, or receipts from selling an asset.

Where a government is concerned, revenue refers to the receipts they obtain as a result of fees, taxation, fines, securities sales, transfers, intergovernmental grants, resource rights and mineral rights, or any sales of government assets or state-owned and -run companies which they might make.

In the world of not for profit organizations, such revenues are commonly referred to by the phrase of "gross receipts." Among the components that make up these receipts are donations from companies, foundations, and individuals; investment returns; grants out of governmental agencies and entities; membership dues and fees; and fundraising endeavors.

Risk Management

Risk Management refers to the identifying, calculating, analyzing, and prioritizing of risks. When used here, risks mean the effect of uncertainty on objectives, as the ISO defines in its ISO 31000. These risks must then be dealt with in such a manner as to lessen the impact of them. This is done through deploying resources in order to monitor and effectively control the dangers presented by the unfortunate events. In other cases, the ultimate goal is to maximize the opportunities which are presented alongside the risk. The objective of such risk management is to make certain that this uncertainty will not interfere with or hinder the company's or project's goals.

Risks can arise from a variety of sourses. This includes project failure threats, financial markets' risks, credit risk problems, legal liabilities, natural disasters or so-called acts of God, accidents, adversarial sponsored attacks, and other events which cannot be easily predicted. Such events are called "Black Swan" events. Two different kinds of negative events are classified as risky at the same time that positively occurring events are called opportunities.

The Project Management Institute, ISO, National Institute of Standards and Technology, and various actuarial societies have come together to develop a few different sets of standards for effective risk management. The difficulty comes from how vastly the definitions, methods of dealing with, and goals for handling risk management differ based on if the project is security, project management, industrial process, engineering, actuarial assessments, financial portfolios, or even public safety and health.

There are a wide range of accepted strategies for managing the various threats (defined as uncertainties that have negative consequences). These include reducing the probability or negative effects from the threat, avoiding it altogether, retaining a part of the consequences from it, transferring some or all of the risks to another third party, and trying to turn the threat into an opportunity (defined as the uncertain future benefits by risk managers).

There have been criticisms of a great number of the standards for risk management as they do not present any quantifiable way of measuring improvement of risk. One particular study identified one out of six IT projects as "Black Swans." These showcased huge budget and time over runs. The cost over runs ran an average of 200 percent while the schedule over runs averaged 70 percent.

Dealing effectively with risk involves choosing the most appropriate counter measures to first size up and then quantify the risk. Mitigation requires the highest levels of appropriate management to approve the strategy which is most appropriate. A corporate image risk should be addressed by the highest levels of management every time. However computer virus risks and threats would be best addressed by only the IT levels of management, which already possess the authority to handle these problems on their own.

Per the ISO 27001, that next stage following completing the risk assessment phase involves coming up with the best Risk Treatment Plan. This must document the actions on how every one of the ascertained risks will be treated. Mitigating risks typically involves picking the right security controls that have to be specified under the Statement of Applicability. This sets out the specific control objectives and other controls that were chosen and why they were selected.

Whichever plan is selected for risk management, the plan must propose effective and relevant security protocols and solutions to manage said risks. As an example, computer virus risks can be effectively mitigated through buying and installing the right antivirus software. The best plans for risk management must have a schedule of times and events to be implemented as well as the individuals who bear the responsibility for getting these things done.

Run Rate

The Run Rate refers to a company or corporation's financial performance. It utilizes the present financial information in order to forecast the firm's future time frame performance. This then allows analysts and accountants to extrapolate going forward based upon the present day financial performance. Naturally this rate takes as a granted the belief that the current financial conditions for the economy in general and the firm in particular will continue. It is also possible for the run rate to mean the company's average stakeholder ownership dilution on a yearly basis as a result of grants of stock options which the company has parceled out during the past three years and as featured within their annual report.

The idea of extrapolating such a future performance is based on the assumption that the current performance will indeed continue over the longer term. It always helps to consider a clear cut example to shed more light on difficult concepts like this one. If Nestle has sales of $10 billion in its last quarter, the Chief Executive Officer could reasonably extrapolate based on this data that the corporation is functioning on a $40 billion run rate. As such, the financial information is deployed in order to develop a year-long projection for the firm's likely performance. Analysts would then call this process annualizing.

Run rates are often useful for coming up with good performance estimates for those corporations which have only a short corporate history behind them, as in under a year. Alternatively, they are particularly helpful for assessing the longer term extrapolations of new departments, divisions, or even profit centers in a well-established firm. This is often the case for any company that is enjoying its first quarter in profits in a long time or ever. This run rate can similarly prove to be useful if fundamentals in the operation of a given business were shifted in some meaningful way that will have a major impact on the future performance and results of the business in question.

The problem comes in with the run rate often proving to be an ultimately deceptive measurement. This is particularly the case in seasonal industries. A useful example pertains to retailers considering the profits in the wake of the important winter holiday season. This proves to be the crucial time period where a great number of retailers make their greatest volumes of sales. When such information is utilized to develop a run rate, then the resulting estimates of the future forecast will likely be flawed and over inflated.

Another weakness to the run rate is that it is usually dependent on only the most recent information. This means that it might not fairly compensate for changes in circumstances which can lead to a false bigger picture. With technology producers like Microsoft, Google, Samsung, and Apple, they often bring in far greater sales surrounding the launch of one of their new products. If they employ only the data from the time frame following a substantial product release, this will likely result in falsely skewed data.

Another limitation to run rates is that they do not take into consideration any big one-time only sales. It might be that a factory receives a big contract and is fortunate enough to be paid upfront for the order. Whatever their delivery timetable for the services or goods, this will lead to higher sales figures for a single reporting period because of this unusual one-off purchase.

It is easy to calculate up a run rate if the company has quarterly data. All that must be done is to multiple the numbers by four. When monthly data is being analyzed, the number has to be multiplied out by 12.

S Corporation

S Corporation refers to the Subchapter S Corporation type of company filing which measures up to certain requirements set by the IRS Internal Revenue Service. This status provides a corporation which possesses a hundred or fewer shareholders all of the advantages of incorporation while also keeping the benefits of only being tax treated like a partnership.

One of the many benefits to this type of incorporation is that it is able to pass all of the company income straight through to the shareholders, thus avoiding the problems of double taxation which are a real issue with shareholders of public companies. There are some particular requirements that must be met to enjoy these advantages. The firm must be domiciled as a domestic corporation. It cannot possess over a hundred shareholders, and it may only count a single class of stock.

Such S Corporations can pass all of their credits, deductions, losses, and any income straight through to the various shareholders. They may then report this loss or income directly via their own personal tax returns. It allows them to pay out their taxes at generally considerably lower individual income tax rates. There are some built in gains on which the S Corporation will pay the taxes at the corporate level, but these are few and far between.

These S Corporations have to be domestically headquartered firms whose shareholders are estates, certain kinds of trusts, and individuals. A corporation, partnership, or non-resident alien can never qualify for this category of shareholder. There are also some financial institutions, domestic international sales firms, and insurance outfits that are not allowed to incorporate as an S Corporation.

There are some significant advantages to establishing an S Corporation. It builds up real creditability with employees, possible customers, investors, and suppliers as it proves the owner is seriously committed to the firm. Employees may also be shareholders in the company, which allows them to enjoy company salaries while also receiving any corporate dividends and distributions which are tax-free as compared to the investment in the company. This is certainly beneficial for morale.

Paying out distributions in the form of dividends or salaries allows the owners to lower the self-employment tax liability at the same time as it creates wage and expense deductions for the firm. Since this S Corporation will not pay any federal taxes at company level, such losses can be utilized to offset other forms of income for the tax returns of the shareholders. It is always helpful to save money on the onerous American corporate income taxes, particularly for new firms. It is another benefit to these companies that the various interests within the corporation can be easily transferred without creating tax liability events and consequences. Complicated accounting rules do not create restrictions nor does the company have to adjust the basis of property either.

Yet there are also a few downsides to establishing a company as an S Corporation. The IRS closely examines any and all distribution payments made to shareholders in the forms of either dividends or salaries to make sure that they are really employees working in the firm. If wages become characterized as dividends, then the company will lose its compensation paid deduction. Should dividends be characterized as wages, then the company will pay a greater amount of employment taxes. It is also easy for mistakes to be made in the areas of notification, consent, election, filing requirements, or stock ownership requirements that lead to the S Corporation being untimely terminated. There is considerable money and time investment in such a corporate structuring as well.

The owner will have to begin by filling in and filing articles of incorporation to the Secretary of State, get a registered agent on board for the company, and pay any relevant fees and costs involved. Owners often have to pay yearly reporting fees and franchise taxes along with ongoing types of fees. These may be inexpensive, but they can still be deducted under the cost of doing business category. Even if the investors possess non-voting shares of stock in this form of corporate structuring, they will still get distribution and dividend rights.

Salary

Salary refers to the monetary component of a job's arrangements. Companies provide this as compensation for employees delivering specific services in their capacity on the job. The figure usually pertains to the amount of money the employees receive for a year's worth of work. It is also the amount of money which the workers earn in regular pay intervals, such as weekly, bi-weekly, or monthly pay periods. Such payment arrangements are commonly negotiated between the employee and employer when the working relationship begins. Salary details and agreements will often change with time and experience on a job.

Employers make the determination on offering a salaried job to a prospective employee. The individuals only provide their consent to such a role. After they begin the new job, such employees will typically be required to work a bare minimum number of hours every work week. This form of compensation is not reliant on how many hours the employees work on a weekly basis. Instead it relates to an employee successfully completing expected work tasks every week and month. In order to hold on to such a salaried position, the workers have to measure up to minimum performance standards and periodic reviews.

One thing salaried employees can count on with a high degree of certainty is that their supervisors will expect them to do more work when required. The United States is particularly concerned about how many hours employees have to work. The Congress passed the Fair Labor Standards Act to ensure that all by the hour employees receive overtime pay as appropriate. This however never applies to employees who are exempt.

Exempted employees are those working in executive, administrative, and professional level positions. Many computer and sales employees are also exempted from the overtime pay requirements. Exempted employees have to receive a minimum amount of weekly compensation, receive the identical salary even when they work a different amount of hours, and provide certain services and fulfill particular duties.

Those employees unfortunate enough to be considered exempt from this Fair Labor Standards Act will occasionally be expected to work late at night or weekends, and all without receiving additional pay. Wise employers realize that keeping such hard working employees motivated in these scenarios requires special incentives. Among these are end of year financial bonuses and holiday allowance and pay. Other employers will provide "comp time" a compensation-based time arrangement that rewards those employees who work on a Saturday with another day off in the next work week.

Many employers which can afford to do so will decide to raise their better performing employees' salaries from time to time. These pay increases commonly come after an annual, semi-annual, or quarterly performance review which will typically be conducted by a member of the management or the principal management team and the employee. Companies realize that hard working and effective, talented employees need raises in order to ensure they do not switch jobs for better opportunities at another company and to tangibly reward them for a job well done.

A number of positions at firms have pre-determined salaries arranged. Yet a highly qualified individual will generally be able to negotiate a higher salary. Qualified employees can similarly negotiate raises in salary, particularly in cases where additional work or responsibilities have been delegated to an employee.

Salary should never be confused with wages. Pay that employers provide based on the quantity of hours which the employees work is called wages. These employees are compensated for the numbers of hours they actually work. They also have the advantage of generally receiving overtime pay for putting in extra hours than those which are typically expected in a given work week.

While wage employees have the advantage of earning overtime pay, salaried employees often receive special benefits unique to this form of compensation. Among this is paid vacation time and paid sick day accrual. Sometimes wage or hourly employees will be moved up to salaried positions once they have proven themselves effective workers for the company.

Sarbanes-Oxley Act of 2002

The Sarbanes-Oxley Act of 2002 is also properly called the Public Company Accounting Reform and Investor Protection Act of 2002. It is more typically referred to by its abbreviation SarbOx or even SOX. Congress passed this much needed reforming federal law of the United States because of a variety of significant accounting and corporate scandals that successively rocked the nation. Among these were Enron, WorldCom, and Tyco International. Such scandals eroded the already low public trust Americans held in both accounting and reporting procedures.

The law became named after its two sponsors the democratic Senator Paul Sarbanes of Maryland and the republican Representative Michael Oxley of Ohio. The vote on the act proved to be nearly unanimous as the Senate passed it 99 – 0 while the House approved it 423 – 3. The legislation proved to be far reaching. As such it created improved or new standards for every publicly traded U.S. company management, board, and public accounting company.

Congress was also hoping to safeguard investors from fraudulent accounting practices that corporations had been increasingly engaging in over the years. The SOX decreed strict major structural changes that were intended to step up corporate financial disclosures and stop accounting fraud.

The numerous early 2000s years accounting scandals prompted Congress to act to improve the deteriorating situation. The failures at Enron, WorldCom, and Tyco had severely shattered investors' confidence in public financial statements. These led to a massive overhaul of the standards that regulated reporting in the industry.

The act itself is comprised of 11 sections or titles. These run the whole spectrum and range from criminal penalties to the responsibilities of Corporate Boards. The SEC Securities and Exchange Commission is charged with implementing the new rulings and requirements for compliance with the provisions in the new and improved corporate governance law.

Some observers felt the new legislation turned out to be important and helpful. Others believed that it actually created more economic harm than it stopped. Still others claimed that the act itself was more modest in its scope and reach than the tough rhetoric that surrounded it proved to be.

The initial and most crucial ruling of the act set up a new semi-public agency. This Public Company Accounting Oversight Board was tasked with regulating, overseeing, inspecting, reprimanding, and disciplining any accounting firms who failed in their critical jobs as public company auditors.

The SOX Act also deals with important matters like corporate governing, auditor independence, and improved financial disclosure practices. Some analysts have called this among the most substantial changes to United States laws dealing with securities since President Franklin D. Roosevelt's New Deal in the 1930s.

These regulations and accompanying policies for enforcement, which the SarbOx laid out, changed and supplemented legislation that already existed and pertained to regulating securities. Two key provisions emerged from the SOX Act. In Section 302, a mandate was established requiring upper level management to personally certify and sign off on the accuracy of the financial statement as reported.

Section 404 provided a new requirement regarding internal controls and methods for reporting that auditors and corporate management were required to establish. The controls had to be determined to be sufficient enough to ensure accuracy. Publicly traded companies were less than pleased by this section. It implied costly changes would be required from companies which would have to create and build the necessary internal controls from the ground up. This proved to be expensive to implement.

Sequestration

Sequestration refers to the package of cuts to the Federal government's budget which became effective on March 1st of 2013. More precisely, the phrase pertained to the method of budgeting in which the drastic cuts would be put into place. The sequester, or super committee sequestration as it was fully known, also extended beyond 2013 from 2014 to 2021.

Congress set themselves up for the fiscal devastation of the Sequestration with their short-sighted Budget Control Act of 2011, also known by its acronym of BCA. Most people simply called it the debt ceiling compromise. The original idea behind such a wide ranging and long-term effects bill was to goad the Joint Select Committee on Deficit Reduction, better known as the Super committee, to arrive at a compromise on cutting out $1.5 trillion in spending over the period of ten years. Had the committee succeeded with this goal and Congress approved it by December 23rd of 2011, then no Sequestration would have taken effect.

Instead, as many would expect, Congress could not pull itself together to approve the recommended cuts from the Super committee. This resulted in the Sequestration taking effect in 2013, much to the undying regret of both Republicans and Democrats in the House and Senate. What resulted was a series of severe cuts which became evenly split between defense and domestic programs. Half of them affected defensive discretionary spending such as base operations, weapons systems purchases, and military facility construction work, reducing the military's fighting edge in many ways. The remainder impacted discretionary domestic spending along with mandatory programs which potentially included Medicaid, the unemployment trust fund, and Social Security payments.

In practice, they agreed that Social Security and Medicaid along with low income programs such as the SNAP Supplemental Nutritional Assistance Program (food stamps) and TANF Temporary Assistance for Needy Families (welfare) would be exempt from the Sequestration. Other low income programs though were potentially targeted in the cuts. These included WIC the aid for Women, Infants, and Children along with Section 8 housing vouchers and LIHEAP the Low Income Home Energy Assistance Program.

For 2013, the following programs were cut by these drastic dollar and percentage amounts. Defense suffered from a $42.7 billion cut for 7.7 percent. Domestic discretionary cuts amounted to $26.1 billion for 5.1 percent. Medicare took an $11.1 billion hit amounting to two percent that year. Other mandatory program cuts equaled $5.4 billion for a 5.2 percent cutback. This equaled the total required $85.3 billion of mandatory cuts which the Congressmen had set forth in their own Sequestration.

The worst of the news did not even take effect in 2013 though. The caps for the budget years from 2014 to 2012 were set to cut out even more at $109.3 billion per year. Congress each year got to determine whether they would pinpoint the cuts by agreement or simply suffer the mandatory pre-programmed across the board drastic reductions to which they had unintentionally agreed back in 2011.

On the positive side, no programs actually suffered from elimination because of the notorious Sequestration. The goal was instead to scale back the scope and price tag of the already existing programs, not to completely obliterate any of them. Despite this better news, the bad news came from the think tank Third Way. It estimated that around 1.8 million people lost or will lose their positions because of the non-defense category cuts.

Here are some of the larger specific program cuts for 2013. Military operations across the four branches of the service plus the National Guard and the Reserves were slashed by $17.1 billion. Military research for the year saw its budget crushed by $6.1 billion. The National Institute of Health suffered from a $1.6 billion cut as well. Border security took a hit to the tune of around $595 million, while airport security suffered a loss of $276 million and immigration enforcement saw $295 million eliminated.

The Centers for Disease Control and Prevention similarly lost $303 million in Federal funding for 2013. FEMA disaster relief lost $928 million, while public housing support suffered a drop of $1.74 billion. NASA lost $896 million, while the Energy Department's Securing Nuclear Weapons programs lost $903 million.

Special Education lost $827 million and the Head Start program suffered a drop of $400 million. The FBI lost $556 million while the diplomatic functions of the State Department lost $665 million. Even Global Health programs dropped by $411 million, while the National Science Foundation lost $361 million.

Small Business

Small Business refers to any company that has a maximum of 500 employees, per the definition set by the United States' own SBA Small Business Administration. According to this definition of small business, the majority of companies within the United States are actually small businesses. SBA states that 99.7 percent of the around six million U.S.-based business with employees fall into this category. In point of fact, fully eighty percent of all American businesses employ less than ten people. Yet despite this, the larger corporations still employ a greater share of the American work force.

Yet U.S. Presidents often refer to statistics for small businesses that include those who employ only under 50 workers. This is why when someone (like a politician for example) mentions small businesses, one should understand to which definition of small they are referring. Yet qualifying for the various federal programs does not clarify the situation of what a small business is either. This is because the legal standard of this status will vary per each and every industry.

It always helps to consider some real life examples of a challenging concept in order to better grasp it. Consider the definitions set by the BLS Bureau of Labor Statistics. According to their industry by industry cutoffs, "cookie and cracker makers" have a maximum threshold for small businesses classification of as many as 750 employees. Yet in the "cereal manufacturing business" or for those firms engaged in "specialty canning" operations the limit is 1,000 workers. "Smaller oil refiners" are allowed to employ as many as 1,500 workers to qualify for the designation. Still other industries do not possess a hard and fast limit to the numbers of employees if their average company receipts in dollars are under a certain threshold limit. With "egg or chicken producers," they are allowed to realize as much as $12.5 million yearly in receipts and still be considered as a small business under the all-important guidelines of the SBA.

Understanding whether or not they are a smaller business is similarly important because of Obama-care regulations and rules. Provisions for these companies in the health care laws will vary. Smaller businesses who employ under 25 employees with average annual wages of less than

$50,000 will receive subsidies. Those employers who maintain staffs of less than 50 employees however are exempted from all of the penalties for not offering standard health care coverage to their workers.

Forbes magazine publishes a list called the "Small Giants." In this ranking, they reveal the best of the not so big companies every year. These top ten recipients of this ranking for the year 2017 were as follows: Barefoot Books with 20 employees, Basecamp with 52 employees, Dansko with 150 employees, Dutch Brothers Coffee with 170 employees, Essential Ingredients with 66 employees, Fresh Books with 248 employees, Fusion OEM with 55 employees, Galileo Learning with 80 employees, GYK Antler with 85 employees, and H.B. McClure with 500 employees.

The criteria to be considered a small business by Forbes are obviously quite different from the various departments of the government, though it does seem to agree with the Small Business Administration limit of 500 employees or less. Forbes says about these respected companies that they opted to be great firms instead of big ones.

Special Drawing Rights (SDR)

Special Drawing Rights are currency units of the International Monetary Fund. These units were originally worth .888671 grams of gold and $1 when they were initially created under the gold standard in 1969. In 1973 the pegged currency system set up at the Bretton Woods conference collapsed.

The IMF then re-defined these SDRs as a basket of the major world reserve currencies. Until October 1, 2016, SDR baskets are comprised of U.S. dollars, euros, British pounds, and Japanese yen. On October 1 this definition will be broadened to add in the Chinese renminibi. The IMF created these unique currency units in order to supplement the existing currency reserves of countries who are members.

Every day the IMF figures up the SDR value and puts it up on their website. The value is a composition of its various parts. They figure the value as measured in U.S. dollars by adding up the value of each currency in the basket in dollars. To do this, they utilize the noon time exchange rates from the London market fixing.

Every five years, the IMF has an Executive Board meeting to review the components of the Special Drawing Rights. They have the ability to hold this meeting earlier should financial circumstances call for it. The idea is to make certain that the basket continuously mirrors how important various currencies included are in the financial and trading systems of the world. The review that ended in November of 2015 decided that the Chinese renminbi currency had become freely usable enough to include as the basket's fifth currency alongside the dollar, euro, British pound, and Japanese yen.

They also adopted a new method for determining how much of each reserve currency will make up an SDR. Equal weighting is now being given to the exports of the currency issuing nation and a composite financial indicator. With the financial indicator, each of the components is being given an equal weighting. It is based on the reserves in the currency held by other countries, the amount of foreign exchange turnover for that currency, and the total of international debt securities and bank liabilities which are held in that currency.

Until October of 2016, the Special Drawing Rights components are U.S. dollars at 41.9%, euros at 37.4%, British pounds at 11.3%, and Japanese yen at 9.4%. As of October 1, 2016 the new SDRs are instead comprised of U.S. dollars at 41.73%, euros at 30.93%, Chinese renminbi at 10.92%, Japanese yen at 8.33%, and British pounds at 8.09%. This represents the new SDR value in a change more significant than any made in decades. The next scheduled review for the SDR is set to occur on September 30 of 2021.

Special Drawing Rights can be given out to member states of the IMF as a proportion of their IMF quotas. This gives every member an international reserve asset that will not cost them anything. Charges are made on allocations and then utilized to cover any interest owed on SDR holdings. Member countries that do not utilize their holdings which are allocated do not pay since any charges equate to the interest they receive. Members whose holdings become greater than what they are allocated receive interest on the extra ones.

SDRs today are only used in limited capacity as reserve assets. Their main purpose is to function as the account unit of the IMF and a few international organizations. The SDR is not actually a claim against the IMF or a true currency. Instead it represents a possible claim against the IMF members and their currencies.

Standard Deduction

A Standard Deduction refers to the minimum amount of income which will not be subjected to taxes. This deduction may also be utilized to decrease the AGI adjusted gross income of the tax payer in question. Such standard deductions are only allowed to be employed in cases where the tax paying individual elects to skip the itemized deductions for figuring up income which is taxable.

Standard deductions are ultimately dependent on a number of personal factors that are particular to the filing individual. Among these are the age, filing status (married or single), any disabilities, and ability of any other taxpayer to claim them as dependent on their tax return.

Naturally, not every tax payer will elect to go with the standard deductions. Many do however. The single most compelling reason that they choose this over the itemized deduction route has to do with the fact that the majority of tax paying individuals (in the nation) will not accrue receipts for all of their potential deductible expenses as they go through a given year.

Besides this fact, a great number of individuals decide that the government's standard deduction is reasonably generous. When they examine the comparisons between the two, they discover that the standard deductions will usually provide them a better reduction to their taxable income than the alternative method of figuring up the sum total of their allowable expenses and entering these instead. For one thing, such standard deduction amounts receive an adjustment for inflation every year. For another, if tax payers cannot supply evidence of such allowed expenses upon request to the Internal Revenue Service, then they may not choose to proceed with the itemized deductions method in any case.

The ultimate idea behind such standard deductions is to make certain that every tax payer will receive at least a portion of their income which will not be assessed by the federal income taxes. These standard deductions also apply to many different states which levy a state income tax. They generally permit individuals to claim some kind of deduction like this on the income tax return of the given state.

Each person's level for standard deduction varies based on the filing status that they have particular to their situation. It always helps to look at a clear and real world example to understand challenging concepts like this one. Take the tax year of 2016. Those single tax payers along with married filing separately tax payers were allowed to take the standard deduction of $6,300. For those who filed as married filing jointly, they received $12,600, exactly twice the deduction of the single filers. For those who file as the head of a household (which are single individuals that can claim at-home dwelling dependents), the deduction rises to $9,300.

There are also higher standard deductions available to those taxpayers who have blindness, are at least 65 years old, or who are both. For those who are totally or partially blind, the Internal Revenue Service gives this special adjustment. Such filers require an eye doctor-certified statement to reinforce their claim. A great number of the various states throughout the country also give these kinds of adjustments based on blindness or old age.

Though there is little doubt that it proves to be significantly simpler to just take the standard deduction than it is to go through the trouble and time to itemize specific deductions, this could cost filers tax-reducing deduction amounts. Many individuals who gave large amounts of money to churches or charities, encountered major medical costs, paid property taxes or interest on mortgage, or who suffered from uninsured losses because of natural disasters or theft will find itemizing pays off. This is why the IRS suggests individuals spend some time to work their tax deductions both ways to learn which one will provide a larger deduction. For people who utilize a good tax program like Turbo Tax, it will do it on the behalf of the filer.

Subordinated Debt

Subordinated Debt refers to a security or alternatively a loan which has a lower ranking to other debt securities and loans. This pertains to the claims on a corporation's earnings or assets in the event of repayment default. Analysts also call this a subordinated loan or a junior security alternatively. When the borrower defaults on the loan or security in question, those creditors who extended the loan or investment and who are only holding a subordinated security will not receive any compensation until after all of the senior most debt holders have received payment in full. In principal this means that they will get little if anything at all back in the event of an actual default. Subordinated Debt proves to be the precise opposite of unsubordinated debt.

It helps to explain why such Subordinated Debt is always riskier for creditors or investors than comparable unsubordinated debts prove to be. Those firms which borrow on a subordinated debt basis generally turn out to be huge corporations and other businesses. Their size gives them the air of likelihood to repay a less sure loan or security.

As corporations take on more debt, they will typically issue at least two types of bonds as subordinated and unsubordinated debt. Should the huge corporation later default and then file for bankruptcy, it will be the responsibility of the bankruptcy court to decide on the priority of loan repayments according to seniority of the creditors. They will order the firm to pay off its debts using the proceeds from the sale of the corporate assets according to a certain order of repayment. Lower priority repayment debt turns out to be the unlucky Subordinated Debt. Greater priority debt will be the unsubordinated debt.

As the term implies, the liquidated assets through bankruptcy sale will first pay off the unsubordinated debts. If there is any cash remaining after these creditors are made whole first, then the unsubordinated debt holders will receive a portion of their funds back according to the schedule set out by the bankruptcy court. In the unlikely event that enough cash remains, the Subordinated Debt becomes completely repaid. It is more likely that the subordinated holders will get a payment in part or nothing whatsoever.

This explains why Subordinated Debt is so very risky in practice. Potential lenders or investors always have to be aware of the solvency prospects of the company in question as well as its total assets and other more senior debt obligations when they are considering investing in a given bond issue. Yet risky or not, these less senior bond holders still have seniority over all classes of stock holders in the company, even the preferred stock holders. Subordinated Debt bondholders will receive a greater rate of interest than the unsubordinated ones in order to make up for the possible default risk, which is very real.

Like with any debt obligations, such Subordinated Debt will appear on the principal company balance sheet. First the balance sheet will actually list out the firm's current liabilities. Next comes the senior most debt, the unsubordinated issues, which will appear as longer term liabilities. Lastly, the subordinated issues appear as the longer term liabilities ranked according to their payment priority. As firms issue such subordinated bonds and then bring in the cash from the lender or investor, the cash account goes up, or alternatively the PPE property, plant, and equipment account. The firm's accountants simultaneously record a liability for the exact amount.

Tax Accountant

Tax accountants are professionals who help clients with finances. One of their main tasks is to prepare tax returns for individuals and businesses. They complete taxes for local, state, and federal levels. These agents can do this because they have great knowledge of governmental regulations and business rules. The Internal Revenue Service established tax accounting with the section Title 26 of its Internal Revenue Code.

Tax accountants also perform a variety of other functions. They help their customers minimize the amount of taxes owed. They assist them in meeting tax filings and requirements. Accountants also update their clients on any changes to the tax code that will impact their business. When there are government audits or disputes over taxes, companies turn to their tax accountants for representation to help resolve them.

Tax accountants' work schedules are different than those of many professionals. This is because much of their business is seasonal. From mid April thru end of December, they keep busy with typical work weeks. Starting in January through mid April, these professionals see their work hours go up dramatically. The first four months of the year they are doing individual and business tax returns for clients.

Becoming a tax accountant requires significant amounts of education and licensing. These professionals generally need bachelor's degrees either in accounting or a related field. Business administration is another major that individuals can take to become an accountant. It makes a good base for a master's degree in accounting. Other master's programs that help with this line of work involve taxation, auditing, business statistics and calculus, or financial planning.

The professional qualification that sets accountants above many of their peers is the CPA. To obtain the official Certified Public Accountant status they must put in another 30 educational hours and obtain experience in accounting. Finally, accountants take an exam to gain this designation. Having a CPA credential with their state board allows them to file financial reports with the Securities and Exchange Commission.

Each state has its own requirements for the CPA license. One hundred and fifty semester hours of college or university credit is usually necessary. Most states also require a candidate to demonstrate minimally two years work experience in the field.

The American Institute of Certified Public Accounts is the governing body that administers the CPA exam. After candidates have met the other educational and experience criteria they may take this. Gaining the certification is not the end of the process. CPAs are usually required to stay caught up with various continuing education courses. Otherwise they will not be allowed to keep their designation.

There are several questions that business owners should ask before hiring a tax accountant for their enterprise. It is good to know the types of clients these professionals count. Finding one that understands their business is important. Companies also need to make sure a potential accountant is available all year round.

Finally, companies should determine that their potential financial planning company has real experience dealing with the IRS. Sometimes CPAs are a more impressive designation. This does not give them the experience that an Enrolled Agent has with the IRS. The Federal Government actually certifies EAs precisely to handle taxes. Another advantage that EAs have is that many of them have been IRS agents. As such they possess real and valuable experience in performing and handling business and personal tax audits.

Tax Bracket

A tax bracket refers to a certain income range against which the government levies a specific income tax rate. With the majority of income taxing systems in the world today, lower incomes fall under lower income rates tax brackets. At the same time, higher incomes are taxed at greater rates. The idea behind such brackets is to ensure that a progressive income tax system remains in place.

In the tax year for 2016, the Internal Revenue Service decreed there would be seven different tax brackets. Each of these offers minute variations on the theme for married filers, single filers, and head of household filers. This led to the de facto establishment of 21 real tax brackets for the tax year.

Importantly, the tax bracket thresholds did increase a little for tax year 2016. As an example, the lowest bracket proves to be under $9,325 for individual taxpayers, which was raised from $9,275 back in tax year 2015. The highest possible tax bracket for this tax year 2016 is now $418,041, itself raised from the 2015 tax bracket high of $415,051. This changes every year, so it is important to consult the IRS.gov website for current information annually.

Those individuals whose incomes are under the minimum bracket of $9,275 have income which is taxed according to the minimum 10 percent tax rate. For everyone filing singly who earns over this amount, the first $9,275 becomes taxed at the rate of 10 percent. Earnings which exceed this on up to $37,650 are then taxed at 15 percent. From $37,650 to $91,150 the earnings become taxed at a steeper 25 percent rate. Income beyond the $91,150 is taxed at still higher rates. This means that many tax filers actually fall into several tax brackets and not only the first one.

The tax bracket should never be confused with the tax rate. Tax rates represent the actual percentage at which the given income becomes taxed. All tax brackets possess their own unique tax rates. Many people simplify and call their tax rates the bracket at which they are taxed as if they were identical. The comparison is not valid since the majority of Americans have earnings which fall into more than one tax bracket.

An example helps to make the tax bracket concept clearer. Consider an individual who earns a hefty $500,000 every year. At such a lofty level as this, the filer will have income that goes into each of the single filing tax brackets. This means the person will pay many different tax rates (seven in fact). This will depend on which part of his or her income is being considered. On all earnings which exceed $406,751 the tax rate will be a punishing 39.6 percent. On the initial $9,075, the rate will merely be the 10 percent rate of the first tax bracket. This means that the actual tax rate of such an individual will lie somewhere in the middle of the two tax rate extremes of 10 percent and 39.6 percent, making it closer to 25 to 35 percent effectively.

The opposite of such a progressive income tax system as this one is a flat tax system. In these taxing arrangements, every individual becomes taxed on all income at the identical rate. It does not matter how much people make in this type of tax setup.

Those analysts and economists in favor of the tax bracket system in particular and progressive tax systems in general argue that the people who make higher incomes can bear a heavier taxing burden and still enjoy a comfortable, high standard of living. Lower income earners will struggle to cover their basic human needs at any tax rate.

The other argument is that such a system will cushion and stabilize against losses in after tax income. The reason is because a real salary decrease becomes counterbalanced out by a drop in the effective tax rate. In this way, people who suffered a pay cut would feel the blow to their post-tax income less severely since the tax rates would drop alongside the income decline.

It is worth noting that such tax brackets do not only apply to individuals who file their income taxes. The IRS also sets the rates and brackets for trusts, companies, and corporations. They adjust both these and the personal tax brackets for the impacts of inflation from time to time.

Tax Credits

Tax credits refer to different sums of money which taxpayers may deduct from their total tax bill that they owe the federal, state, or local government. The amount of a given tax credit will naturally depend on the type of credit involved.

Some kinds of credits accrue to businesses or individuals who operate (or live) in particular locales, industry segments, or specific classifications. These credits are different from exemptions and deductions that lower the amount of income the IRS considers to be taxable. Instead, a tax credit will actually decrease the amount of tax which the business or individual owes.

Governments often provide such tax credits to foster certain patterns of behavior and actions. This could be to lower the aggregate cost for certain taxpayers' housing, or for replacing appliances which are older with newer and more efficiently operating appliances.

Generally speaking, such tax credits prove to be more beneficial than an exemption or deduction since they diminish the amount of taxes the entity or individual must pay on a dollar for dollar basis. These other types of expenses and exemptions do lower the ultimate tax liability. Their limitation is that they only reduce this based on the marginal tax rate of the individual or business. This means that those individuals who are considered to be a member of the 15 percent tax bracket only receive 15 cents in tax savings for each marginal tax dollar deduction. On the other hand, the credit decreases such tax liabilities by a whole dollar.

These credits can be broken down into refundable, partially refundable, or nonrefundable tax credits. Refundable credits prove to be the most helpful form since they are refundable in their entirety. No matter how high (or low) the tax liability or income of particular taxpayers may be they will receive the full dollar credit amount. This is still the case even when such a refundable tax credit decreases the tax liability to under $0. In such a scenario, the taxpayers will receive a negative tax liability, which the IRS calls a refund.

Per the year 2016, the most typical refundable tax credit remains the EITC

Earned Income Tax Credit. There are similarly other types of refundable tax credits which taxpayers may claim for health care insurance and coverage, for educational expenses and costs, and for raising children.

Other tax credits may be partially refundable. This means that they can reduce taxable income and also decrease the individuals' (or businesses') tax liability. In 2016, a partially refundable form of tax credit proved to be the American Opportunity Tax Credit. When taxpayers manage to lower their liabilities to below zero and still have part of the $2,500 (as of 2016) tax deduction remaining, they may apply 40 percent of what is left as a refundable credit.

The final type of such a credit is the nonrefundable tax credit. These the taxpayers may deduct directly from the liability of taxes all the way to the point where the liability then equals zero. The remaining nonrefundable tax credit can not be deployed to take refunds. These types of credits have a negative effect on lower income taxpayers, since they can not gain the full benefit from the credit amount. Such credits which are nonrefundable will only be valid for the particular reporting year too. They also expire once the return has been filed and can not carry forward to future years. Specific examples of such nonrefundable tax credits for 2016 include raising children, adoptions benefits, realizing foreign income, and paying interest on mortgage.

Tax Deductions

Tax Deductions prove to be a legal method for reducing income which the taxing authorities consider to be taxable. They typically arise because of expenses, especially such costs as taxpayers or businesses experience in the course of producing income or earning profits. This differs from exemptions and credits as both exemptions and deductions actually reduce the amount of income which can be taxed, while the credits applied actually reduce the total tax individuals and business will have to pay.

Two categories into which tax professionals often divide tax deductions are above the line and below the line. Above the line deductions benefit all taxpayers regardless of how much income they earn. Below the line ones only provide value if they surpass the individual taxpayers' standard deductions. For 2016, this deduction turned out to be $6,400 for single taxpayers without families or dependents.

Tax deductions also differ according to business and personal types. For the United States, (as well as most business taxing jurisdictions), businesses may take both trade and business expenses off of their taxable income. These allowances vary widely from one type to another and are often restricted. In order to be permissible, said expenses have to be realized in the operations of the business on an activity the owners undertake in an effort to make profits.

Cost of goods sold is a nearly universally accepted tax deduction for most every system of income tax regardless of the jurisdiction. This reduces the gross income, and tax authorities typically consider it to be an expense. In the United States, the Internal Revenue Service permits "all the ordinary and necessary expenses paid or incurred during the taxable year in carrying on any trade or business" as typical business tax deductions. These will be governed by any applicable limitations, enhancements, and qualifications.

Limitations do exist with regards to these types of business deductions. This is the case even though the necessary expenses may pertain directly to the business in question. Some of these limitations apply to activities which include lobbying expenditures, key employees' compensation packages, the use of vehicles, and entertainment related to the business. Besides this, deductions which exceed the income of one enterprise can not necessarily offset income earned in other ventures. The U.S. limits those deductions from one passive activity to being used against income from another such passive activity.

Depreciation is another key tax deduction which the U.S. permits businesses and sole proprietors. This mechanism for cost recovery happens through deductions in the form of depreciation. It applies to most any tangible asset. The IRS permits such depreciation throughout the potential useful life of the asset, which they estimate.

The government assigns most depreciation (useful life) time-frames using the nature and utilization of such assets and the type of business as their guidelines. For example, they may allow three years of depreciation for tax deductions on a laptop or desktop computer. This means that the cost of the purchase can be divided by three and each resulting third of the price may be used as a specific tax deduction for three consecutive years.

Personal deductions are the other principal type of tax deductions. These pertain to individual taxpayers. Some intrinsically personal goods, costs, or services may be deducted from taxable income, per the IRS. The standard and set allowance for taxpayers and also some of their family members or dependents which they support is determined by the Internal Revenue Service and varies most every year.

The IRS calls these personal exemptions. In the United Kingdom and other British English-speaking jurisdictions throughout the world, these are known as personal allowances. In both types of systems, such exemptions and allowances become reduced and finally eliminated for those married couples or individuals whose income surpasses preset maximum levels.

Among the types of personal exemptions (which the U.S. and many other systems allow) are property taxes and local or state income taxes paid, medical costs, primary home loan interest charges, contributions to charitable organizations, contributions to either health savings or retirement savings plans, and some educational costs or interest paid on education-related student loans. The U.S. and Britain also allow payments to other individuals to become deductible in many cases, such as with child support or alimony.

Tax Evasion

Tax Evasion refers to the illegal actions undertaken by an individual, company, or other organization on an often international scale to get out of paying their fair tax burden in their home tax jurisdiction. Individuals who get caught evading their taxes often suffer from criminal charges and penalties that can even include several years in real and served out jail time. The Internal Revenue Service in the United States classifies such tax avoidance as a serious federal offense under its national tax code.

The idea behind tax evasion covers both an illegal underpayment of owed taxes as well as the illegal non-paying of taxes in their entirely. The way that such individuals become caught when they do not at all submit their tax forms to the IRS is through the IRS Internal Revenue Service's ability to figure out that their taxes are owed in utilizing the third party submitted base information including 1099s and W-2s from the employer of the individual in question. Such parties will not usually be convicted of deliberate tax evasion unless they are able to successfully and conclusively determine that it was done willfully and deliberately.

Deliberately not paying correct federally owed taxes though is a very serious matter. In fact it often ends with criminal charges being filed by the IRS or another national taxing authority in other developed nations. For such charges to actually be filed, the agency must first ascertain conclusively that the tax avoidance was done intentionally by the offending taxpayer. This means that the individuals may be forced to pay the taxes which were properly owed at the same time as they are found guilty of deliberately not paying their taxes and then made to spend time in jail.

In determining that the failure to pay their fair taxes proved to be intentional, many factors will be contemplated. The most common of these is the financial situation of the payer in an effort to learn if not paying resulted from deliberate fraud or otherwise attempting to hide reportable income from the tax authorities. Failing to pay can be deemed to be fraudulent in those scenarios where the taxpayer endeavored to hide assets by assigning them to a third party or lodging them in overseas bank accounts.

Examples of this are by reporting earned income using a fake name or other person's social security number. This might also be considered to be identity theft by the appropriate legal authorities. People can be judged as hiding income by not reporting work that did not pay according to traditional means. This might involve receiving cash payments in exchange for services and goods sold. When these sums are not properly reported to the IRS as income in the annual tax filing, then this constitutes willful and deliberate fraud.

There is an important and real distinction between tax evasion and tax avoidance as well. Tax evasion entails illegally making efforts to sidestep paying taxes which are actually owed. Tax avoidance is an entirely legal means of reducing the amounts of taxes owed by a taxpayer. Among these activities could be giving charitably to approved not for profits as well as investing income into tax deferred instruments like IRA individual retirement accounts. With IRAs, no taxes will be owed or paid on invested funds or their returns earned on them unless the funds are withdrawn early before retirement age is fully attained.

Tax Exempt Income

Tax Exempt Status means that certain transactions or earnings in the form of income will not be taxed at either the local, state, or even federal, (or a happy combination of all three) level. As taxpayers earn their income or sell some of their assets to realize a gain before the end of a given tax year, then they create a tax liability for themselves with the government. Tax deductions should never be confused with tax exemptions, since these deductions only lower the residents' tax liabilities.

Tax exempt items are those which are entirely excluded from any forms of tax computations. Items which are tax exempt income might be reportable on the individuals' (or otherwise business or not for profit organization entities') tax returns only as information. It is important to note that these exempt items are not included in the tax calculations.

A common example of tax exempt income is municipal bonds which pay interest. Such bonds are those which cities and states issue in order to generate money for particular projects or general operations. For those taxpayers who gain interest income off of such municipals which are sold from the state in which they reside, this income becomes exempted from both state and federal taxes for them.

In these cases, taxpayers will be given a 1099-INT form to be utilized for all investment interest which they earned throughout the year. All tax-exempt interest will be reported on box eight of the tax form. Such interest earnings will only be reported for the purposes of providing information. It would not be covered in the calculations for personal income taxes. In other cases, interest earnings are fully taxable events.

There are some kinds of capital gains which can be classified as tax exempt income as well. For instance, these capital gains could be offset against other cases of capital losses in the same taxable year. As an example, investors who make $10,000 in capital gains and who also realize $5,000 in capital losses at the same time on a different asset or investment will only pay their taxes on the $5,000 net capital gains which remain after subtracting the capital losses from the capital gains in the same taxable year.

In many cases, when there are significant capital losses, these can be "carried forward" into the future to offset any capital gains for those coming years. American Federal tax codes also permit taxpayers to take a part of their capital gains from home sales and exclude them from federal taxes. This is permissible up to a specific and pre-set dollar amount. The rule became set up in order for those homeowners who sell their homes to be able to protect these gains from taxes so that they can help to fund their future retirements.

Another factor which affects tax exempt income is a calculation known as AMT, or alternative minimum tax. This secondary tax calculation can be required on some individual tax returns. Alternative Minimum Tax considers some previously ruled out as tax exempt items and puts it back into the personal tax calculation. As an example, income from municipal bonds is put back into the mix when using the AMT calculations. Taxpayers are often required to use an AMT calculation on their original tax returns so that they can be made to pay the higher amount of tax from the larger tax liability.

Tax Exemptions

Tax exemptions are special monetary exemptions that decrease the amount of income which is taxable. This can take the form of full tax exempt status that delivers 100 percent relief from a certain form of taxes, partial tax on certain items, or reduced tax rates and bills. Tax exemption can refer to particular groups such as charitable outfits (who receive exemption from income taxes and property taxes), multi-jurisdictional businesses or individuals, and even military veterans.

The phrase tax exemption is commonly utilized to refer to specific scenarios where the law lowers the amount of income that would fall under the taxable label otherwise. With the American Internal Revenue Service, there are two kinds of exemptions which are available to individuals. One example of a tax exemption concerns the decrease in taxes the IRS gives for any dependent children who are under age 18 (who actually live with the head of household income tax filer).

For the year 2015, the Internal Revenue Service permitted individuals who were filing taxes to receive a $4,000 exemption on every one of their permitted tax exemptions. This simply means that any individuals paying taxes who count on three permissible exemptions are able to deduct fully $12,000 off of their taxable income level.

In the cases where they make a higher amount than an IRS pre-determined threshold, the amount in tax exemptions which they are able to utilize becomes phased out slowly and finally eliminated completely. For the tax year 2015, those individuals filing taxes who earned in excess of $258,250, as well as those married filing jointly couples who earned more than $309,900, received a lower amount for their exemptions. This complicated sliding scale with seemingly random numbers in place is all part of the reason why observers claim the American tax system is outdated and overly complex.

There is an important caveat for individuals filing taxes. They can not claim their own personal exemption when someone else claims them as a dependent on their tax return. This is one of the elements that separate exemptions from deductions in the world of tax terminology. Each individual filing is permitted to claim his or her personal deduction.

Looking at a real world example helps to clarify the complicated rules. Young college students who have a job while they go to school will typically be claimed by their parents like a dependent on the parents' income tax return. Since the parents are claiming them as a dependent, the students are not permitted to claim their own personal exemption. They can take the standard deduction however. This means that the students who earn $13,000 will be allowed to take the $6,300 standard deduction. This lowers their taxable income to $6,700. If their parents did not claim them, it would mean they were able to also claim the personal exemption, which would reduce their taxable earnings down to $2,700 (derived by subtracting the $4,000 exemption amount from $6,700).

In the majority of cases, individuals who file are also able to obtain a personal deduction for their husbands or wives. This does not apply if the spouse turns out to be claimed by their parents as a dependent on the parents' tax return.

There are many scenarios where the dependents of an income tax filer prove to be minor aged children of the primary taxpayer. Regardless of this fact, individuals who pay their taxes may also have other kinds of dependents they can claim for exemption purposes against their income. These dependents are typically relatives of the payer in question, such as a child, parent, sister, brother, uncle, or aunt. They must be truly dependent on the person paying the taxes in order to live for the IRS to accept them as dependents for income tax filing purposes.

It is possible for a person to have no tax liability whatsoever thanks to the combination of personal deductions, personal tax exemptions, and exemptions and deductions for his or her dependents. When this is the case, these individuals are allowed to request an official exemption from withholding tax from their employers. When they do so, their payroll department will only withhold Social Security and Medicare contributions (but not income tax contributions) from their paychecks.

Tax Rates

Tax Rates refer to the percentage of their income that corporations or individuals will have to pay in taxes to their governing authority or authorities. In the United States, this proves to be the percentage rate that both the federal government and many state governments assess against the taxable income of an individual or the earnings of a corporation. In the U.S., the system utilized is a progressive tax system. This simply means that as the amount of taxable income rises, so will the percentage rate at which taxes are levied on the income or earnings.

Another way of looking at the Tax Rate is that it is the percentage rate that a company or individuals owe form their respective earnings or income. They must pay this to at least the central authority (federal government in the United States), sometimes the state government (or provincial government), and occasionally the municipal governments as well (counties or cities). This makes the tax burden extremely high on these residents and companies. It explains why as much as more than half of earnings or income can be easily taxed in the United States today.

Another feature of these tax rates in progressive systems like the U.S. is that the tax rates are further grouped into tax brackets. There are seven of these brackets. In each of the brackets, the dollar threshold depends on the filer status. These could be single, head of household, married filing jointly, or married filing separately. The two most common statuses for tax filing are single and married filing jointly.

The seven tax brackets include 10 percent, 15 percent, 25 percent, 28 percent, 33 percent, 35 percent, and 39.6 percent. Every tax payer falls into one of these categories in the U.S. As the individuals' incomes rise, so too does their tax bracket. This means that those who make the most money should in theory pay the most taxes. Yet the way it works is that on the particular income above each threshold, they pay that specific tax rate.

As an example, consider the year 2016. Those individuals who were single filers and earned $450,000 would pay the largest bracket rate of 39.6 percent on only their income in excess of $415,050. On each lower bracket amount, they would be levied the appropriate tax rates on the money earned in that bracket.

For their first $9,275 in income, they would pay 10 percent on this. On the next income up to $37,650, they would be assessed 15 percent. The money from that point up to $91,900 would be levied at 25 percent. The next amount of money up to $190,150 would be assessed taxes at the rate of 28 percent. Money earned up to $413,350 taxes at 33 percent. To $415,050 pays at 35 percent. The remaining money up to the total income of $450,000 would be taxed at 39.6 percent, the top income tax bracket.

If the people were married filing jointly, the bracket threshold amounts would be higher in the example above. For their first $18,650 in income, they would pay 10 percent on this. On the next income up to $75,900, they would be assessed 15 percent. The money from that point up to $151,900 would be levied at 25 percent. The next amount of money up to $231,450 would be assessed taxes at the rate of 28 percent. Money earned up to $413,350 taxes at 33 percent. The remaining money up to the total income of $450,000 would be taxed at 35 percent. If they had earnings above the $466,951 threshold maximum tax bracket income level, this would be assessed at the the top income tax bracket of 39.6 percent.

If this sounds like a complicated and confusing mess, that is because it is. It explains why the United States requires over a million employees at the Internal Revenue Service alone to keep up with the most complicated tax systems in the history of the world.

Tax Refund

A Tax Refund refers to money which the IRS Internal Revenue Service gives back to a tax payer for overpayment of their taxes in a given tax year. For the eight out of ten Americans who receive them most every year, they evoke feelings of wild celebration. The truth of the matter is it simply means that this majority overpaid their income tax out of their payroll tax withholding with their employer throughout the calendar year. This is not a good thing in reality.

Self-employed people will also receive a refund if they have overpaid their estimated taxes. This does not represent free money or additional income when a tax check arrives in the mail or is alternatively direct deposited. Instead, it signifies that the recipient cheerfully agreed to loan Uncle Sam money without charging him any interest for the service.

It is also possible for tax refunds to be issued out of refundable tax credits. This can occur if any money remains from such credits after the taxes due from the federal income have been covered. After the federal government receives and processes all of the return for the tax year in question, it must formally sign off on a refund before the money will be dispatched.

The amount of time that this requires varies according to the means which individuals employ in filing their taxes. Electronically filed taxes-refund processing times are usually sent in under 21 days from the Internal Revenue Service accepting the return. It is possible for delays to hinder this by as much as 12 weeks, though it is highly unlikely that this would happen. Paper tax returns which are mailed typically take from six to eight weeks to be issued and arrive in the mail in the form of a traditional paper check.

If individuals wait until peak tax return season to file, their refunds will commonly be delayed. Tax preparers at the IRS can and do become overwhelmed as easily as any person at this busy time of the year. After all, the IRS is not guaranteeing the time frame for the refunds to be sent out, only estimating their best guess. This is why those waiting for a tax refund should never wait on such a payout to fund a critical purchase or make a time sensitive payment (on a house, mortgage, or other credit card bill).

For those who do find themselves in desperate straits to receive such a refund though, there are loans against imminent refunds which taxpayers can apply for and receive. Some tax preparers, such as H&R Block, will issue refunds against owed refunds as well, in exchange for a small percentage convenience fee. All delay liabilities then transfer to the tax preparing firm and away from the individual tax filer.

Where electronic tax refunds are concerned, individuals have three choices. They can have the IRS deposit them to a checking account, savings account, or retirement account (such as an IRA). Besides this, one could have the IRS purchase a $5,000 or less Series I savings bond if he or she fancies receiving less than a single measly one percent per year in interest.

People have up to three years from the point of filing to claim their refund. This means that now in 2017, filers could still apply for a refund from the tax year 2014. When the IRS grants an extension for any reason, the deadline for the three years starts at the end of the deadline extension.

The sad news is that sometimes people are not allowed to keep their whole refund. The IRS could make a tragic mistake and overpay a refund. They will get this back eventually one way or the other. Any individuals who owe back payments on child support will also have this seized, as they would for back taxes of overdue student loan bills. It is also possible to get a smaller than expected check. In the event that the remaining money does not show up within two weeks of the incorrect amount, it is always a recommended idea to contact the Internal Revenue Service directly.

Total Public Debt

Total public debt refers to all of the national debt which the United States owes to its various creditors and other agencies within the government to whom it owes money. This amount grows in years where there are deficits as the government spends more funds than it receives in taxes.

The aggregate national debt shrinks in surplus years as the federal government receives a greater amount of money that it spends. Every year of the Obama administration has been a deficit year that increased the debt. As of the end of Fiscal 2016, the government's total public debt amounted to $19.7 trillion.

The total public debt includes all money owed to Americans and foreigners as well as other agencies within the government. As such, the gross national debt for the country is made up of two components. The first of these is marketable debt which the public and foreign countries hold. This includes instruments such as Treasury bills, bonds, and notes.

Investors regularly buy and sell this debt on the bond markets. Any investor who is not a part of the federal government is considered to be a part of this class of debt. This means T bills held by consumers, companies, banks and financial institutions, the Federal Reserve, and local, state, and foreign governments are all included in this category of debt. As of July 29, 2016 this portion of the debt amounted to $14 trillion.

The other category of the total public debt is the debt which other government accounts hold. This is also called intra-governmental debt. These debts are also comprised of Treasuries, only these can not be bought and sold. This category of debt is like IOUs kept in federal government administered accounts. The country owes it to beneficiaries of programs, as with the Social Security Trust Fund or the Medicare Trust Fund. These government accounts once had surpluses and invested them over time in Treasury securities. The amount which they are owed includes principal plus interest earnings. On July 29, 2016, this category of the total public debt equaled $5.4 trillion.

Together, the two categories which make up the total public debt equaled

$19.4 trillion on the July 29, 2016 date. This represented fully 106% of the prior twelve month national GDP for the United States. Foreigners held $6.2 trillion worth of the debt at this point equivalent to about 45% of the debt which the public held or 32% of the aggregate public debt. The largest foreign holders proved to be China and Japan. As of May 2016, China owned about $1.25 trillion while Japan held $1.15 trillion worth of U.S. government debt.

Usually, the government's debt goes up as and when the government spends monies on entitlements, interest on the debt, and budgetary programs. It similarly decreases as taxes and other monetary receipts accrue. Both categories change throughout the months of the fiscal year.

The government does not in practice issue Treasury debt itself on a day by day basis as it spends money. Instead, this is issued or redeemed according to the government's money management operations. The total amount of money which Treasury is authorized to borrow is restricted by the debt ceiling of the United States. Congress conveniently lifts this every time the ceiling is hit.

Trade Balance

Trade balances are used to describe the difference between the value of goods and services that are exported versus those that are imported into a country. Countries might have positive trade balances, where they export a greater value than they import. They might also have negative trade balances, or trade deficits, when they import a larger value of goods and services than they export.

Positive trade balances create cash stockpiles and investment surpluses. Nations like Singapore, South Korea, Taiwan, and most of the Gulf Oil states like Saudi Arabia, Kuwait, and the United Arab Emirates continuously run positive trade balances. Negative trade balances create currency outflows or government debt that must be issued and sold domestically or exported as payment for the extra imports. Countries like the United States and Great Britain commonly run negative trade balances.

Positive trade balances are beneficial and constructive to a nation. They can be run forever in theory, so long as other countries continue to purchase their goods and services at high levels. Negative trade balances, or trade deficits, are harmful to a country over long periods of time. They can not be carried on forever, since eventually the negative trade balance running countries will reach a point that they have spent all of their money covering the imports or issued an amount of debt that finally becomes unsustainable and undesirable to investors any longer.

The United States' trade balance specifically refers to the differences between the value of American goods and service exports versus goods and services imported into the United States. This trade balance proves to be among the largest Balance of Payment components. America's Balance of Payments is constantly pressuring the U.S. dollar's value. These deficits minimally bring down the value of the currency for a country that continuously runs them.

Trade balances are reported in the United States and other advanced economies. The problem with such reports is they commonly come out some time after the data is current. This means that most of the information contained within such trade balance reports has already been anticipated and affected the markets. The Foreign Exchange markets do move based on these trade balance reports though, since trade balance data helps to form or support foreign currency trends. To this FOREX market, the Trade Balance report has proven historically to be among the most significant released from the United States.

Trade Credit

Trade credit refers to special financing terms which are many times given to a business by a supplier. This situation arises when a business buys supplies or goods and the financial officer or owner of the vendor agrees to provide either all or half of the purchased order on credit. In the case of half on credit, the balance half would become payable on delivery of the merchandise to the business.

When businesses receive a half order trade credit, they have several possibilities for paying for the balance on delivery. If they have ample resources, they can simply pay with cash. Otherwise, they can borrow the money to pay for the other balance on the inventory. This is why such credit remains among the most critical means of lowering the amount of working capital smaller businesses especially require. It is even more common and necessary with retail operations.

Suppliers normally extend such trade credit to a purchasing business once they have been a regular client for anywhere from 30 days, to 60 days, to 90 days. This trade credit has the advantage of being interest free. An example of this concept helps to make it clearer. Perhaps a supplier ships the Great Sweater Company knitted hats. The bill might normally be due within thirty days. Since Great Sweater Company enjoys these special credit terms, they would have an additional 30 days to cover the cost of the knitted hats which the vendor supplied.

When companies first start a new business, it is difficult to obtain such credit from the suppliers and vendors. In fact they will initially require each order to be paid by either check or cash on delivery. This will be the case until the new business demonstrates that it can successfully pay its bill in a timely fashion. It is a common practice in the business world. For those startups that need to raise money to make the operations work in the early days, it is important for them to be able to negotiate some form of this credit with their suppliers. It becomes easier earlier if the business owner can provide a well-developed financial plan.

It is important for businesses to properly utilize this trade terms credit. When they become trapped in the mentality of it being a necessary means of permanently financing the operations, then the business is in trouble. Instead it should be viewed as a useful source of funding for covering shorter term and smaller needs. This credit is not really a longer term solution to the funding problem.

For businesses who do not avoid this trap, they often times become heavily committed to working with the supplier who generously extends such trade credit terms. The end result of this is that the business is not able to choose a more aggressively competitive supplier that provides better prices, more timely deliveries, and/or a higher quality product because they do not offer such generous credit terms for their buyers. There is a trade off for everything in business.

It is important to realize that trade credit is rarely free. Every supplier may have its own terms. Yet most of them will provide a significant cash discount for those businesses that pay their invoices in 10 days or less. The same as cash price may be for 30 days. By waiting for the 30 days to pay the invoice, it is costing the business the two percent discount. If a business chose to do this for 12 months a year, it would mean the merchandise was costing an additional 24 percent versus the price of paying the 10 days same as cash terms.

When a business pays after the 30 days credit expires, most vendors charge from one to two percent interest in penalties. By being late for a year, this could cost an additional from 12 to 24 percent. This is why effectively utilizing trade credit means that a business will need to plan intelligently ahead so it does not lose cash discounts consistently or pay late fee penalties needlessly. Little details like this separate successful businesses from ones which fail.

Trade Deficit

Trade deficits are unfavorable balances of trade. With a trade deficit, a greater valued amount of goods and services are being imported than are simultaneously being exported. This stands in contrast to trade surpluses that occur when a larger amount of goods and services are exported by a nation than are imported in return. Trade deficits are also called trade gaps.

These trade deficits and trade surpluses are a part of the balance of trade, or net exports, which proves to be the total difference between imports' and exports' tangible value within a country's economy during a particular time frame. The balance of trade results from the relationship of the country's exports and imports.

Economists have held varying opinions on how negative or non important that trade deficits might be. Some have said that issuing paper money not backed by anything other than faith and credit of a government in exchange for valuable produced goods is not a bad thing. Professor Milton Freedom, the founder of monetarism, is one of the main proponents of this particular point of view. He felt that what would likely happen is that high exports would raise the U.S. currency value, while high imports would lower the U.S. dollar value.

Friedeman said that the worst case scenario for running trade imbalances would be that easily and inexpensively printed U.S. dollars would leave the country in order to pay for the excess imports versus exports. Friedman claimed that this produced the same result as if the country that earned the dollars through exports simply set them on fire and did not send them back to America. His policies became influential in the late 1970's and early years of the 1980's.

Other influential investors and businessmen have made opposite arguments. Warren Buffet is perhaps the greatest investor in American history. He claims that the constant U.S. trade deficit proves to be the biggest financial threat facing the national economy. He says that it is worse than the enormous annual national budget deficit and consumer debt levels together.

Buffet has said that other countries in the world own three trillion dollars more of America than we own of their countries. This investment imbalance has only increased since Buffet made these arguments nearly five years ago. Buffet and his followers are so worried about the imbalanced trade deficit that they have suggested instituting import certificates as an answer to the American problem and to bring balanced trade back to the country.

Trade Misinvoicing

Trade misinvoicing, or simply misinvoicing, refers to a means of illegally moving large amounts of money over national borders via misreporting or misrepresenting the total value of a given commercial transaction exchange. This sleight of hand form of money laundering which is trade based is actually done using an incorrectly filled out invoice which the perpetrators submit to customs. Of the various kinds of illegal financial outflows which world organizations monitor, this trade misinvoicing is among the biggest components.

In general, there are four main reasons for why businesses and criminals deliberately misinvoice their trade. These are money laundering, claiming tax incentives, evading customs duties and taxes, and avoiding capital controls. Money laundering is a way in which either criminals or even government officials try to wash their funds which they obtain through either crime or graft and corruption.

Where claiming tax incentives is concerned, there are many nations in the world today which provide generous taxation incentives to those domestic exporters who export and sell their services or goods overseas. Criminals are able to take advantage of such tax incentives through inflating their export amounts in the local currency.

Evading customs duties and taxes are two separate issues that are still related. When an importer lies about its goods and services values, it is successfully able to straight away avoid significant import duties. There can be a range of other taxes, including corporate or personal income taxes and VAT taxes which the company or individual is able to avoid as well.

Avoiding capital controls is a controversial issue which different cultures value independently of each other. There are numerous developing nations which restrict the value of capital which businesses or individuals are permitted to either withdraw from or bring into their national economies. Seeking to get money moved into or out of their native country is a strong reason behind trade misinvoicing. This is still considered to be an illegal means of moving money out of the country in question. It does not matter to enforcers of a country's laws that it may seem unfair or unreasonable to restrict the rights of individuals and businesses to move their own funds across borders and currencies.

Because great numbers of countries try to rapidly process their customs transactions so that they can increase their economic growth and encourage international trade, it is easy and with little risk for criminals to engage in trade misinvoicing. This is particularly the case for such enterprises that only choose to slightly misinvoice their trade transactions by amounts ranging from five percent to 10 percent.

An example of how this trade misinvoicing works in practice helps to understand the illegal practice. An Indian importer purchases $1 million in cars from an American exporter. He utilizes an intermediary locate in Mauritius to re-invoice the cost of the cars as $1,500,000. The Indian importer then pays his American exporter the fair $1 million. The remaining half a million dollars which remains the Indian importer then quietly diverts to an offshore bank account, probably also located in Mauritius, which the importer owns. By engaging in this practice, the Indian importer has been able to illegally smuggle half a million U.S. dollars out of India to Mauritius. This firm will not pay taxes or import duties on the half million dollars either, since to Indian customs it does not exist.

Tax avoidance and trade misinvoicing should not be confused, though they both utilize mispricing to accomplish their nefarious ends. International corporations often engage in aggressive schemes of tax avoidance. In and of itself, this is not misinvoicing, even though many multinationals do practice such illegal and incorrect invoicing.

Valuation

Valuation refers to the method for ascertaining the present worth of any companies or assets. A range of techniques exist to decide this value. When analysts assign values to a firm, they consider the corporation's capital structure, the firm's management, and the potential of future earnings as well as the various assets' market values.

Securities' market values will ultimately be decided by the amount that buyers will voluntarily pay to sellers. This assumes that the two sides willingly choose to engage in the transaction. As securities become traded on exchanges, the sellers and buyers together set the true market value for the bonds or stocks in question. There is also the idea of intrinsic value. It means that the believed value for securities centers on either future earnings or another characteristic of the company that is not dependent on the going market price of the relevant security.

It is critical to understand the value of an asset in order to begin to make smart decisions for the organizations or the investors. They can not determine how much to pay or accept in takeover bids or investments, decide on which investments to include in a portfolio, determine how much and how to finance operations, or decide on dividends as part of running their operations without this foreknowledge.

The central concept behind valuation proves to be that investors, accountants, and analysts are able to engage in reasonable and realistic estimates in value on the majority of assets. This allows them to place values on financial and physical assets. It will always be the case that some kinds of assets are simpler to value than are other ones. Valuation details are not the same with every asset either. Uncertainties concerning the estimates of value will also be different with various assets. Yet in the end, what remains constant are the central principles for valuing assets.

There are basically three separate approaches for valuing any asset. The first method is using discounted cash flow valuation. Following this method of assigning value means that the asset's value must be correlated to the current value of the anticipated future cash flow for the asset in question.

The second means is relative valuation. In this method of determining asset value, The given asset value may be estimated by considering the relative pricing of like assets which have characteristics in common. Important characteristics in this consideration are cash flows, earnings, sales, and book values.

The third method analysts call claim valuation. This method works with pricing models of options in order to determine a value for the assets which have characteristics in common with such options. Each of these three attempts to provide values will often provide varying value estimates on the assets. This is why valuing models always provide their explanation for why they valued an asset in a given way at a different value from the rival other two models for valuing. It makes it easier for economists, investors, accountants, and analysts to choose the best model for valuing a particular asset.

Discounted cash flows prove to be a very popular method for assigning value to many financial or company held assets. Analysts and investors will work primarily with the outflows and inflows which the asset in question generates with this method. They must discount the cash flows with an appropriate discount rate to effectively value the assets based on future anticipated cash flows.

This discount rate adjusts for the future interest rates, inflation time value on money, and investor-required returns. When a corporation purchases a new machine, they will first contemplate the purchase price cash outflow and measure the anticipated cash inflows of the new asset. Whether they are inflows or outflows, they must all be discounted down to a current value so that the firm can come up with an NPV Net Present Value. When the NPV turns out to be positive, it makes sense for the corporation to go ahead with the investment into buying the given asset.

Wash Sale

The Wash Sale refers to an IRS Internal Revenue Service code rule that outlaws any taxpayers from utilizing loss sales on securities in what they cleverly call a "wash sale." The rule essentially explains such a sale as any that occurs as the investor trades or sells securities at a loss within 30 days before or after this particular sale, buying a stock or other security that is deemed to be substantially identical, or otherwise obtaining an option to do the same. Such a sale will also occur when investors sell the security and their spouse or a company which they own subsequently purchases the same or substantially the same security back.

Where stocks are concerned at least, one company stock and another is never considered to be substantially the same to the IRS. They also do not count preferred stocks or bonds of one company and another as materially the same. Yet there are cases where the preferred and common stocks of a single company could be considered to be basically the same investment. This is especially true when the preferred stock can be freely converted into the company's common stock with no restrictions, or if they both possess voting rights, and if they trade for a price that is near the official conversion ratio of the preferred stock issue.

When such a loss becomes disavowed by the IRS thanks to the wash sale rule, it means that the taxpayer investor will be forced to add his loss back on to the cost of the newer stock. This would then be known as the cost basis on the new stock. Consider an example to help demystify what is at best a confusing topic. An investor might buy 100 shares of JP Morgan common stock at$35 per share, then sell them for $30 per share in a loss, and in less than 30 days later purchase another 100 shares of JPM common stock for $33. The $500 ultimate loss in this scenario would not be permitted for claiming by the IRS thanks to the wash sale rule. Yet it can be added back in to the $3,300 cost of the newer shares. The basis for the new cost then would be $3,800 as the 100 shares times $33 equals $3,300 plus the $500 loss on the prior trade equates to a total new cost basis position of $3,800.

In truth, the only silver lining to a stock or mutual fund trade that goes bad is that the capital loss can help to offset other more profitable investments elsewhere.

The ironic part is that there is no such wash rule for any investor who cashes out on profits on a trade then reenters the trade within 30 days. Tax professionals call this unfair scenario the "heads I win, tails you lose" IRS is the master rule. Options are similarly included under the wash rules which mean that you can also have your options loss disavowed if you repurchase the identical ones within 30 days.

Many investors will wonder where the IRS draws the lines on the ever popular newer index mutual funds such as the S&P 500 ones. The IRS throws sand in the eyes of the investor by stating that all circumstances have to be considered when evaluating if securities are in fact substantially identical. No one knows what this really means in point of fact. The general interpretation though is that no two mutual funds are "substantially the same" to each other. Yet selling a single S&P 500 index fund for a loss then purchasing another different S&P 500 index fund in 30 days or less would likely be disavowed by the tricky rule.

Withholding Tax

Withholding Tax refers to the U.S. Federal income tax which they withhold from the wages of any employee. Employers pay these taxes which they collect from their employees' payrolls straight to the government. All amounts which they withhold become credited against the employees' income taxes. This offsets the amount the employees owe throughout the calendar year. This tax is similarly assessed on other forms of income, including dividends, capital gains, and interest earned by any securities the individual holds. Even non-residents who are American citizens will have to pay these taxes.

The Internal Revenue Service utilizes two different forms of Withholding Taxes in their efforts to be certain that the correct amount of taxes become withheld in various scenarios. By far and away the most commonly utilized and talked about one is the standard means of withholding against personal income. All U.S.-based employers are required to do this on behalf of their employees, whether they are part time or full time. The second and less common method pertains to those nonresidents of the U.S. who earn money in the United States. Their income similarly must be levied to ensure that Uncle Sam receives his full due.

By engaging in Withholding Tax procedures, the United States Department of the Treasury is able to go straight for their share of taxes right at the income source, instead of trying to collect their income taxes after the fact once they are already earned (and potentially spent). They originated this clever, forward thinking system back in 1943 as they instituted a massive tax hike on Americans. Back in the day, the government pondered the issue and believed that they would find it hard to gather up such a huge percentage of income in taxes if they did not get them upfront.

The vast majority of employees fall under the legislation that withholds the taxes when they become hired. The IRS requires all employers to obtain a completely filled in Form W4 at this point before their new employees can receive their first paycheck. This form is utilized to estimate the proper amount of taxes the employee will owe throughout the year and per payroll.

For the majority of people in normal circumstances, they need to have approximately 90 percent of their estimated income taxes be withheld by the Internal Revenue Service this way. Otherwise, they will probably fall behind on the taxes. This oversight comes with stiff penalties. The system is also designed to not overtax individuals as they are paying along the way throughout the year.

Both independent contractors and investors have an exemption from the tedious procedures of Withholding Tax. This does not in any way exempt them from paying the income tax though. When such taxpayers as these get behind on their tax withholding and payment, they can be subjected to backup withholding. This involves a steeper tax rate of withholding that the government sets at a punishing 28 percent.

As if this was not difficult and confusing enough, fully 41 of the individual 50 states utilize a similar withholding scheme for their state income taxes. This way they are sure that they will be able to levy and collect on their own taxes from the state residents. The states rely on both their own worksheets as well as the IRS' Form W4 in order to estimate state income tax withholdings for the year and per paycheck. Nine of the states do not collect an income tax.

Such withholding tax is mandatory for the overwhelming majority of Americans or nonresidents who earn income off of a business or a trade within the U.S. Even Americans who live and earn money overseas cannot escape from their income tax obligations. Even nonresident American citizens living and working abroad will be assessed on foreign earned income as well.

Working Capital

Working Capital is a company metric. This proves to be a useful corporate measurement for two significant purposes. On the one hand it is a metric for discerning shorter-term financial health. On the other hand, it is also a means of ascertaining the firm's efficiency. The equation for working capital is current assets minus current liabilities. The working capital ratio is defined as current assets divided by current liabilities. This reveals if a corporation possesses sufficient shorter term assets to cover its shorter term time frame debt liabilities. Sometimes this concept is also referred to as net working capital.

When the number comes in at less than one, this reveals a negative working capital (also known sometimes as W/C). Any number which proves to be higher than two means that the company does not sufficiently invest its excessive assets. The most highly desired ratio proves to be a figure between 1.2 and 2.0.

The sobering facts are that when the firm's current assets are not greater than its current liabilities, it can run afoul of its creditors and the ability to repay them over the shorter term. In the worst case, bankruptcy can ultimately result. Decreasing working capital ratios throughout an extended time frame serve as a prescient warning that should be carefully and thoroughly investigated by analysts and would-be investors alike. It might be that the critical company metrics of sales volumes are steadily declining over time. This would mean that the account receivables amounts would go down and continuously deteriorate little by little.

This figure also reveals to investors and analysts alike the underlying operational efficiency of the firm. Money which is tied down in the form of inventory or which other clients still have not paid to the firm in due receivables will not be available to pay down company bills and other obligations. This means that if a company has consistently slow collections, it will be revealed as a rising number in the working capital figure. The best way to understand this is through contrasting the figure from one time period through to another one or even several like time periods. Slower collections can mean that the company and its operations have potentially fatal flaws.

It is important for investors to remember that high working capital ratios do not signal good things for the company in question. Instead, it means either that they are not sufficiently investing their excess reserves, or that they possess too large an inventory. Investors know all too well that they can quickly ascertain the company balance sheet strength by considering three important categories of quality. These include asset performance, working capital adequacy, and capitalization structure.

This means that analysts can discern the real liquidity of the firm and its efficiency with regards to the current position of the firm. Companies utilize an analytical tool to successfully accomplish this. It is called the firm's cash conversion cycle. Still, while companies like to bandy about this number in such important arenas as their annual reports, the quantity of working capital does not provide much insight on the quality of the liquidity position of the firm in question.

The cash conversion cycle proves to be the gold standard analytical tool for assessing the investment grade quality for the two crucial assets of the firm, the accounts receivable and the inventory. This CCC cycle is made up of three standards. These include the trade receivables category, the trade payables category, and the associated ratios pertaining to the inventory turnover. The three parts may be detailed in a number of days or a number of times each year.

Yield to Maturity (YTM)

Yield to Maturity is also widely known in investment and analyst circles by its acronym YTM, as well as by the phrases book yield and redemption yield. This represents the aggregate return which investors can expect to receive for a bond if they keep the security until the end of its actual life. This is why YTM is generally called a longer term bond yield even though it is still expressed as a rate per year. Another way of saying this is that this proves to be the investment's internal rate of return for the bond if the owner keeps it all the way through maturity. This assumes of course that the bond issuer makes all of its payments both on time and in the full amounts contracted.

In order to understand the Yield to Maturity calculations, it is critical to realize that the formula assumes all coupon payments the issuer makes will be exactly reinvested for the rate of the current yield of the bond. The formula similarly considers the bond's par value, current price on the market, term to maturity, and coupon interest rate. All of this makes the YTM a complicated yet good formula for determining the return of a bond. It allows investors to effectively compare and contrast those bonds which possess varying coupon rates and maturity dates.

There are several different ways to figure out the Yield to Maturity. It is a complicated formula so many investors simply fall back on pre-printed and -figured bond yield tables. Determining the exact YTM requires either a software program or the use of a financial or business calculator. This is because the value for a basis point drops as the price for a bond increases in an inverse manner. Many firms actually calculate YTM for six month time frames as well as on an annual basis. They do this because most coupon payments take place twice per year.

A significant difference between Yield to Maturity and the current yield lies in the fact that the YTM takes into account money's time value, while the simplified current yield computations will not. This is why investors often prefer to utilize the YTM instead of the current yield when they are crunching number on bond returns to compare and contrast with other bond issues and different types of investments.

There are a number of similar yet still variations on the classical Yield to Maturity figure. These should never be confused with the true YTM. Among these are the Yield to call (YTC), Yield to put (YTP), and the Yield to worst (YTW). Yields to call go with the assumption that the bond issuer will recall the bond by repurchasing it in advance of it reaching maturity. This assumes that the resulting cash flow period will be shortened. Yield to put is much like the YTC, only the seller is allowed to and may sell the bond back to its issuer on a specific date for a pre-determined price. Finally, Yield to worst means that the bonds in question can be put, called, or even exchanged. This is why YTW bonds usually have the smallest yields from the three variations on YTM and the YTM rate itself.

There are some important limitations to the utility of Yield to Maturity as a measurement for comparing and contrasting various bonds against other bonds and other forms of investment classes as well. With YTM, these calculations never take into account the actual taxes which investors will have to pay on the bonds. This is why YTM is sometimes called the gross redemption yield. These calculations for yield also do not factor in either selling or buying costs for the bonds themselves.

It is also important to keep in mind that YTM is limited by the fact that both it and current yields are estimate calculations. They can not ever be 100 percent accurate or reliable. The true returns will vary with the realized price of a bond when a holder sells it. The prices of such bonds can vary significantly as the market actually determines them (and not the issuer). Such variations in the value of a bond and the price for which it is sold may impact the YTM substantially. They more drastically impact the current yield calculations and measurement in the end.

Zero Balance Account (ZBA)

The zero balance account, also known by its acronym ZBA, refers to the type of checking account which maintains a permanent balance of zero. The account does this through an automatic transfer of funds out of a master account. The amount which transfers over only proves to be sufficient enough to cover any and all checks which other financial institutions present to the bank where the holder's account resides.

Corporations utilize these zero balance accounts in order to draw down excessive balances from separate accounts. It also helps them to keep better and stricter control over amounts they disburse in the ordinary everyday course of business operations.

These accounts will therefore only have a zero balance within them. The only exception to this zero balance account status is when checks are written against them and presented to the bank in question. In this way, companies are able to keep the balances as close to zero for accounts that do not have any reason to hold excessive reserves. The activity in these ZBA's is restricted to only processing payments. This is why they do not maintain any ongoing balances.

Because of this, a larger sum of funds will remain available for the company to deploy. They can instead put them to work in investments and company cash flow purposes rather than keeping low dollar amounts lying idly by in a number of sub-accounts. It does not present a problem when checks must be paid off from these special zero balance accounts, since the electronic clearing system recognizes that these accounts are in fact ZBA's and they will move the necessary funds over from the master account at the financial institution in the precise dollar amount needed to clear the check.

Companies and other organizations can also rely on a zero balance account to fund purchases which employees make with their debit cards. This allows them to carefully monitor all of the financial transactions and any activities which take place on the cards, since the debits must be pre-authorized. This works well for companies and charitable not for profit organizations which are protected by not maintaining any idle funds within the ZBA's.

The debit card transaction will not be approved by the bank which backs them until and unless the requisite funds become available to the account by a transfer from the authorized account representative at the firm or NGO. This means that debit card transactions simply can not be run without prior authorization by the appropriate superior in the organization. Businesses are able to reduce their risks of activities which are not approved of occurring.

This is critically important to especially larger organizations with many employees and numerous sub accounts and associated corporate debit cards. There is no better spending control oversight for these types of situations than the zero balance account. Incidental charges can be monitored throughout the sizeable operations.

Since incidental expenditures are variable in nature, it is harder to fund and control them without such an account. Large companies and not for profits effectively reduce rapid access to the company or charitable funds with these debit cards. In this way, they have put into place the best practices for approval procedures. It ensures that such procedures will be adhered to in advance of a purchase being made by an employee.

As budget monitoring tools, these ZBA's are also ideal. They may be established as one account per department or business operation. This allows the accountants at the company an easy and fast means of monitoring annual, monthly, and even weekly to daily purchases. The company book keepers are also able to effectively track particular shorter term projects and their financial expenditures by utilizing such a ZBA. Projects which are in jeopardy of running significantly and rapidly over budget also benefit from such accounts. The overseers can maintain control of all purchases by requiring proper approval and notification before the charges take place.

The master account of such zero balance accounts is the critical component of this entire concept. As the central operational center for all fund management in the organization, the account will be employed to disperse funds to all ZBA subaccounts as needed. These master accounts typically include other benefits like better interest rates for balances which they hold.

Other Financial Books by Thomas Herold

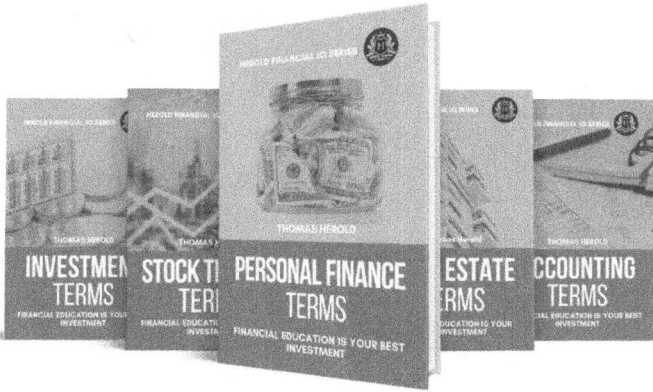

Herold Financial IQ Series
Financial Education Is Your Best Investment

Get Smart with the Financial IQ Series
The Herold Financial IQ series covers all major areas and aspects of the financial world. Starting with Personal Finance, Real Estate and Banking term. Covering Corporate Finance, Investment as well as Economics.

It also includes Retirement, Trading, and Accounting terms. In addition, you'll find Debt, Bankruptcy, Mortgage, Small Business, and Wall Street terminology explained. Not to forget Laws & Regulations as well as important acronyms and abbreviations.

Available on Amazon as Kindle, Paperback and Audio Edition
Go to Amazon.com and search for 'Herold Financial IQ' or copy and paste this link below.

http://bit.ly/herold-financial-iq

High Credit Score Secrets - The Smart Raise And Repair Guide to Excellent Credit

Poor Credit Score Could Cost You Hundreds of Thousands of Dollars
A recent financial statistic revealed that increasing your score from 'fair' to 'good' saves you an average of $86,200* over a lifetime. Imagine what you could do with that extra money?

Improve Your Credit Score in 45-60 Days or Even Less
This practical credit compendium starts off by demonstrating over 50 guaranteed methods of how you can almost immediately boost your credit score. Follow these simple, effective and proven strategies to improve your credit score from as low as 450 points to over 810.

Don't let bad credit hold you back from achieving financial freedom. Your credit score not only influences all your future choices, but it also can save you thousands of dollars.

Available on Amazon as Kindle, Paperback and Audio Edition
Go to Amazon.com and search for 'High Credit Score Secrets' or copy and paste this link below.

http://bit.ly/high-credit

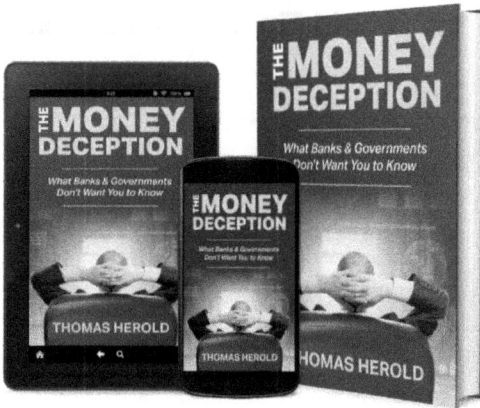

The Money Deception
What Banks & Governments Don't Want You to Know

„It is well enough that people of the nation do not understand our banking and monetary system, for if they did, I believe there would be a revolution before tomorrow morning." - Henry Ford

The Catastrophic Results of Money Manipulation
This money has been souped up by the 1% that now controls 50% of the world's wealth. The fastest and biggest wealth transfer in history is underway. Money evaporates from the middle class, leaving them struggling and without hope for retirement.

What's Happening to Your Money?
Going all the way down into the rabbit hole, it shows you the root of the problem and also lays the foundation for the future. It describes the most likely transition into a new worldwide crypto-based currency, which will become the new basis of our financial system.

Available on Amazon as Kindle, Paperback and Audio Edition
Go to Amazon.com and search for 'Money Deception' or copy and paste this link below.

http://bit.ly/money-deception

Other Books in the Herold Financial IQ Series

99 Financial Terms Every Beginner, Entrepreneur & Business Should Know

Personal Finance Terms

Real Estate Terms

Bank & Banking Terms

Corporate Finance Terms

Investment Terms

Economics Terms

Retirement Terms

Stock Trading Terms

Accounting Terms

Debt & Bankruptcy Terms

Mortgage Terms

Small Business Terms

Wall Street Terms

Laws & Regulations

Financial Acronyms

www.ingramcontent.com/pod-product-compliance
Lightning Source LLC
Chambersburg PA
CBHW071543210326
41597CB00019B/3103